The Big Anxiety

THINKING IN THE WORLD

Series editors: Jill Bennett and Mary Zournazi

Thinking in the World combines the work of key thinkers to pioneer a new approach to the study of thought. Responding to a pressing need in both academic and wider public contexts to account for thinking as it is experienced in everyday settings, the series explores our thinking relationship to everything from illness, to built environments, to ecologies, to other forms of life and technology.

Other titles in the series

Thinking in the World, ed. Jill Bennett and Mary Zournazi
Practical Aesthetics, ed. Bernd Herzogenrath
An Anthropological Guide to the Art and Philosophy of Mirror Gazing,
Maria Danae Koukouti and Lambros Malafouris

The Big Anxiety

Taking Care of Mental Health in Times of Crisis

EDITED BY
JILL BENNETT

BLOOMSBURY ACADEMIC
LONDON • NEW YORK • OXFORD • NEW DELHI • SYDNEY

BLOOMSBURY ACADEMIC
Bloomsbury Publishing Plc
50 Bedford Square, London, WC1B 3DP, UK
1385 Broadway, New York, NY 10018, USA
29 Earlsfort Terrace, Dublin 2, Ireland

BLOOMSBURY, BLOOMSBURY ACADEMIC and the Diana logo are trademarks of
Bloomsbury Publishing Plc

First published in Great Britain 2022

Cover design by Ben Anslow
Cover images: Edge of the Present (Photo © Jessica Maurer); Parrragirls Past,
Present (Photo © Silversalt)

A catalogue record for this book is available from the British Library.

A catalog record for this book is available from the Library of Congress.

ISBN: HB: 978-1-3502-9778-4
PB: 978-1-3502-9779-1
ePDF: 978-1-3502-9775-3
eBook: 978-1-3502-9776-0

Series: Thinking in the World

Typeset by Deanta Global Publishing Services, Chennai, India
Printed and bound in Great Britain

To find out more about our authors and books visit www.bloomsbury.com and
sign up for our newsletters.

CONTENTS

List of figures viii
List of contributors x
Acknowledgements xvii

Introduction 1

1   The politics of experience – and the function of art in the expanded field of mental health *Jill Bennett* 3

PART I Suicide, felt experience and what works 15

2   Why do art therapies work? *Siri Hustvedt with Jill Bennett* 17

3   *Edge of the present:* Mixed reality, suicidality and future thinking *Chloe Watfern, Jill Bennett, Stephanie Habak and Katherine Boydell* 28

PART II Culture and experience 39

4   Knowing from the inside *Lynn Froggett and Noreen Giffney* 41

5   Radical creativity: Breaking the cycles of trauma *Marianne Wobcke with Jill Bennett* 55

PART III Dialogue and embodied encounters 67

6   *The Eradication of Schizophrenia in Western Lapland* and Open Dialogue in the work of Ridiculusmus *David Woods and Jon Haynes* 69

7   The Visit: A collaborative confabulation *Gail Kenning,*
     Jill Bennett and Volker Kuchelmeister 80

PART IV Designing for experience 91

  8   Facilitating environments: An arts-based psychosocial
       design approach *Jill Bennett, Lynn Froggett and*
       Lizzie Muller 93

  9   I have a thing about tables *Lois Weaver with Laura*
       Hunter Petree 112

PART V Resistance, racism and decolonization 123

10   Narratives of resistance from indefinite detention:
      Manus Prison Theory and Nauru Imprisoned Exiles
      Collective *Omid Tofighian, Behrouz Boochani, Mira* and*
      Elahe Zivardar 125

11   Poetic solidarities *Claudia Rankine with*
      Evelyn Araluen 139

PART VI Reparative action 151

12   Designing reparations: Creative process as reparative
      practice *Andrea Durbach, Jill Bennett and Pumla*
      Gobodo-Madikizela 153

13   EmbodiMap I: Trauma survival and refugee
      experience *Lydia Gitau* 166

PART VII Thinking in action with creative resources
            after trauma 179

14   Unnerved *Anita Glesta* 181

15   *Wau-mananyi:* The song on the wind *Pantjiti*
      Imitjala Lewis, Rene Wanun Kulitja, Angela Lynch
      (Uti Kulintjaku), translated by Beth Sometimes 191

16   EmbodiMap II: An auto-ethnography *Sophie Burgess* 197

PART VIII Soundwork/earwork 209

17 *Held Down, Expanding:* An exchange on trauma
through acousmatic sound art practice *Thembi
Soddell* 211

18 *Hold me in a circle of tender listening:* Entangled
encounters with women survivors from the Mental
Health Testimony Project archive *Amanda McDowell* 223

PART IX Lived experience, activism and survival 237

19 Being together in a neurodiverse world: Exploring
with Project Art Works *Kate Adams, Sonia Boué and
Chloe Watfern* 239

20 Pathologize this *Dolly Sen* 250

21 Super-fast augmented anxiety *Clive Parkinson* 260

Index 275

FIGURES

3.1   *Edge of the Present*, mixed reality installation, 2019. Photo by Jessica Maurer/Alex Davies, courtesy The Big Anxiety 30

5.1   Left: Marianne Wobcke, *Grandmother Dreaming* 2011; Lino cut, 30 × 30 cm, edition 2/10. Photo courtesy of Jenny Sanzaro; Right: Marianne Wobcke, *Baby in a Cage – The Second Matrix – No Way Out,* 2009. Polystyrene, felt and wire sculpture. Photo courtesy the artist 56

6.1   *The Eradication of Schizophrenia in Western Lapland* at Battersea Arts Centre, 2014. Left to right: Jon Haynes (patient), Patrizia Paolini (Mum, through window) and David Woods (doctor). Photograph by Richard Davenport 70

7.1   *The Visit*, immersive media (still), 2019. Courtesy fEEL UNSW 81

7.2   *The Visit*, 3D LiDAR (Light Detection and Ranging) scan of a physical kitchen with props created using photogrammetry, 2019. Courtesy fEEL, UNSW 81

8.1   Left: *Awkward Conversations* in Customs House; Right: Debra Keenahan's *Awkward Conversations* walk. The Big Anxiety, 2017; photographs by Gisella Vollmer, Skyline Productions 96

8.2   *Parragirls Past, Present*, 2017 (viewer in immersive 3D film). The Big Anxiety, 2017; photograph by Saeed Khan/AFP 104

10.1   Film still of Behrouz, Manus Island (left) and poster (right), *Chauka, Please Tell Us the Time* (2017), Sarvin Productions 2019 131

10.2   Left: Render image of a 3D model of the Nauru detention centre created by Elahe Zivardar for the film *Searching for Aramsayesh Gah* (2022); Right: 'What am I?/ Nothing. A number? Maybe. The number of a boat/IVL-57', Elahe's ID card. Both images courtesy Elahe Zivardar 135

13.1   EmbodiMap, felt Experience and Empathy Lab (fEEL), 2020. Courtesy fEEL, UNSW 169

14.1   *Untitled*, oil on canvas, 48 inches × 72 inches. Anita Glesta, 2017 182

14.2   Still from the animation, *UNNERVED*. Anita Glesta, 2021 187

15.1   Uti Kulintjaku, 2019. Photo Volker Kuchelmeister; courtesy fEEL Lab 192

15.2   *Wau-mananyi: The song on the wind*, Stills from VR and
       installation, 2019. Photo Volker Kuchelmeister; courtesy fEEL
       Lab 195
16.1   EmbodiMap, fEEL Lab (screenshot from VR session). Photo: Sophie
       Burgess/Volker Kuchelmeister; courtesy fEEL Lab, 2021 200
19.1   *The Not Knowing of Another* (Adams 2008), still and installation
       view at MK Gallery, 2011, Courtesy Project Art Works 240
19.2   *Illuminating the Wilderness* film still (Project Art Works 2019).
       Courtesy Project Art Works 242
20.1   *The Lost Sheep*, 2017. Courtesy Dolly Sen 256
20.2   A young girl telling Dolly that her brother made her mad, *Bedlamb*,
       Bethlem Hospital, 2019. Courtesy Dolly Sen 258
21.1   Vic McEwan and Clive Parkinson, Boree Creek, 2019. Courtesy Vic
       McEwan 261
21.2   Still from *Still Life*, Sam Taylor-Johnson, 2001. Courtesy Sam
       Taylor-Johnson 272

CONTRIBUTORS

Kate Adams, MBE, is an artist, advocate, activist and artistic director and CEO of Project Art Works, which she co-founded in 1997. Her highly personalized studio research practice explores an expanded conception of art, influenced by her son Paul Colley who has complex support needs, and involves collaborations with many individuals, caregivers and their circles of support. Project Art Works were joint winners of the Film London Jarman Award 2020; shortlisted for the Turner Prize 2021; and commissioned for DOCUMENTA 15 (Kassel 2022). In 2012 Kate was awarded an MBE for services to art and disability.

Evelyn Araluen is a First Nations Australian born in Dharug country, descendant of the Bundjalung nation; poet, researcher and co-editor of *Overland Literary Journal*. Her award-winning poetry, criticism and fiction have been published in *LitHub*, the *Guardian*, the *Western Humanities Review*, the *Australian Poetry Journal* and more. In 2019, Evelyn was festival Poet for The Big Anxiety. Her poetry and essay collection *DROPBEAR* was published in 2021.

Jill Bennett is Scientia professor, Australian Research Council laureate fellow and director of The Big Anxiety Research Centre and felt Experience and Empathy Lab (fEEL) at the University of New South Wales (UNSW). Her books include *Empathic Vision: Affect, Trauma & Contemporary Art* (2005), *Practical Aesthetics* (2012) and the edited collection *Thinking in the World: A Reader* (Bloomsbury 2020). Her work on trauma encompasses psychosocial design and the development of creative media. She founded the award-winning The Big Anxiety – festival of people + art + science in 2017.

Behrouz Boochani is a Kurdish-Iranian journalist, human rights defender, writer and filmmaker. He was detained in Manus Island and in Port Moresby for over six years under the Australian government's policy to deter people seeking asylum by boat (2013 until 2019). He managed to escape to Aotearoa, New Zealand, was granted protection in July 2020 and is a senior adjunct research fellow at the Ngāi Tahu Research Centre, University of Canterbury. His book *No Friend but the Mountains: Writing from Manus Prison* won the Victorian Prize for Literature.

Sonia Boué is a multiform artist whose research and practice is at the forefront of neuro-inclusive participatory arts practice in the UK. She has published in *Disability Studies Quarterly* and on Disability Arts Online; has created a BBC Radio 4 programme *The Art of Now: Return to Catalonia*, a film collaboration with Tate Britain, *Felicia Browne: Unofficial War Artist* in 2016; and was commissioned to make the short film *Dual Identity* for the Barea Archive at the Bodleian Library. Sonia proudly identifies as a neurodivergent person.

Katherine Boydell is professor of mental health at the Black Dog Institute and adjunct professor within the Dalla Lana School of Public Health, University of Toronto, and in Theatre at York University, Toronto. Katherine was awarded a Suicide Prevention Australia Innovation Grant for her work on the *Edge of the Present* virtual reality (VR) project to determine the impact of the VR experience on positive future thinking for individuals with a history of suicidality. She has published over 250 papers and book chapters, and recently edited a book, *Body Mapping* (2020).

Sophie Burgess is a postdoctoral fellow in Psychosocial Practice in the fEEL Lab, UNSW. She is a clinical psychologist working concurrently in private practice and has been an analysand in long-term psychoanalysis. Her research (published in such journals as *Clinical Psychologist*) focuses on therapeutic applications in trauma recovery.

Andrea Durbach is professor emeritus at UNSW where she was director of the Australian Human Rights Centre (now Institute) from 2004 to 2017. Born and educated in South Africa, she practised as a political trial lawyer under apartheid. Her book *Upington* (1999) is an account of her representation of twenty-five Black defendants in a notorious death penalty case which formed the basis of the 2011 documentary *A Common Purpose* (dir. Mitzi Goldman). She has conducted research and written on historical harm and the potential and limitations of reparations and reconciliation, primarily in relation to Australia's 'Stolen Generations' and victims of apartheid South Africa.

Lynn Froggett is professor of Psychosocial Research and co-director of the Institute for Citizenship Society and Change at the University of Central Lancashire, and chair of the Association for Psychosocial Studies (APS). Her methodological innovations include the development of the visual matrix, a group-based experiential method of facilitation and evaluation. Her books include *Social Work and the Visual Imagination* (co-edited, 2018) and *Love, Hate and Welfare* (2002).

Noreen Giffney is a psychoanalytic psychotherapist and psychosocial theorist, currently lecturing in Counselling at Ulster University, Northern

Ireland. Her research explores the importance of cultural objects in the unconscious lives of patients and clinical practitioners. She is the author of *The Culture-Breast in Psychoanalysis: Cultural Experiences and the Clinic* (2021) and co-editor of *Clinical Encounters in Sexuality: Psychoanalytic Practice and Queer Theory* (2017).

Lydia Gitau is a postdoctoral fellow (Psychosocial Practice) in the University of New South Wales' fEEL Lab. She has published on trauma and peacebuilding, including a monograph, *Trauma-sensitivity and Peacebuilding: Considering the Case of South Sudanese Refugees in Kakuma Refugee Camp* (2018). Lydia has worked as a counsellor in Kenya and as a trainer and trauma counsellor with NSW Service for the Treatment and Rehabilitation of Torture and Trauma Survivors (STARTTS).

Anita Glesta is New York-based multimedia artist, best known for her public installations (such as *WATERSHED* 2016–17, National Theatre, London; Ellis Island and New York Public Library). Her work has been included in numerous group exhibitions and her solo exhibitions in New York City and throughout the world. Her PhD research (UNSW) explores the impact of trauma on the body and physical health.

Pumla Gobodo-Madikizela is professor and research chair for Historical Trauma and Transformation at Stellenbosch University. Her work focuses on intergenerational repercussions of oppression and institutional violence, and what she terms "reparative humanism." The latter draws on her work on South Africa's Truth and Reconciliation Commission, and builds on her earlier research on the psychoanalytic interpretation of remorse and forgiveness in the context of gross violations of human rights. Her award-winning book, *A Human Being Died That Night: A South African Story of Forgiveness*, 2003 has been transformed into a theatre work performed internationally.

Stephanie Habak is a researcher in the arts-based knowledge translation (AKT) lab at the Black Dog Institute, as well as the Maridulu Budyari Gumal – Sydney Partnership for Health Education Research and Enterprise (SPHERE). Her work focuses on the use of the arts, specifically virtual reality and gaming media, in health translation. She has published results of studies in journals such as the *International Journal of Environmental Research and Public Health*.

Siri Hustvedt is the author of a book of poetry, three collections of essays, a work of non-fiction and six novels, including the international bestsellers *What I Loved* and *The Summer Without Men*. Her novel *The Blazing World* was long-listed for the Man Booker Prize and won The Los Angeles Book Prize for fiction. In 2012 she was awarded the International Gabarron Prize for Thought and Humanities. She has a PhD in English from Columbia University and is a lecturer in psychiatry at Weil Cornell Medical College, New York. Her work has been translated into over thirty languages.

Gail Kenning's research and art practice focuses on participatory arts and health with a focus on ageing and dementia. Her research projects span the UK, Netherlands and Australia. Her publications include the book *HCI and Design in the Context of Dementia* (2020). Gail is a postdoctoral research fellow with fEEL, the Big Anxiety Research Centre and Ageing Futures Institute, UNSW, Sydney.

Volker Kuchelmeister is an expert in presence, embodiment and place representation for immersive applications. As lead immersive designer at the UNSW felt Experience and Empathy Lab, he has developed research tools and immersive media productions, including the award-winning The Visit; EmbodiMap; Parragirls Past, Present; and Wau-mananyi. He has published papers in many arts, digital media and technology journals.

Mira is a writer and researcher who was detained in Nauru from 2013 until 2019.

Amanda McDowell is an artist and PhD student in Arts and Humanities at the University of Kent. Her doctoral research examines women's psychiatric experience in twentieth-century Britain, with particular reference to trauma, affective listening practices and voice. She exhibited her most recent sound work at The Big Anxiety festival, 2019, and is currently making a sound piece for the Mental Health and Justice Project.

Lizzie Muller is associate professor at UNSW Art & Design, teaching Curating and Cultural Leadership. She researches audience experience, reflective-curatorial practice and participatory knowledge creation in museums. Recent books include *Curating Lively Objects: Exhibitions beyond Disciplines* (with Caroline Seck Langill, 2021). Her curated exhibitions blending art, science and technology include *Human non Human* (Powerhouse Museum, Sydney 2018) and *A Working Model of the World* (Dundee, New York and Sydney, 2017).

Clive Parkinson is the director of the Manchester Institute for Arts, Health and Social Change. His research takes a critical lens to the arts and health community through film, spoken word, text and performative practice. Until 2021 he was reader in Arts, Health and Social Justice and director of Arts for Health at Manchester Metropolitan University. A diagnosis of multiple-myeloma piqued his curiosity, leading him to refocus on work that blurs the arts, community and environmental health. Following his *Manchester Declaration* (2019) he published *A Social Glue* (2021), a five-year plan for Greater Manchester.

Laura Hunter Petree is a New York-based artist, writer and producer of performance. She has worked with Split Britches since 2017, serving as a collaborative writer, archivist and producer. Her research interests include immersive performance, space, whiteness and the American psyche.

Claudia Rankine is professor of Creative Writing at New York University, previously Frederick Iseman professor of Poetry at Yale. She has authored five books of poetry, including *Citizen: An American Lyric* and *Don't Let Me Be Lonely*; three plays including *HELP* and *The White Card*, and a 2020 essay collection, *Just Us: An American Conversation*. Rankine is co-editor of several anthologies including *The Racial Imaginary: Writers on Race in the Life of the Mind*. In 2016, Rankine co-founded The Racial Imaginary Institute (TRII). Among her numerous honours, Rankine is the recipient of fellowships from the Guggenheim Foundation and the MacArthur Foundation.

Dolly Sen is a writer, filmmaker, artist, performer and mental health activist based in the UK. She is interested in the madness given to us by the world. She has published widely on mental health, activism, creativity and the mental health system.

Thembi Soddell is a sound and installation artist, electroacoustic composer and practice-based researcher with an interest in psychology, perception, extreme emotion and the subjectivity of experience. Thembi's practice-based PhD thesis (RMIT, 2019), titled 'A Dense Mass of Indecipherable Fear: The Experiential (Non)Narration of Trauma and Madness through Acousmatic Sound', investigated the use of acousmatic sound in representing and understanding lived experience of so-called mental illness and trauma from a patient perspective, including critique of the mental health system.

Omid Tofighian is adjunct lecturer in Arts and Media, UNSW; honorary research associate in Philosophy, University of Sydney; and honorary research fellow in Birkbeck Law, University of London. His published works include *Myth and Philosophy in Platonic Dialogues* (2016); he is the translator of Behrouz Boochani's multi-award-winning book *No Friend but the Mountains: Writing from Manus Prison* (2018); and co-editor of journal special issues *Literature and Aesthetics* (2011), *Alphaville: Journal of Film and Screen Media* (2019) and *Southerly* (2021).

Uti Kulintjaku (UK) (represented by artist/healthworker **Pantjiti Imitjala Lewis**, artist/community advocate **Rene Wanun Kulitja** and manager/social worker **Angela Lynch**) is a multi-award-winning arts and social innovation project, initiated and led by senior Anangu women artists and *ngangkari* (healers) from within the Ngaanyatjarra Pitjantjatjara Yankunytjatjara Women's Council's (NPYWC) in the Australian Central Desert. UK works to address cycles of trauma and improve the mental health and well-being of Aboriginal people in remote desert communities, developing innovative arts and media to explore the psychosocial experiences of trauma and depression.

Chloe Watfern is a researcher, writer and artist, currently Scientia PhD scholar in the School of Art and Design and the Black Dog Institute at the University of New South Wales, Sydney. Drawing on her academic background in art history and psychology, her research is focused on the use of arts-based methods to investigate and communicate complex health and social issues. She has published in *Art/Research International* and the *British Journal of Learning Disabilities*, and literary platforms including *Overland* and *Running Dog*.

Lois Weaver is a New York/London-based artist, activist and professor of Contemporary Performance at Queen Mary University of London. She has been a writer, director and performer with Peggy Shaw and Split Britches since 1980. She is a 2014 Guggenheim fellow and a 2016–18 Wellcome Trust Engaging Science fellow. Her experiments in performance as a means of public engagement include Long Tables, Care Cafés, Porch Sittings and her facilitating persona, Tammy WhyNot. Her most recent book is *The Only Way Home is through the Show* (2015), edited by Jen Harvie.

Marianne Wobcke is a trained nurse, midwife and professional artist. Born on Turrbal land, and connected to the Girramay people from North Queensland, she is of Stolen Generations lineage. Marianne has developed a new programme of culturally connected birthing practices and trauma recovery and has brought together a practice called Perinatal Dreaming. Currently a PhD candidate at Griffith University, Marianne was awarded the 2021 Australia Council for the Arts Ros Bower Award for Community Arts and Cultural Development.

David Woods and **Jon Haynes** are co-artistic directors of Ridiculusmus, a multi-award-winning performance company, established in1992. The company has created over twenty-five original theatre productions and is regularly commissioned by venues including the Barbican, National Theatre, Royal Court, Soho Theatre, BAC and Arts House, Melbourne.

Elahe Zivardar, aka Ellie Shakiba, is an Iranian artist, architect, videographer, photographer and documentary maker who was imprisoned by the Australian government in Nauru from 2013 to 2019. She was accepted as a refugee by the United States in 2019 and currently lives and works in Washington, DC. During her detention in Nauru she used photography and video to document the horrific treatment and conditions endured by people seeking asylum, and the impact of Australia's policies on local people. Elahe's recent work includes her series of paintings, *Border-Industrial Complex*; she is co-director and executive producer for the film *Searching for Aramsayesh Gah*.

ACKNOWLEDGEMENTS

The projects discussed in this book involve large-scale collaborations. Readers are invited to view these on The Big Anxiety website – thebiganxiety .org – where full production and supporter credits are listed.

We acknowledge and thank all the participants and collaborators who have contributed in various ways to these projects.

A previous version of Chapter 8 was published under the title 'Psychosocial Aesthetics' in the *Journal of Psychosocial Studies*. The revised version is included by kind permission of Policy Press.

Chapter 6 has been developed from a shorter piece by David Woods, published in *Context* magazine in 2015: 'Breakthrough Moments: Open Dialogue in the Ridiculusmus Play, "The Eradication of Schizophrenia in Western Lapland"'.

An epigraph in Chapter 18 appears courtesy of © Brandon LaBelle, 2014, *Lexicon of the Mouth: Poetics and Politics of Voice and the Oral Imaginary*, Bloomsbury Academic, an imprint of Bloomsbury Publishing Inc.

Research for this book has been supported by the Australian Research Council under the Laureate and Linkage programmes, and by UNSW.

Thanks to Ally Bisshop for her always excellent management and copy-editing of the book; also to Melissa Neidorf, Chloe Watfern and Mark Tredinnick for their help with preparation and editing.

Introduction

CHAPTER 1

The politics of experience – and the function of art in the expanded field of mental health

Jill Bennett

Art is a means to communicate experience – the sense and feeling of what it is to be in a particular embodied relationship to the world. It is an activation of aesthetic intelligence ('aesthetic' deriving from the Greek *aisthetikos*, pertaining to sense perception), capturing what is known by sensory, affective and emotional means, while at the same time engendering new forms of experience. Unlike more conventionally scientific methods, which isolate and examine their object from the outside, an exploratory art process may engage with experiencing from the inside, with the internal dynamics of what happens, and with the unfolding interplay of emotions rather than with their classification. In this respect, art does not simply represent experience but frames and investigates the subjective as a mode of knowing, in turn shifting perspectives and proliferating vantage points onto the symptoms and pathologies that constitute 'mental health'. Lived experience, once articulated and elaborated by such means, transforms the object of mental health discourse, giving rise to new forms of expression that are neither classificatory nor diagnostic but concerned with the texture of feeling, and with interpreting, sharing and transforming what is felt.

The everyday words we use for emotion – 'anxiety', 'depression', 'love' or 'hate' – are often vastly inadequate to the description of experience, and insufficient to its sharing, the psychoanalyst Christopher Bollas has observed (1995: 29). When we share an emotional reality, 'it is as if unconscious communication takes place by means of our separate senses, communication devoted to knowings derived from feelings' (1995: 29). To the extent that art realizes and enacts such a sense-based connection, it is the basis for a potentially therapeutic encounter by which experience (anxiety, distress, trauma) may be placed in the world, shared and potentially transformed. For Bollas, whose work resonates throughout this volume, the transformation of trauma or psychic pain can occur through art, insofar as it involves a generative process, developing 'a new psychic structure' and perspective, which allows 'a certain mastery over the effects of trauma' (1992: 78–9). There is, in other words, a psychosocial force to creative action, its impact felt internally and within the world.

The radical existentialist writer and psychiatrist R. D. Laing (1967: 17) writes in *The Politics of Experience* that 'experience is not "subjective" rather than "objective", not "inner" rather than "outer", not psychic rather than somatic'; it is at some level always located within a social nexus, a material environment or ecological niche. Rather than an individualized response to the world, it is necessarily relational, shaped within what Jacques Rancière (2004) later termed a regime of the 'sensible' – referring to the normalization of experience that determines what is perceived or imperceptible, visible or invisible, audible or inaudible within the social order. By reconfiguring what is sensible (able to be sensed) and thereby known, art has the potential to transform relationships within the institutionalized order. It is therefore integral to the politics of lived experience – a politics that elaborates marginalized, excluded or unspoken experience, and which exposes the power relations suppressing such experience. Moreover, a bottom-up approach that remains focused on the elaboration of lived experience creates the conditions for new experiences and opportunities for action, as well as for evolving practices of care and psychosocial support. In this way, much art operates in the field of 'mental health' through diverse collaborations and pragmatic interventions both within and outside the formally constituted health sector.

The distinctive contribution of art does not lie in its instrumental use nor in the overt expression of politics, however; art operating in a didactic form (correcting, informing, mediating rather than creating) is potentially the least conducive to a politics that relies on elaboration of experience. The art that is 'useful' in the expanded field of mental health – a field that is or seeks to be fully engaged with lived experience – is that which functions most effectively to express and transform experience. This art, this field and this process of transformation is the focus of the current volume.

The 'demand to experience the "evidence"' (Laing 1967: 15)

In 2016 I attended a session of the intriguing UK Parliamentary inquiry into arts, health and well-being in the House of Lords. Around the table, leading exponents of the field produced dossiers of 'evidence', including the results of randomized controlled trials (RCTs) designed to establish that art really does have health benefits and no downside. Still, it seemed, doubt lingered in the face of this mounting evidence; the researchers were commonly asked for more studies, more data. As I recall the discussion, the session chair (Michael Bichard, a former chair of the UK's Design Council) cut in to dismiss the naysayers at this point, questioning the basis of these demands for more. He said: 'It's not about evidence (we have the evidence here!); it's about belief', which felt like an encouraging pronouncement from the core of the establishment. Recourse to the measures and metrics of the health sector was evidently obscuring the scope of the paradigm shift on offer. But clearly new ground was being established, if not within the sphere of health itself, then in the more conceptually interesting 'third space' at the intersection of different disciplines and practices (Muller, Froggett & Bennett 2020).

The irony in the optimistic but double-edged adoption of the RCT is that the notoriously rigorous exclusion criteria and 'inclusion biases' of such rule-bound studies (justified in clinical trials by the need to subject variables to scientific control) render them 'of limited applicability' (Rose 2019: 123; Greenhalgh 1997: 244). Not only do few of those who are the imagined beneficiaries of a given procedure meet all the various criteria for selection in such studies, but the mental health sector faces an even greater challenge of engagement insofar as it has no contact with *most* of the people it estimates to be in need of clinical support (a recent study across ten English-speaking countries determined that over 50 per cent of those with 'clinical level mental health risks' do not seek help; the World Health Organization estimates that up to 80 per cent of those with mental health needs may not seek help, the figure being far higher in disadvantaged populations).[1]

By virtue of the freedom to operate outside the tight bounds of 'evidence-based medicine', by engaging with feelings, affects and emotions rather than clinical diagnosis, the arts may connect directly with people, tapping into a broader range of lived experiences. In so doing, the arts generate rich experiential engagements which not only contribute to a knowledge base but open up an area of therapeutic action, which (as the chapters of Part I establish) extends into an area of embodied practice, untapped by cognitive behaviour therapies. In this respect the arts are a natural resource for activists and survivors, for those ill-served or marginalized by institutionalized practice, or disinclined to 'seek help' – but potentially also for a health field that acknowledges very limited reach across the populations it seeks to engage.

'Art therapies work. What is needed is a subtle, rigorous, interdisciplinary understanding of why they work', writes Siri Hustvedt in Chapter 2. But how and where do we create space to do this concerted interdisciplinary work, evolving not only new practice but new methods of evaluation and forms of collaboration? With this goal in mind, The Big Anxiety began in Sydney, Australia, in 2017 as a festival – a place for developing experimental arts projects in the public domain – for inviting public use, testing and adaptation.

This 'place' was envisaged in the gap between art and mental health, though not simply as the joining of two entities, 'Arts & Health' (a designation which does not in itself capture the hybrid practice emerging from integration).

The deliberately amorphous concept of The Big Anxiety makes room for what arises in experience and in the world, for anxieties at large as well as those defined through clinical practice, and for envisaging mental health in a nexus of psychosocial relations. As an attempt to curate a 'third space' at the intersection of arts and science, the festival asks not only what disciplines have to say to one another but how collaborative practices might evolve in relation to communities of lived experience. To reflect this working principle, the event was initially tag-lined, 'festival of arts + science + people', flipping to people + art + science, when it emerged that an inverse hierarchy was in play – not just conceptually but in the methods of art projects in which lived experience was a foundation, art a means to communication and the psy-sciences a point of reference and dialogue, rather than a source of classification. The chapters that follow each exemplify this mode of bottom-up thinking in practice.

The turn to experience, foreshadowed in its radical philosophical form in the 1960s by the figures associated with 'anti-psychiatry' (famously, R. D. Laing in the UK, Franco Basaglia in Italy, Félix Guattari in France) and in activism by the service-user movement, has now permeated mainstream mental health, which embraces 'lived experience' in research and service design. 'Person-centred' service provision is an aspirational goal, though frequently flagged as a deficit (see, for example, Productivity Commission 2020) and the practice of 'co-design' is now embedded in much institutional research and practice, with the objective of ensuring that services are designed *with* rather than on behalf of those now called mental health 'service users' or 'consumers'.

Yet if there is a shift at the centre towards inclusion and even collaboration, there is no established *methodological* base for bottom-up or experience-focused research within the mainstream mental health disciplines. The reasons for this – flowing from a structural exclusion of experience – are well established by historians of psychiatry and mental illness. In Michel Foucault's famous passage from *Madness and Civilization*:

> The constitution of madness as a mental illness . . . thrusts into oblivion all those stammered, imperfect words without fixed syntax in which the exchange between madness and reason was made. The language of psychiatry, which is a monologue of reason about madness, has been established only on the basis of such a silence. (Foucault 1967: xii)

Established in this way as a 'highly normative discipline' (Rose 2019: 17), psychiatry has since its inception pathologized those who deviate from social norms, updating diagnostic categories as those norms change.[2] If there is general acknowledgement of its historical wrongs, mainstream psychiatry remains wedded to a medical model of mental disorder, which many argue is ill-founded and the cause of ongoing iatrogenic harm.[3] Clinicians and service users advocating the abandonment of the diagnostic model offer alternatives that emphasize lived experience and trauma narratives in place of individual pathology ('what happened to me, not what's wrong with me') (Johnstone et al. 2018), while critical psychiatry recognizes 'tensions between [psychiatry's] social control functions and patients' best interests' (Middleton & Moncrieff 2019).

These arguments within psychiatry are extensively examined elsewhere (Rose 2019). Here our particular concern is with the means and techniques for amplifying experience, and with understanding the structures that allow experience to be known. As artist-activist Dolly Sen notes, medical archives are filled with observational data of 'inobservable worlds', which require first-hand experiential description from those who live in such worlds.[4] If there is interest in 'outsider art' and even in expanding the archive to make room for experience, its impact within a field bound to a medical 'hierarchy of evidence' (Greenhalgh 1997) is often circumscribed. In a recent discussion in *Psychology Today* (Pierre 2020), a psychiatrist equates critical psychiatry or 'anti-psychiatry sentiment' with the anti-vaccination movement. Both are 'opposed to medical interventions that they see as ineffective and harmful', he reasons, and 'both rely primarily on the subjective anecdotal experiences of those that have claimed "harm" and "damage", whereas that harm is, for the most part, not reflected in the clinical experience of physicians, research studies, or in FDA reporting databases' (Pierre 2020). The retreat to the logic of gatekeeping and truth-testing highlights the pervasive difficulty of perceiving the evidence-base on any other terms.

The question is, how does harm meet the threshold of the sensible? Dolly Sen (Chapter 20) writes here of her annihilating experience of psychiatry as a child survivor of rape; the Parragirls project (discussed in Chapter 8) similarly functions to redress the experience of institutional abuse and a lifetime of being disbelieved by authorities; in Chapter 11, poets Evelyn Araluen and Claudia Rankine discuss the widespread disregard of the material evidence of the experience of people of colour; in Chapter 12, Andrea Durbach, Pumla Gobodo-Madikizela and I reflect on the work of truth commissions that explicitly recognize the long-suppressed truth of systemic violence and oppression. In all these instances, the evidence of experience is not only contested but suppressed by instruments of the state – by what Omid Tofighian (Chapter 10) refers to as a *kyriarchal* regime, a system of oppression permeating all areas of social and institutional practice. Creative practice is the resource of resistance; Sen says creativity is 'armour' in a fight against an inhumane system; in Chapter 10, writer Behrouz Boochani says of his experience as an asylum seeker in detention, 'writing is a weapon', a means to present refugees as human; and Elahe Zivardar in the same chapter says her art was both healing and a 'weapon to fight and survive'. These are not poetic metaphors, just facts of survival. As both Rankine and Araluen and Boochani suggest, the political imperative is to make space for the 'evidence' to be seen, heard and perceived; for the evidence to be experienced.

The aesthetic (i.e. sense based) dimensions of the politics of experience are increasingly foregrounded in public discourse; terms such as 'gaslighting' (for the complex procedures by which experience is denied) and 'tone deafness' (for the failure to perceive disruption in the order of the sensible) are now part of the popular lexicon. The force of these descriptions lies in the ascription of affect to the relationship by which power is enacted – rather than simply to harmed individuals.

In his 1961 book *Self and Others*, Laing (1961: 27) wrote that it was 'premature to speak of an already existent systematic method of investigating the field of inter-experience, let alone the phenomenology of such a method', the term 'inter-experience' referring to 'the relation between my experience of you and your experience of me' (1961: 16–17). In this volume such a concept is implicitly activated in the various discussions of empathy and the ways in which experience is met or negated. It is advanced methodologically in the dramatizations, discussed by their creators in Part III (both theatre duo Ridiculismus and my own fEEL Lab colleagues develop productions drawing on therapeutic protocols and lived experience, in relation to psychosis and dementia, respectively). Inter-experience is also the focus of Chapter 19's reflection on 'The Not Knowing of Another' – a work produced by Kate Adams and Project Art Works: a neurodiverse group collaborating with people with complex support needs. Challenging paradigms of inclusion and assimilation, their slow processes of attunement, adaptation and accommodation were for many years marginalized under the banner of community arts, then feted as social practice within the high concept artworld of documenta and the Turner Prize. This shift in artworld interest may also be read as a (re)turn to experience. If the arts have always been a space for articulating complex subjective experience and 'diversity of perception', progressive politics has often resisted practical engagement in the 'less glamourous' work, argues Adams, whose practice addresses the microaggressions and defensive reactions of the social field.[5]

In the foreword to the report of the UK Parliamentary inquiry, 'Creative Health' (APPGAHW 2017), Alan Howarth laments the persistence of a 'chronic and sterile' stand-off between two camps: the proponents of art for art's sake vs. those who promote the practical, community benefits of art. The failure to conceptualize practical aesthetics within the arts – and within institutional practice – is as much a problem as the reduction of art to its instrumental value. The revolution (or redistribution of sensible) that takes place in the museum is of little practical import unless it translates into practice, just as the 'arts on prescription' programmes mentioned in Chapter 21 by Clive Parkinson (a radical thinker and practitioner in the field) are the easy pickings of Arts & Health if there is no deeper investigation of the politics of exclusion (of who is in the building, who perceives its affordances or possibilities for action).

It is at this practical juncture that this volume aims to make inroads. The Big Anxiety does not start with artworks but with the problem, the experience itself, from which derives the practice. It is concerned with the mechanics and design of practice, as well as with its outcomes – whether with the psychosocial design of a facilitating space (Chapters 4, 5 and 8), the use of art as a means to address trauma within communities where the longer-term effects of conflict are manifested (Chapters 4, 5 and 12), with the use and adaptation of creative media 'tools' (Chapters 13 and 16), or with the design of engagement which, as leading US performance artist Lois Weaver shows, may begin with putting out the tables (Chapter 9).

Within psychosocial aesthetics, design is focused on the provision of material and psychological resources as a means to internal and external transformation; as we suggest in Chapter 8, this may be the conscious expansion of our capacity to perceive what psychologist J. J. Gibson (1979: 127) called affordances for action, 'either for good or ill'. It is here in the generation of aesthetic experience that the field of politics (redistribution of the sensible) intersects with therapeutic practice (procedures for psychosocial transformation) – and that a deeper understanding of the 'use' of art emerges (linked by a number of authors to D. W. Winnicott's (1971: 128–39) conceptualization of cultural experience).

The chapters that follow examine this meeting point in various instances of experimental practice across diverse media. As with The Big Anxiety festival from which many of the conversations and artworks arise, they mobilize a creative framework for psychosocial work – whether understood as art, therapy, resistance or some combination of the above – that is in the first instance a presentation of experience, and a means for experience to be perceived and met. This endeavour attends to the ecological niche in which experience materializes; it is necessarily an argument for an expansion beyond disciplines and institutional boundaries.

Rather than limiting inquiry to the role of arts *in health*, we envision mental health as an expanded field and the emergent creative work that might advance it – an inquiry that is grounded in lived experience, rather than defined by the object of mental health. As Bruno Latour (1991) argues, 'Modern' Western knowledge systems (which are strong on specialization, weak on interconnection) are characterized by a disciplinary purism according to which disciplines own their own objects. Mental health, which might be understood as a complex cultural amalgam, is thereby defined through the disciplinary lens of psychiatry around its traditional object of the unhealthy mind or mental pathology. Social, environmental and cultural practices may be understood as factors affecting mental health and well-being – but the nature of mental health itself (and the way that it is measured) is internally secured.

The alternative might be a system in which 'mental health' is understood as an evolving object at the centre of a nexus of practices, including but not limited to psychology, psychiatry and mental health science. Collaboration would span incommensurable paradigms that contest the very nature of the object; health research would encompass rich concepts of well-being and models for integrating knowledges and practices, beyond the medical model. Such frameworks are not only the logical extension of the recommendations of government reports (from the UK's Creative Health (APPGAHW 2017) to the Australian Productivity Commission's (2020) call for more people-centred services) but the basis for (inter)cultural engagement, particularly in the context of legacies of violence. In Australia, First Nations concepts of mental health and well-being are predicated on an attunement to Country. In English, the word 'country' is limited to a concept of physical place – a nation state or a non-urban environment. It carries none of the ontological meaning to which Marianne Wobcke alludes in Chapter 5, where she explains that being 'on Country' for First Nations peoples evokes a sense of belonging to place, culture and community that is the working definition of well-being. Within this lifeworld, as the Uti Kulintjaku (Chapter 15) collective affirm, art is embedded, integral to mental health, indivisible from the whole.

The connection of art and health is, in this model, axiomatic – not a hypothesis to be proven. The question of how we might 'measure' an art intervention arguably makes little sense if this entails isolating variables and mechanisms to determine the causal chain of what acts upon what to achieve which outcome. As Hustvedt (Chapter 2) points out, these mechanistic metaphors are not fit for purpose in the study of a human emotional ecology.

From a cultural perspective we might ask the 'aesthetic' questions: How do we look, see, listen, hear, attune, perceive? How do we experience? Psychoanalyst Noreen Giffney and psychosocial researcher Lynn Froggett (Chapter 4) address the challenge of cultivating the capacity for experience itself, discussing the potential for using cultural objects. Turning to the psychoanalyst Wilfred Bion, they ask how we might have an experience so that we can 'take it in, metabolize it, make meaning of it'.

In psychoanalytic terms this is not a trivial question. *Being in* an experience is not available to all. In a given setting, social exclusions, and what we call 'psychosocial affordances' (Chapter 8) are always already in play 'for better or worse'. An encounter may give rise to an internal feeling of emptiness, boredom, disappointment or inadequacy. But in a facilitating environment, anxieties can be held and metabolized; a given artwork or participatory experience may then be taken up or taken in.

For this reason, we start with the blocks to experience: with trauma and with hopelessness; with the immediate practical challenge of how one moves forward from the 'edge of the present' (Chapter 3), how one enters a space when conditioned to anticipate exclusion. This is not the macro-politics of revolution but the micro work of resistance and repair that makes change, step by step. Thus psychologist Sophie Burgess (Chapter 16) works through a creative process from a position of 'not experiencing', failing to 'potentiate'; and artist Anita Glesta (Chapter 14) works from an experience of the 'unthought known', tracking in painting an unfolding medical event of which she is not yet conscious. Amanda McDowell (Chapter 18) articulates a similar process of disconnection and discomfort, mobilizing listening and 'earwork'. Thembi Soddell (Chapter 17) explores the phenomenology of acousmatic sound as a means to the intersubjective communication of trauma; and Lydia Gitau (Chapter 13) considers how creative media resources might support her work with trauma survivors in the context of refugee camps and resettlement programmes.

Trauma is 'untransformable truth' as Adam Phillips (2019: 26) reminds us – and in this framework 'any handed down knowledge, is always potentially a dead end'. It is this that makes creativity the necessary solution. As Marianne Wobcke (Chapter 5) reports, there is no recourse to expert outside advice against a backdrop of intergenerational trauma and colonial violence – no authority can be trusted, nothing taken in. Creativity is the ground zero of change since it begins from the proposition that the only way beyond trauma is the restoration of agency, the capacity to create one's own meaning. Almost before art is concerned with expressing experience it is concerned with opening up possibilities for action (these two functions are theorized through the practice discussed in Chapter 8).

This volume interweaves theories of experience but is in essence an exercise in applied thinking, deriving ideas from their use in practice. Its writers come not from an established field with shared protocols or theoretical base but from different areas of practice in a field which is emergent. In the spirit of the 'Thinking in the World' series, they are each engaged in some way in ground-up, experience-oriented creative thinking and practice.

Unlike after-the-fact theoretical commentary on art, the chapters are *formative* reflections from within an unfolding inquiry, which in most cases has produced finished works but is nevertheless 'reflection in action' as Donald Schon (1983) puts it – practice that is carried forward, so that the thinking in the book may be further tested in practice, in artworks that will emerge alongside the chapters (and that can be accessed by readers online or in exhibitions).

The book, like the art within, is intended to be of 'use'. Rather than offering definitive 'readings' of works, it is about working through difficulties with art and artfulness –whether this be in the making or viewing of a film, performance or virtual reality (VR) experience, the reflective act of painting, or simply finding a means to communicate (Behrouz Boochani writing in detention, sending each line of a book by SMS to a receptive translator as discussed in Chapter 10), or the act of taking something in – of going from the emptiness of trauma and depression to sensing, feeling and connecting.

This is what is at stake when in mental health settings we talk of care that is 'trauma informed'. The term signifies a corrective step, less dependent on being 'informed' in fact than on sensing and recognition, on a set of capacities, and a responsive system attuned to lived experience. Such an approach to care will embed new aesthetic practices; it will design with awareness of psychosocial affordances, expanding perception and opportunities for action; it will listen and hear the 'unobservable', and actively design away the barriers to connection. Art is a means to do all this.

*   *   *

A note on the artworks associated with the book

One of the distinctive features of the volume (and of The Big Anxiety festival) is its focus on immersive media, as well as on traditional art forms. The experimental use of VR and immersive installation arises directly from the various authors' interest in investigating and communicating embodied experience – and in examining the ways in which immersive experience can have a powerful effect on the way we feel. Readers will find visual/media resources relating to such works on The Big Anxiety website (thebiganxiety .org) – including links to video material.

Lydia Gitau (Chapter 13) and Sophie Burgess (Chapter 16) discuss the applications of a particular VR programme, EmbodiMap, created in our felt Experience and Empathy Lab (fEEL). Those with an Oculus Quest VR headset may download EmbodiMap from the Oculus app store.

Clive Parkinson's reflections as an academic in one of the UK's leading Arts & Health programmes have taken the form of a series of performance lectures ('part rant, part tone poem'), combining lived experience narratives with polemic, performed live with a synchronized video backdrop (such as dis/ordered, commissioned for The Big Anxiety, 2017). In this spirit, he has conceived Chapter 21 with a video accompaniment, also available on the website.

Notes

1 The main reason cited being a lack of confidence in mental health treatments (United States and United Kingdom) and preference for self-help (ten countries) (Newson et al. 2021).

2 The American Psychiatric Association removed the diagnosis of 'homosexuality' from their Diagnostic and Statistical Manual (DSM) in 1973, and apologized in 2021 for the use of racialized theories to confirm the deficit status of people of colour; in 2019 the World Health Organization voted to no longer classify 'gender nonconformity' as a mental disorder in its International Statistical Classification of Diseases (ICD), acknowledging the iatrogenic harm that results from pathologizing gender identity within a disease model (Papenfuss 2019).

3 Lithuanian psychiatrist Dainius Puras, in his role as United Nations Special Rapporteur, argued: 'there is now unequivocal evidence of the failures of a system that relies too heavily on the biomedical model of mental health', calling for 'a shift in investments in mental health, from focusing on "chemical imbalances" to focusing on "power imbalances and inequalities"' (United Nations 2017).

4 See press release for Sen's 'Birdsong from inobservable worlds': https://
   weareunlimited.org.uk/commission/dolly-sen-birdsong-from-inobservable
   -worlds/ (accessed 26 September 2021).

5 See Kate Adams' video within The Big Anxiety's web-based Course of Empathy
   app (2019). Available online: courseofempathy.org (accessed 26 September
   2021).

References

All-Party Parliamentary Group on Arts, Health and Wellbeing (2017), 'Creative
   Health: The Arts for Health and Wellbeing', Inquiry Report 2nd edition.
   Available online at: https://www.culturehealthandwellbeing.org.uk/appg
   -inquiry/Publications/Creative_Health_Inquiry_Report_2017_-_Second_Edition
   .pdf (accessed 26 September 2021).
Bollas, C. (1992), *Being a Character: Psychoanalysis and Self-experience*, New
   York: Hill & Wang.
Bollas, C. (1995), *Cracking up: The Work of Unconscious Experience*, London:
   Routledge.
Foucault, M. (1967), *Madness and Civilization: A History of Insanity in the age of
   Reason*, London: Routledge.
Gibson, J.J. (1979), *The Ecological Approach to Visual Perception*, Boston:
   Houghton Mifflin.
Greenhalgh, T. (1997), 'How to Read a Paper. Getting Your Bearings (deciding
   What the Paper is About)', *BMJ (Clinical Research Ed.)*, 315 (7102): 243–6.
Johnstone, L. and M. Boyle with J. Cromby, J. Dillon, D. Harper, P. Kinderman,
   E. Longden, D. Pilgrim and J. Read (2018), *The Power Threat Meaning
   Framework: Towards the Identification of Patterns in Emotional Distress,
   Unusual Experiences and Troubled or Troubling Behaviour, as an Alternative to
   Functional Psychiatric Diagnosis*, Leicester: British Psychological Society.
Laing, R.D. (1961), *Self and Others*, London: Tavistock.
Laing, R.D. (1967), *The Politics of Experience*, Middlesex: Penguin.
Latour, B. (1991), *We Have Never Been Modern*, Cambridge, MA: Harvard
   University Press.
Middleton, H. and J. Moncrief (2019), 'Critical Psychiatry: A Brief Overview',
   BJPsych Advances, 25 (1): 47–54.
Muller, L., L. Froggett, and J. Bennett, (2020), 'Emergent Knowledge in the Third
   Space of Art-Science', *Leonardo*, 53 (3): 321–6.
Newson, J., V. Pastukh, J. Taylor and T. Thiagarajan (2021), *Mental Health has
   Bigger Challenges Than Stigma: Mental Health Million Project 2021*, Sapien
   Labs. Available online: https://mentalstateoftheworld.report/wp-content/uploads
   /2021/05/Rapid-Report-2021-Help-Seeking.pdf (accessed 26 September 2021).
Papenfuss, M. (2019), 'World Health Organization Removes Gender
   Nonconformity From List Of Mental Disorders', *Huffington Post*, 31 March
   2019. Available online: https://www.huffpost.com/entry/transgender-right-world
   -health-organization-no-longer-mental-disorder_n_5cf0ade0e4b0e346ce7bbd93
   (accessed 26 September 2021).

Phillips, A. (2019), *Attention Seeking*, London: Penguin.

Pierre, J. (2020), 'Taking a Critical Look at Critical Psychiatry', *Psychology Today*, 02 October 2020. Available online: https://www.psychologytoday.com/au/ blog/psych-unseen/202010/taking-critical-look-critical-psychiatry (accessed 26 September 2021).

Productivity Commission (2020), *Mental Health*, Report no. 95, Canberra: Australian Government.

Rancière, J. (2004), *The Politics of Aesthetics: The Distribution of the Sensible*, translated by Gabriel Rockhill, London: Continuum.

Rose, N. (2019), *Our Psychiatric Future: The Politics of Mental Health*, Cambridge: Polity.

Schon, D. (1983), *The Reflective Practitioner: How Professionals Think in Action*, New York: Basic Books.

United Nations (2017), 'World Needs "revolution" in Mental Health Care – UN Rights Expert', *Press Release*. Available online: https://www.ohchr.org/EN/ NewsEvents/Pages/DisplayNews.aspx?NewsID=21689 (accessed 26 September 2021).

Winnicott, D.W. ([1971] 1991), *Playing and Reality*, London and New York: Routledge.

Part I

Suicide, felt experience and what works

CHAPTER 2

Why do art therapies work?

Siri Hustvedt with Jill Bennett

Siri Hustvedt's writing offers insight into a number of philosophical concerns underpinning the conceptualization of the therapeutic benefits of arts and the means by which these are achieved. In this piece, she elaborates on her work on mechanisms, the limits of cognitive-behavioural models of mental health and the meaning of suicidality.

Jill: Interest in the psychosocial benefits of creative writing, and of arts engagement more generally, has led researchers to look for 'mechanisms' that may lead to positive change.

What is the problem with mechanistic thinking?

Siri: The word 'mechanism' is ubiquitous in biology and psychology. Its continual appearance in neuroscience papers sent me back to its origins in seventeenth-century philosophy – Descartes, Hobbes, Newton and others. In the early modern period, nature became a great machine of inert matter that functioned according to causal laws that could be described mathematically. Every natural machine (including the human body) was reducible to its component parts, and a close analysis of each part would bring an understanding of the whole. Criticism of mechanistic thought has been part of science ever since. Among the notable voices are Margaret Cavendish (1623–73), Gottfried Leibniz (1646–1716), Giambattista Vico (1668–1744), eighteenth-century defenders of vitalism (Montpellier group), Goethe (1749–1832), Alfred North Whitehead (1861–1937) and the twentieth-century biologists C. H. Waddington, J. B. S. Haldane and Barbara McClintock. Some contemporary criticisms of mechanism turn on emergence theories. What if the whole is more than its parts? What if some processes emerge from other processes and once they have emerged go on to exercise further influence on those processes? Complexity theory challenges mechanistic models by asserting that complex adaptive systems emerge through self-organization, are nonlinear, and thrive at the edge of chaos (Mazzochi 2008).

In psychology, calling on 'mechanisms' may simply reveal a desire for the precision and cultural value of the 'hard' sciences. Neither biology nor psychology has laws, only regularities, a fact that has compromised attempts to give either discipline the certainties of chemistry and physics. Stephen Jay Gould called this longing in biology 'physics envy'. Although Gould's wit turns on Freud's penis envy, he does not mention that Freud, who hoped to root psychology in biophysics, had physics envy too. He imported *mechanism* into psychology, most famously *Abwehrmechanismus* – defence mechanism.

In the *Encyclopedia of Personality and Individual Differences*, Ulrich Koch and Kelso Cratsley (2020) write: 'In the most inclusive sense psychological mechanisms offer causal explanation of mental states and behavior, often with reference to underlying systems, activities, or entities. . . . However, the concept has been deployed in dramatically different ways with very different meanings depending on the school or particular tradition of psychology.'

Mechanistic models have been successful at isolating and identifying biological processes, which explains their endurance. Francis Crick's central dogma in genetics (often reduced to DNA to RNA to protein) is an example of a triumphant mechanistic model. A number of contemporary scientists, however, believe the model's linear neatness belies the complexity of the molecular processes involved (Woese 2004; Koonin 2012; Camacho 2019). A scientific model's success suggests only that something has been uncovered by using it, not that it is an accurate depiction of what is actually happening in nature. Mechanistic models explain how the larger machine works through the movements and interactions of its parts, but biological processes do not always follow a clear sequence and may be stochastic (randomly determined).

In psychology studies of art therapies, the use of the word 'mechanism' gives a 'scientific' gloss to the research, but the term is rarely defined, and its use may actually impede developing interdisciplinary approaches that might uncover why art has therapeutic value.

Jill: Applications of the mechanistic model in the arts and health field are often striking for their failure to account for the specificities of an aesthetic process or practice. You make this case in 'The writing self and the psychiatric patient' (Hustvedt 2016a), in which you discuss a paper (Baikie and Wilhelm 2005) that proposes four 'mechanisms' to explain the beneficial effects of expressive writing. Since that time, the search for causal mechanisms has gathered momentum, especially in the field of music and health. A recent UK study (Perkins, Yorke & Fancourt 2018) identifies multiple 'clusters of mechanisms' (the term 'mechanism' ascribed loosely to effects or benefits identified by the respondents) but offers little precision. While it validates 'participation in singing' as a generic activity, there is no consideration of the salience of the content, form or aesthetic qualities of what is created or performed.

My concern is that such an approach instrumentalizes arts participation without elaboration of the means by which a creative process may support growth or 'repair'. You refer to a writer in one of your classes feeling 'alive' after a writing exercise. In Chapter 8 of this volume we discuss a film project that a participant describes as having 'given me back my reality' (she had been subjected to ongoing abuse in a child welfare institution, the reality of which had been denied by perpetrators and institutional authorities). The experience for her was one of 'being believed'. While this outcome relies upon a well-supported, extended engagement, it is the effect of creating a film that encapsulated (the feeling of) what happened, crafted to achieve stated communicative goals ('to explain what happened to us to our children'; to take control of the story and how it is told; to ensure that this never happens again; to hold social services accountable).

The process, it seems to me, entailed finding a form to achieve not only these goals but the fusion of felt and narrated experience (of 'the narrating I and the experiencing Me', as you put it (Hustvedt 2016b: 375)) in a manner that is not possible through the other, sometimes available, channels of legal testimony or media reporting. We might also observe that the processing of emotion or distress in a creative collaboration is clearly not an individual reaction, precipitated by a discrete mechanism. It is the outcome of a relational process in which expression is enabled, elaborated, received and 'held' within a containing space (in which one may come to experience 'being believed'). Distress is thereby potentially co-regulated in a collaborative process, which sets itself the task of creating a scaffold for narrating experience. The process of fashioning an expressive form and giving shape to a narrative (in this case through collaborative storytelling, performing, recording, scripting, text/film editing and so forth) itself enabled a titration process, through which the recounting of trauma and felt experience could be modulated and directed to an extent that is not possible when one gives testimony in formal contexts.

The evaluation of the reparative dimension of such a creative process might, then, trace the transformation of felt experience into expressive form throughout a particular work's coming into being. But this implies a phenomenological aesthetics rather than a mechanistic model. By what methods or with what approaches do you think we can advance insight into a creative process and its psychosocial outcomes with sufficient subtlety and precision?

Siri: The qualitative study you cite on postnatal depression (Perkins, Yorke & Fancourt 2018) compared two groups of women and their babies, both under supervision; one sang together, the other played together. They concluded the singing group did better. After 'an inductive thematic analysis of participants' transcripts', the authors identify four 'overarching themes' which then mysteriously become 'mechanisms': psycho-emotional, activity, social and environmental (Perkins, Yorke & Fancourt 2018). The following comment falls under psycho-emotional: 'Everything is for the baby. You go to a class and it's always for the baby. . . . This [singing] is good for the baby but at the same time it's something for us as well' (Perkins, Yorke & Fancourt 2018). Is this a causal mechanism? Doesn't this woman also address a *social* bias in her *environment*: new mothers are often regarded as props for their children's development (in ways fathers are not) and expected to fulfil a fantasy of maternal sacrifice and self-abnegation? Falling short of this ideal risks moral condemnation not only from others but also from the self that has internalized the fantasy, which then contributes to depression. Isn't the psycho-emotional also social and environmental?

The reputed emotional benefits of choral singing have produced a host of papers on the subject, including those that have measured cortisol, a stress hormone, and oxytocin, a hormone linked to labour, nursing and social bonding in the participants (Schladt et al. 2017). However, there is no one-to-one correspondence between the subjective experience of 'feeling anxious' and cortisol concentrations (O'Brien, Tronick & Moore 2013; Linz, Singer & Egbert 2018; Vlenterie et al. 2021) or between 'feeling good' and oxytocin (Guzman et al. 2013; Olivera-Pasilio & Dabrowska 2020). Reduction from first-person reports to biological 'mechanisms' is at best riddled.

I do not think investigating connections between subjective reports and biological processes is futile. The interdisciplinary field of psychoneuroimmunology links social-psychic factors such as 'lack of social support' to nervous, endocrine and immune functions to demonstrate how stress can result in chronic inflammation and increased vulnerability to disease. Understanding the effectiveness of art therapies requires investigative tools from several disciplines.

The problems you identify are ones of omission:

(1) Lack of attention to the salience of artistic content;

(2) Ignoring the particular (as opposed to the generic) form of the art in question;

(3) Forgetting dynamic processes that occur during a project, a temporal movement that can be represented as a narrative;

(4) Failure to adequately treat the intersubjective or relational (as opposed to purely subjective) qualities of collaborative, therapeutic art-making.

A general suspicion that subjective qualities (lived experience, Husserl's *Erlebnis*) pollute scientific objectivity has led to the avoidance of personal and interpersonal meaning. In neurology, for example, anosognosia – the failure to recognize illness or deficit – has been widely studied. A neurological patient may refuse to acknowledge that his arm is paralysed and may even attribute it to someone else; and yet, a patient's *particular* explanation for the immobile limb – it's my pet rock, it's the arm of my dead brother and so on – has been largely ignored in the field with significant exceptions (Sacks 1985; Solms & Kaplan-Solms 2000; Feinberg 2001). When a physician ignores a patient's story, he treats her as a biomedical object, a collection of mechanisms, rather than an embodied subject with a history.

Every story represents time and creates meaning by linking events in a causal chain. Time – invisible, intangible, mysterious – is often conceived spatially. In contemporary Western cultures, the timeline moves from left to right according to the conventions of reading (in Arabic, the direction is reversed). The past is also understood as *behind* a body not *in front* of it. Because every story is dialogical, part of intersubjective linguistic reality, told to and for another (even when the teller and the listener are incorporated in the same person) it is inherently social. When an 'I' addresses a 'you', the alienation in the symbols of language allows the speakers to leave the present and move into the past or imagined future. The narrating 'I' takes 'control of the story' because the speaker-writer has a requisite distance from represented experience and integrates memory fragments into a cohesive whole.

Traumatic experience has no reflective distance: it is always immediate. The events have no narrating 'I', no agent, and cannot be situated in an autobiographical past with a particular time and place. Pierre Janet, the French philosopher and neurologist, described this lack in traumatized people in *Psychological Healing* ([1919] 1925): 'a person is unable to make the recital which we call narrative memory, and yet he remains confronted by a difficult situation.' Trauma returns in a speechless present as an involuntary symptom (Van der Kolk 2000). The flashback, a motor-sensory-affective and sometimes visual eruption, is the most dramatic example of a somatic volcano.

Although Maurice Merleau-Ponty did not write about trauma, his idea of 'vertical time' in *The Visible and the Invisible* (1968) and its link to what he called wild being (*être sauvage*) is a useful concept. Traumatic memory takes place in vertical time, a prelinguistic, pre-literate, pre-personal, preconceptual, pre-reflective mammalian reality (Hustvedt 2016d). Healing from this kind of memory requires leaving the vertical and assigning it to a place on the symbolic horizontal timeline, or 'putting it behind you'. This trick is not achieved through conscious decision, but by working through an unspeakable reality with at least one other person to create a translation of it into a representative, meaningful, external *form* – words, gestures or objects. Art necessarily enacts this translation because it is, as philosopher Susanne Langer (1953) argued, a form 'symbolic of human feeling'.

Parragirls Past, Present, a film made by and about women who were subject to brutal abuse at Parramatta Girls Home in Australia as teenagers, creates a projected, virtual space from the architecture of the now shut-down institution, a space at once *like* the actual buildings and *unlike* them because it is rendered with point-cloud digital effects (see Chapter 8). The women narrate their memories and reflect on their pasts, but do not appear. Through the medium of immersive images, the film constructs a memory architecture like the mental buildings used in the ancient mnemonic techniques of artificial memory, during which a person takes an imaginary walk inside a building marked by powerful emotional imagery (Yates 1966), but in this case, the remembering is collective: a 'for us' artform, into which once secret stories are articulated, deposited, contained and assigned to the autobiographical past.

As far as I know, artificial memory was not consciously evoked, but the filmmakers took narrative possession of traumatic experiences by lodging them in virtual spaces that echo the loci of explicit memory. Notably the film's title includes the words 'past' and 'present'. As the film opens, the viewer is taken on a virtual walk down a driveway towards the institutional buildings. It is night. Animal sounds mingle with musical tones. A woman speaks: 'They won by putting me in here, but they didn't beat me, okay. They were the winners. They got to shut the door, but I am standing here, and it hasn't beat me.' I am here. I am speaking. They tried to destroy me as a person with a will of my own, but they did not succeed.

Jill: The concept of triggering has entered popular discourse. Is this too a problematic effect of mechanistic thinking? The term has been generalized beyond its application to PTSD flashbacks (see Chapter 8) to encompass possible upset as a result of being exposed to sensitive or potentially distressing material; hence, 'trigger warnings' are deployed to pre-empt distress. But the processing of trauma/distress implies a controlled, supported process of 'triggering' or of exposure rather than avoidance. Literature or film may be a useful prompt in this regard – and writing a way of working through a 'triggering' situation.

Siri: As a person who experienced flashbacks in my sleep for four days in a row after a car accident and a fifth time years later (also in my sleep), I am keenly aware of the gulf between those shocking motor-sensory explosions and the distress I have experienced under other circumstances when I retained the ability to reflect on myself and the situation I was in.

While words, images, sounds and sensations may 'trigger' distress, exporting the language of PTSD to the classroom drains it of clinical meaning. Many people who have undergone bad experiences, including the cruelties of racism, sexism, xenophobia and class bias, do not develop PTSD. The acronym is a new twist on an affliction that has been described from ancient texts onward, often in war contexts, and overlaps with hysteria – soldier's heart, shellshock, war neurosis, conversion disorder and functional neurological disorders (Hustvedt 2009).

Jill: You are critical of the rational foundations of Cognitive Behaviour Therapy (CBT) and of the reduction of suicide to a behaviour that results from maladaptive thinking ('The faith that an application of reason can neaten up disordered minds assumes that once a person is confronted with "true" mental representations rather than "false" ones, he will see the error of his ways and conform to "reality"' (Hustvedt 2016c)).

Neuropsychologist Allan Schore and others have inferred that suicide is not in fact irrational but an exercise of pure rationality without affect or emotion (in Schore's (2019) formulation this is an effect of 'right brain shut down'). There is further support for such a view of suicide as rational in research into overgeneral memory or OGM (for example, in the work of Emily Holmes and colleagues (see Chapter 3), which indicates that severe depression is characterized by an inability to attach affect/feeling/emotion to memory – and hence to an imagined future. Writing or creative practice is surely a potential means of reattaching feeling to events in autographical memory or future thinking?

Siri: CBT inherited the mind/body Cartesian dualism of first-generation cognitive science, which conceived of the mind as symbolic computational software to the body's hardware. Its founders (Ellis, Beck) offer a diluted version of Stoicism: it isn't events that cause suffering but one's attitude towards events. If you straighten out your false, irrational, out-of-step with reality thoughts, you conquer bad feelings. Does a person who has witnessed human slaughter need to realign her thoughts to reality? Isn't reality the problem? The ascendance of CBT in late capitalist culture is hardly surprising. Its focus is on the *individual* who masters his *conscious thoughts*, which in turn control his body and its messy feelings. Although people may improve with CBT, the benefit does not arrive for the reasons its champions claim. Every therapeutic alliance is potentially healing, but the dynamics at work are not about replacing unreasonable thoughts with reasonable ones. Art therapies can be broadly understood through the intercorporeal-intersubjective dynamics at work in everything from shamanic rituals, to hypnotic suggestion, to the transference of psychoanalysis, to placebo effects.

The neuroscientist Fabrizio Benedetti (2011) argues that the multiple physiological effects of placebo are 'made of words, rituals, symbols, and meanings', which crucially includes the relation *between* doctor and patient. A performance, visual artwork or text can occupy the intermediate space between two or more persons as a repository for demons – uncontrollable images and feelings (Charles 1953). In an essay on psychiatric patients and therapeutic writing, I call the 'I' on the page the *alien familiar* (Hustvedt 2016a). Once disembodied in a text, the 'I' is externalized as a visible, material vehicle for communication. This notion can be extended to all symbolic objects that move from internal tumult to external articulation in a dialogical context.

A case study in *The Arts and Psychotherapy* is exemplary (Walker et al. 2016). A military service member, 'Fillmore', diagnosed with PTSD, a mild TBI and depression with psychotic features worked with his art therapist to make a mask of BFIB: 'bloody face in the bunker', his recurring hallucinatory flashback. After finishing the mask, the therapist offered the soldier an oval container for BFIB, which he painted inside and covered with words from newspaper articles on the outside. The therapist then encouraged Fillmore to put BFIB on a shelf in the medical centre 'to make my brain let BFIB go' (Walker et al. 2016). Over time the disturbing hallucination disappeared. Fillmore's therapeutic narrative – creating an object for an internal image, encasing it in a symbolic coffin and letting it rest in peace – carries strong elements of ritual exorcism. Notably, his brain scans showed increased activity in Broca's area, associated with language production.

Jill: As you have written, 'the reasons for suicide are not always mad. In some cases the future has vanished' (Hustvedt 2016b: 372). This is clear in the writing of Holocaust survivors – and of those held in conditions where future possibilities are foreclosed. The longer-term transgenerational impacts of such traumatic deprivation are less well understood. For example, in Aboriginal communities in Australia, youth suicide is alarmingly common and subject to contagion, extending to children as young as nine or ten. Genograms demonstrate that instances of child suicide in remote communities today may be traced back to colonial massacres in the same communities (Atkinson 2002). Such a situation suggests that an increased level of hopelessness is not a function of faulty logic but of the historical conditions that have shaped life in communities.

Hopelessness is one of the measurables addressed by CBT, which as you have suggested offers a training in practical skills/techniques but generally 'fails to grasp the totality of what has gone awry in human beings who are suffering' (Hustvedt 2016b: 375). At a time of global reckoning, in which the effects of systemic racism and sexual violence are emerging into the wider public consciousness through movements like BLM and #MeToo, we surely need to find ways to 'grasp the totality of what has gone awry', precisely in terms of understanding *both the institutional and the lived psychosocial effects* of historic injustice. It is no surprise that neoliberal models of mental health are inadequate to the task of addressing cumulative trauma. The arts have always worked in this void.

Siri: My research into suicide made it clear to me that the automatic link between suicide and mental illness needed to be questioned. The act can be both rational and an assertion of agency in the face of attempts to annihilate it (suicides during or after experiences in the Nazi death camps). I am convinced suicide is dependent on reflective self-consciousness, the ability to represent the self as an *other* to the self, which means it cannot occur in children under four. The youngest documented suicide I found was age seven.

Although I admire Allan Schore's interdisciplinary work, I am cautious about attributing anything to 'right brain shut down' (the right/left brain division is primitive at best), nor would I jump onto suicide as the result of no, rather than too much, affect. Suicide is a diverse phenomenon with multiple causes and cultural variations. Overgeneral memory in depressed and traumatized people appears to be an unconscious strategy to blunt potential affect from specific autobiographical memories, a form of repression. Intrusive imagery, motor-sensory re-enactments and anxiety – all of which are highly emotional – may coexist with OGM.

Biological, psychological and sociological are convenient as categories, but they are not divisible, nor are 'nature and nurture'. The fact that depressive illness occurs far more often in women than in men is frequently viewed as genetic and/or hormonal, as if these biological processes are static and not subject to continual homeostatic adjustment in relation to external and internal stimuli. Feeling depressed in response to sexism and misogyny is not crazy (Bluhm 2011). A recent study connected the experience of racism to gene expression (Thames et al. 2019). The neoliberal approach to all illness eliminates or downplays intersubjective cultural and environmental factors and pays little or no attention to the historical narratives that affect whole groups of people that have been oppressed and marginalized. Illness is viewed as the malfunctioning of an isolated, genetically determined machine body or a chemically 'unbalanced' brain in need of pharmacological balancing. The genome is not a 'code' or 'blueprint' for traits or disease (Dupré 2015; Boyce, Sololowski & Robinson 2020). Gene expression is dependent on myriad environmental variables, from inhaling toxins to the stress of poverty and, while drugs can be helpful in psychiatric treatment, the popular idea of chemical brain imbalances radically distorts the complex dynamics of human suffering.

I think the paradigm shift to embodied models in cognitive science has created greater openness to therapies that acknowledge the intersubjective reality of human experience and the folly of reducing a person to biological machinery. Narrative medicine has surged in recent decades (Charon 2008). In psychiatry the stark failure of neuroscience to deliver cures for mental illnesses has caused many in the field to rethink what works (Kingdon 2020). Art therapies work. What is needed is a subtle, rigorous, interdisciplinary understanding of why they work.

References

Atkinson, J. (2002), *Trauma Trails, Recreating Song Lines: The Transgenerational Effects of Trauma in Indigenous Australia*, Melbourne: Spinifex Press.

Baikie, K.A. and K. Wilhelm (2005), 'Emotional and Physical Health Benefits of Expressive Writing', *Advances in Psychiatric Treatment*, 11: 338.

Benedetti, F. (2011), 'How Placebos Change the Patient's Brain', *Neuropsychopharmacology*, 36: 339–54.

Bluhm, R. (2011), 'Gender Differences in Depression: Explanations from Feminist Ethics', *The International Journal of Feminist Approaches to Bioethics*, 4: 69–88.

Boyce, T.W., M. Sololowski, and G. Robinson (2020), 'Genes and Environments, Development and Time', *PNAS*, 22: 23235–41.

Camacho, M.P. (2019), 'The Central Dogma is Empirically Inadequate … no Matter how we Slice it', *Philosophy, Theory, and Practice in Biology*, 11: 6.

Charles, L.H. (1953), 'Drama in Shaman Exorcism', *The Journal of American Folklore*, 66: 95–122.

Charon, R. (2008), *Narrative Medicine: Honoring the Stories of Illness*, Oxford: Oxford University Press.

Dupré, J. (2015), 'The Polygenomic Organism', in S. Richardson and H. Stevens (eds), *Post Genomics: Perspectives on Biology After the Genome*, 56–72, Durham: Duke University Press.

Feinberg, T. (2001), *Altered Egos: How the Brain Creates the Self*, Oxford: Oxford University Press.

Guzman, Y.F., N. Tronson, V. Jovasevic, K. Sato, A.L. Guedea, H. Mizukami, K. Nishimori, and J. Radulovic (2013), 'Fear Enhancing Effects of Septal Oxytocin Receptors', *Nature Neuroscience*, 16 (9): 1185–7.

Hustvedt, S. (2009), *The Shaking Woman or A History of My Nerves*, New York: Henry Holt.

Hustvedt, S. (2016a), 'The Writing Self and the Psychiatric Patient', in *A Woman Looking at Men Looking at Women: Essays on Art, Sex, and the Mind*, 96–117, New York: Simon and Schuster.

Hustvedt, S. (2016b), 'Suicide and the Drama of Self-consciousness', in *A Woman Looking at Men Looking at Women: Essays on Art, Sex, and the Mind*, 362–91, New York: Simon and Schuster.

Hustvedt, S. (2016c), 'Subjunctive Flights: Thinking Through the Embodied Reality of Imaginary Worlds', in *A Woman Looking at Men Looking at Women: Essays on Art, Sex, and the Mind*, 434–51, New York: Simon and Schuster.

Hustvedt, S. (2016d), 'Remembering in art: The Horizontal and the Vertical', in *A Woman Looking at Men Looking at Women: Essays on Art, Sex, and the Mind*, 452–72, New York: Simon and Schuster.

Janet, P. ([1919] 1925), *Psychological Healing: A Historical and Clinical Study*, New York: Macmillan.

Kingdon, D. (2020), 'Why Hasn't Neuroscience Delivered for Psychiatry?', *British Journal of Psychiatry*, 44: 107–9.

Koch, U. and K. Cratsley (2020), 'Psychological Mechanisms', in V. Zeigler-Hill and T.K. Shackelford (eds), *Encyclopedia of Personality and Individual Differences*, 55–76, Cham: Springer Verlag, https://doi.org/10.1007/978-3-319-28099-8 _1562-1.

Koonin, V. (2012), 'Does the Central Dogma Still Stand?', *Biology Direct*, 7: 27.

Langer, S. (1953), *Feeling and Form*, New York: Macmillan.

Linz, R., T. Singer, and V. Engert (2018), 'Interactions of Momentary Thought Content and Subjective Stress Predict Cortisol Fluctuations in a Daily Life Experience Sampling Study', *Scientific Reports*, 8: 15462.

Mazzocchi, F. (2008), 'Complexity in Biology. Exceeding the Limits of Reductionism and Determinism Using Complexity Theory', *EMBO Reports*, 9: 10–14.

Merleau-Ponty, M. (1968), *The Visible and the Invisible*, translated by Alphonso Lingis, Evanston: Northwestern University Press.

O'Brien, K.M., E.Z. Tronick, and C.L. Moore (2013), 'Relationship Between Hair Cortisol and Perceived Chronic Stress in a Diverse Sample', *Stress Health*, 29 (4): 337–44.

Olivera-Pasilio, V. and J. Dabrowska (2020), 'Oxytocin Promotes Accurate Fear Discrimination and Adaptive Defense Behaviors', *Frontiers in Neuroscience*, 14: 583878.

Perkins, R., S. Yorke, and D. Fancourt (2018), 'Learning to Facilitate Arts-in-health Programmes: A Case Study of Musicians Facilitating Creative Interventions for Mothers with Symptoms of Postnatal Depression', *International Journal of Music Education*, 6 (4): 644–58.

Sacks, O. (1985), 'The Lost Mariner', in *He Mistook His Wife for a Hat and Other Clinical Tales*, 8–22, London: Summit Books.

Schladt, T.M., G.C. Nordmann, R. Emilius, B.M. Kudielka, T.R. de Jong, and I.D. Neumann (2017), 'Choir Versus Solo Singing: Effects on Mood, and Salivary Oxytocin and Cortisol Concentrations', *Frontiers in Human Neurosciences*, 11: 430.

Schore, A. (2019), *Right Brain Psychotherapy*, New York: W. W. Norton.

Solms, M. and K. Kaplan-Solms (2000), *Clinical Studies in Neuro-psychoanalysis*, London: Karnac.

Thames, A., M.R. Irwin, E. Breen, and S.W. Cole (2019), 'Experienced Discrimination and Racial Differences in Leukocyte Gene Expression', *Psychoneuroendocrinology*, 106: 277–83.

Van der Kolk, B. (2000), 'Posttraumatic Stress Disorder and the Nature of Trauma', *Dialogues in Clinical Neuroscience*, 2: 7–22.

Vlenterie, R., P.M. Geuijen, M.M.H.J. van Gelder, and N. Roeleveld (2021), 'Questionnaires and Salivary Cortisol to Measure Stress and Depression in mid-pregnancy', *Plos One*, 16 (4): e0250459.

Walker, M., G. Kaimal, R. Koffman, and T.J. DeGraba (2016), 'Art Therapy for PTSD and TBI: A Senior Active Duty Military Service Member's Therapeutic Journey', *The Arts in Psychotherapy*, 49: 10–18.

Woese, K. (2004), 'A new Biology for a new Century', *Microbiology and Molecular Biology Reviews*, 68: 173–86.

Yates, F. (1966), *The Art of Memory*, Harmonsworth, Middlesex: Penguin.

CHAPTER 3

Edge of the present

Mixed reality, suicidality and future thinking

Chloe Watfern, Jill Bennett, Stephanie Habak and Katherine Boydell

You enter the *Edge of the Present*. There is a headset on a white table. You put it on. You see a facsimile of the room you're in. The room has two windows, one on each wall. It is dark outside. The walls of the room are white. You notice a door. You open it. In comes light. In comes the most exquisite alpine scene of warm sun and green grass and a mountain on the horizon under clouds. There is wind in the grass. You can feel the breeze on your face. You can hear birds chirping. You can hear the wind. You want to lift your arms in the air, so you do, but you can't see them. You want to lie on your back on the floor – you want to lie in the grass, so you do. You stand up. You want to walk out – walk out there, past the barrier of the four walls, but instead, you close and open the door again. Now you see white snow and pine trees and more mountains in the distance. You close and open the door again. Now you are in a rainforest. You turn around, reach over to the window and slide it open. The walls around you fade away. You think to yourself; I don't know where to walk now or what to open. You think to yourself; I don't know where I am. So, you just stand very still and look around. You feel, I can just be here and absorb what is around me: tangled vines, small window of sky through the canopy, falling snow, green grass. You look again for your

limbs but they're not there. You know it's all pixels, all vertices, all bits
of information. But still, you just want to be there. So, you stay there,
standing, until the room returns to white.[1]

Edge of the Present is a mixed reality environment designed by a creative
team led by artist Alex Davies.[2] Its title comes from a phrase used by one of
the participants in development workshops, a man who had lived through
suicide attempts. He described an experience in which the future cannot
be perceived: the feeling of being at the edge of the present, seeing nothing
beyond, no reason to move forward.

Part of an art-science research collaboration focused on memory and
future thinking, the project was informed by collaborators in cognitive
neuropsychology (Conway, Loveday & Cole 2016) but driven through
creative workshops, in which participants with lived experience reviewed
some of the scientific literature. This included the work of Emily Holmes and
colleagues (2007), looking at the mental imagery of suicide survivors during
crises. Mental imagery has been shown to have a causal role in determining
future behaviour – imagining something not only increases the likelihood of
engaging in what is imagined but also makes it appear more probable (Libby
et al. 2007; Pham & Taylor 1999; Carroll 1978). Holmes and colleagues
(2007) established that all fifteen formerly suicidal people they interviewed
had faced intrusive, repetitive suicide-related mental imagery when at their
most depressed and despairing. The researchers described these often vivid
and sensory images as 'flash-forwards' to suicide and death. For example,
one participant explained, 'I could feel it, that cold, damp feeling [of] being
in a coffin' (2007: 5).

Our ability to move through time, to project ourselves backwards and
forwards around the present moment, is tied to the workings of the same
core brain network, one that is also linked to conceiving the viewpoint
of others (Buckner & Carroll 2006). Conway, Loveday and Cole (2016)
have hypothesized a remembering-imagining system that links episodic
simulations of the recent past and the near future. They describe this as 'a
bell curve (of consciousness) moving through time with the peak of the curve
as "now" or the present moment' (2016: 257). Our ability to remember the
past – both near and distant – and the way that we recall it seems to be
intimately linked to how we imagine our futures.

In cognitive psychology, the term 'autobiographical memory' encompasses
both our memory for specific episodes (episodic memory) and more generic
or schematic knowledge of our lives (Conway & Williams 2008). For those
experiencing suicidality, autobiographical memories can become disjointed
and recollected in an 'overgeneral' way (Slofstra et al. 2017). Overgeneral
memory disrupts a suicidal person's ability to recall positive events in rich
detail, or access emotions tied to those events. In place of memories filled
with specific images and sensations, overgeneral memory tends to substitute
abstract and/or broadly thematic verbal content devoid of affect, and not

linked in meaningful ways to the 'story' of a life (Wilson & Gregory 2017; Slofstra et al. 2017). If memory can be understood as 'a trace of the world, it is as much the trace of a sensing/perceiving body as of the object/event perceived' (Bennett 2019). The way that we reconstruct the sensations of living in a past moment can have a powerful impact on our emotions – on how we feel (Salaman 1971 in Bennett 2019; Slofstra et al. 2017).

In her essay 'Suicide and the Drama of Self Consciousness', Siri Hustvedt (2013: 106) writes that 'an intense conscious feeling state of some kind seems to be necessary to trigger the act of suicide'. She distinguishes between a felt, embodied self (the 'me') and a reflective self-consciousness (the 'I' or knower) – 'a self that remembers its past and anticipates its future' (2013: 107). Hustvedt argues that both these parts of a self will contribute to the experience of suicidality – an unbearable feeling, and an internal argument for the deed; the embodied 'me', and the reflecting 'I'.

Later in her essay, Hustvedt wonders, 'what has happened to the suicidal person's future? The word hopelessness implies the future by definition. And the future, of course, is a pure fiction. We do not know what awaits us; our expectations are made from our stories of the past' (2013: 109). If those stories are traumatic, shameful or otherwise distressing, then it makes sense that we bury them, or at the very least regulate their emotional valence. As Hustvedt writes in Chapter 2 of this book, overgeneral memory can be understood as a form of repression.

Perhaps the rumination and/or dissociation that accompany many forms of mental distress also interfere with the formation of rich memories, insofar as they stop us from being *present* in the world: sensing it, feeling it. Stuck at the edge of the present – the past dull, the future dark – sensation and feeling are immobilized.

How, then, do we find a way to reattach affect and sensation to experience? *Edge of the Present* is an attempt to investigate this question. Conceived as an environment to cultivate future thinking, it began with the immediate goal of inventing the next ten minutes of life (Figure 3.1).

FIGURE 3.1 Edge of the Present, *mixed reality installation, 2019. Photo by Jessica Maurer/Alex Davies, courtesy The Big Anxiety.*

Those who enter *Edge of the Present* are invited to dwell in a place that is hopeful and peaceful, where each small action is met by a big reward. *Edge of the Present* blends the felt environment and the virtual environment in a way that encourages openness, curiosity and exploration, inviting its users to cultivate 'future thinking'– to cultivate the next ten minutes of their lives.

In *Edge of the Present*, engaging in doing – opening a window, a door – leads to beauty and calm. You, the user, are having an immediate effect on the space around you, and it is overwhelmingly positive. You, the user, have agency within this mixed reality. For example, if being high up in the mountains triggers a fear of heights, you can simply open a window or door and be transported to a new landscape (there are seven in total).

Feeling a sense of control over self and environment is a commonly theorized feature of emotional well-being. Albert Bandura (1977, 1997) pioneered work on self-efficacy, broadly construed as an individual's belief in their capacity to do things that exert control over their own motivation, behaviour and environment. A related concept is that of learned helplessness (Maier & Seligman 1976), thought to be linked to clinical depression and other mental health conditions, and characterized by the belief that a situation or circumstance cannot be changed or controlled.

Edge of the Present has been demonstrated to counteract feelings of helplessness and hopelessness (Habak et al. 2021). By linking action and choice with positive affect and vivid sensation, the experience also has the potential to counteract the often intensely felt mental images that 'flash-forwards' to suicide (Holmes et al. 2007).

In their manual for designers and users of virtual reality, Fuchs and colleagues (2011) use words like 'immersion', 'real time' and 'sensorimotor channels' to evoke the sense of presence that is felt by the user. For Rizzo and Bouchard (2019: 6), this presence is the feeling of 'being there' in a virtual environment. People tend to act as if they are in a real place, in real time, engaging in real events through a virtual body representation. This sense of immersion, and the agency that a user feels over their virtual body representation, is described as 'virtual embodiment' (Matamala-Gomez et al. 2019). It has the power to induce changes in *physical* bodies. For example, manipulating a virtual body can help with things like pain relief (Matamala-Gomez et al. 2019). However, these changes are often short-lived, in part because virtual realities tend to only engage through sight, sound and proprioception.

Mixed reality technologies like *Edge of the Present* incorporate touch. In mixed reality, users are placed in the real world, and digital content is fully integrated into their surroundings so that they can interact with both the digital and the physical (Flavián, Ibáñez-Sánchez & Orús 2019: 549). In mixed reality, the agency of the user's embodied self is reinforced through visuomotor correlations (Moura, Barros & Ferreira-Lopes 2021). In other words, mixed reality experiences create the feeling of being able to effect change – physically, visually, digitally – in an environment. In *Edge of the*

Present, the more you interact with the room, the more you open the door and windows, the more enriched the bare space becomes by the outside landscape. You don't want to leave. Exploration, openness and curiosity are rewarded. A future, again, might seem possible.

* * *

Cognitive behavioural therapy (CBT) is currently the gold standard intervention for people experiencing major depressive episodes and/or suicidality. However, it is not without its critics. For example, Hustvedt (2013: 110) argues that CBT is founded on a weak theoretical model, which conceives of the mind-brain as 'an information-processing machine'. From this model, suicidal behaviour is ultimately reduced to a set of erroneous cognitions – an information-processing error, which can be addressed through cognitive strategies or changes to an individual's behaviour. While CBT may be effective, the model on which it is founded fails to consider 'the totality of what has gone awry in human beings who are suffering in one way or another' (2013: 110), or the intense imagery and feeling states that accompany suicide attempts (Holmes et al. 2007). Embodied, *felt* experience is a crucial part of suicidality – both the absence of affect in overgeneral memory, and the compelling 'flash-forwards' imagery of suicide. CBT fails to adequately account for this in its focus on changing thought processes. Is it possible, Hustvedt wonders, to find 'another avenue of self-reflection, one more flexible and open to future possibility' (Hustvedt 2013: 111)?

Edge of the Present doesn't ask people to talk. It doesn't intend to engage through words. Instead, it offers relentlessly pleasant imagery and affect through an experience that doesn't appear like a 'treatment'. We need such rich methods of engagement and communication to reach people. Over 50 per cent of those who attempt suicide don't seek help (Stene-Larsen & Reneflot 2019). Even when people do seek help, it is very difficult to provide interpersonal support or solutions for suicidality. Often there is little on offer for people experiencing suicidality, including in our emergency departments (Riley et al. 2020). The invitation to play with technology can be more inviting and achievable than something that requires a very difficult accounting of painful experience. Imagine, then, a suicide prevention 'intervention' that feels like something you might otherwise do for enjoyment. Imagine if in an emergency room (a context where there is little 'to do' while under observation) you could put on a headset, and by performing small actions, transform your immediate environment.

* * *

In 2019, seventy-nine people who experienced *Edge of the Present* during The Big Anxiety festival completed pre- and post-surveys to 'identify improvements and changes in mood, future thinking, and general well-being' (Habak et al. 2021). Fifty-four of those people (68.4 per cent) had previously sought help from a mental health professional. One of the questionnaires they completed was the Beck Hopelessness Scale, designed to measure a person's degree of despair and their risk of suicide (Beck et al. 1974). It includes twenty statements to which a person can agree or disagree along a continuum including 'all I can see ahead of me is unpleasantness rather than pleasantness', and 'my future seems dark to me'. Perhaps unsurprisingly, because of the relentlessly positive nature of the *Edge of the Present* experience, we found a statistically significant decrease in hopelessness, as well as a statistically significant increase in both positive mood and well-being.

But, as we have already established, suicidality encompasses so much more than a thought process or a mood. And in the same way, understanding the effects of *Edge of the Present* requires going beyond measures like Beck's Hopelessness Scale – whose creator Aaron T. Beck, it should be noted, is one of the founders of CBT. These measures are useful in providing a marker of this intervention's potential effectiveness. But they are not enough. They do not tell us about *what it is like* to experience *Edge of the Present*, and they only go so far in explaining *why* experiencing it might help someone who is suicidal. What does an art experience like this *do*? What we need is a method that registers the production of images, sense impressions and affect: a method attuned to aesthetic experience and the way in which it unfolds.

*   *   *

Breath.
Calm.
Nothingness.
Missing. Missing.
Reaching the centre of a maze.
Pathways.
Being trapped in one's own mind.
Out of body.
Loss of body.
Jumping through the worlds.
Holding on.
Natural beauty.
Pixels.
Almost real.
Not real.
A temporary experience.

These words come from the opening of a 'visual matrix' – a psychosocial evaluation process that invites participants to offer associations in response to their experience of an artwork or image, in this case *Edge of the Present* (Froggett, Manley & Roy 2015). In a visual matrix, a group is seated in a snowflake-shaped pattern, no one looking directly at the face of another. Participants speak into a shared space – the matrix. They are encouraged to enter a mode of reverie – 'a form of attuned, sometimes dreamy, attentiveness' (Froggett, Manley & Roy 2015; Manley, Roy & Froggett 2015).

Froggett, Manley and Roy (2015) write that 'the dreamwork of the visual matrix activates aesthetic capacity in the participants, accounting for the imagistic productivity of the matrix, as well as transforming sensory stimuli into communicable thoughts'. The visual matrix is grounded in felt experience, capturing sense impressions, and the way that feelings and thoughts arise in response to images. As a method, it deliberately attempts to avoid the rational ordering of thought to which we often jump when asked to verbally reflect on an experience.

A group of ten people with a range of lived experiences, including suicidality and self-harm, participated in our visual matrix immediately after leaving *Edge of the Present*. Usually, the sense of reverie prompted by a visual matrix leads to an associative flow of impressions, thoughts and images, which extend beyond the original stimulus. But in this matrix, people wanted to stay with the feeling of being in the *Edge of the Present*. It was as though they were reluctant to come out of it; as if the experience hadn't prompted thought so much as a warm bath of positive sensation, which the participants were still intensely attached to. They wanted to discuss and dissect it: what it felt like to look up at the sky ('I like the experience of looking up within the world, not just looking forward and down'), and whether the clouds were moving, and how much they wanted it to be real.

Perhaps the closest they got to accumulating images or emotions or ideas that traversed beyond the work itself was through the acknowledgement that they didn't want to leave, because reality is not so safe or calm or beautiful most of the time. And, one person wondered, what's the future going to hold? Are we only going to be able to access nature through virtual worlds, like the seven landscapes we can witness through this room?

The data from this visual matrix reveals not just what people thought about the experience but how they *felt*, how they wanted to stay in it without interpreting. And perhaps that is the thing about art, or an aesthetic immersive experience like this one – it is the embodied *experiencing itself* that is the paradigm shift, and the 'therapy'.

'*I wanted to stay.*'

The participants spoke about their bodies as a reference point, grounding them – feeling where they were standing and knowing that they were in a game, but then the walls disappeared, and they were both in their body and outside of it at the same time. They spoke about feeling the gap between their embodiment and the virtual environment – touching a wall accidentally, then looking for limbs but they were not there.

The participants spoke about a kind of instant relocation. For one person, 'it took me back to a place which was really magical. . . . It took me back there and it sort of topped-up the tank of awe'. 'Art takes you places', another person agreed. And it's true. They continued, 'I've never seen the snow . . . [it] felt magical. [I was] transported to another world, one that I've never been to before.'

Of course, the places this experience takes us are not intended to be a substitute for the real – for 'being present in a place, and the smells, and knowing that you are really there', as one participant described it – an experience that is already being harnessed by therapy, from forest bathing (Furuyashiki et al. 2019) to nature prescriptions (Koselka et al. 2019).

Instead, one participant said, *Edge of the Present* takes you 'back to the feeling of a place'. And it does so in a way that is instantaneous, without the long car trip or aeroplane journey. In some ways, this has an advantage over nature – it can be accessed anytime, anywhere, including by people who for one reason or another might not be able to leave their home, care or health facility. It is not a substitute for the real; it is something additional to the real, and a different kind of experience to that which we have in nature.

The place this art takes you is hyperreal, perhaps. Certainly surreal, as snow starts to fall in a rainforest – that snow 'that actually did touch you, it felt like it was touching you, in a way', as one participant said. And because of its mixed reality, and because you are both embodied and disembodied at the same time, there is a felt sense of becoming 'one' with this surreal, hyperreal landscape. Small action, big reward: a large, intensely felt response as a white room opens onto landscape.

*   *   *

Formal studies of the use of this mixed reality experience are continuing, and the piece will be adapted and refined. The data gathered to date indicates the potential value of modes of engagement with distress that tap into the embodied, sensory and affective qualities of experience. When you enter *Edge of the Present* you are offered hope. Not hope as an abstract concept but hope as a feeling – prompted by the act of opening a window and letting the light in, of opening a door and passing through it to somewhere else. You are invited to cultivate a sense of the present, of being in an environment that arouses sensation; and then by making a series of choices, to go forward, to have another experience, and another; an immediate future filled, in small ways, with wonder.

Notes

1 This paragraph is an assemblage of accounts of experiencing Edge of the Present, including those of the authors, research participants and journalists.

2 Alex Davies developed the piece in association with workshops led by artist J. R. Brennan with Alessandro Donagh De Marchi, Faisal Sayani and artist/psychologist Michaela Davies. The associated research project led by Jill Bennett was supported by the Australian Research Council Discovery programme.

References

Bandura, A. (1977), 'Self-efficacy: Toward a Unifying Theory of Behavioral Change', *Psychological Review*, 84 (2): 191–215.

Bandura, A. (1997), *Self-Efficacy: The Exercise of Control*, New York: W. H. Freeman.

Beck, A.T., A. Weissman, D. Lester, and L. Trexler, (1974), 'The Measurement of Pessimism: The Hopelessness Scale', *Journal of Consulting and Clinical Psychology*, 42 (6): 861–5.

Bennett, J. (2019), 'Visual Episodic Memory and the Neurophenomenology of Digital Photography', in M. Durden and J. Tormey (eds), *The Routledge Companion to Photography Theory*, 140–54, London: Routledge.

Buckner, R.L. and D.C. Carroll (2006), 'Self-projection and the Brain', *Trends in Cognitive Science*, 11 (2): 49–57.

Carroll, J. (1978), 'The Effect of Imagining an Event on Expectations for the Event: An Interpretation in Terms of the Availability Heuristic', *Journal of Experimental Social Psychology*, 14: 88–96.

Conway, M.A., C. Loveday, and S.N. Cole (2016), 'The Remembering–imagining System', *Memory Studies*, 9 (3): 256–65.

Williams, H. L., Conway, M.A. and G. Cohen (2008), 'Autobiographical Memory', in G. Cohen and M. A. Conway (eds), *Learning and Memory: A Comprehensive Reference*, 21–90, Amsterdam: Psychology Press, https://www.sciencedirect.com/referencework/9780123705099/learning-and-memory-a-comprehensive-reference

Flavián, C., S. Ibáñez-Sánchez, and C. Orús (2019), 'The Impact of Virtual, Augmented and Mixed Reality Technologies on the Customer Experience', *Journal of Business Research*, 100: 547–60.

Froggett, L., J. Manley, and A. Roy (2015), 'The Visual Matrix Method: Imagery and Affect in a Group-Based Research Setting', *Forum Qualitative Sozialforschung / Forum: Qualitative Social Research*, 16 (3): art. 6.

Fuchs, P., G. Moreau, and P. Guitton, (eds) (2011), *Virtual Reality: Concepts and Technologies*, Florida: CRC Press.

Furuyashiki, A., K. Tabuchi, K. Norikoshi, T. Kobayashi, and S. Oriyama (2019), 'A Comparative Study of the Physiological and Psychological Effects of Forest Bathing (Shinrin-yoku) on Working age People With and Without Depressive Tendencies', *Environmental Health and Preventive Medicine*, 24 (1): 46.

Habak, S., J. Bennett, A. Davies, M. Davies, H. Christensen, and K.M. Boydell (2021), 'Edge of the Present: A Virtual Reality Tool to Cultivate Future Thinking, Positive Mood and Wellbeing', *International Journal of Environmental Research and Public Health*, 18 (1): 140.

Holmes, E.A., C. Crane, M.J. Fennell, and J.M.G. Williams (2007), 'Imagery About Suicide in Depression – "Flash-forwards"?', *Journal of Behavior Therapy and Experimental Psychiatry*, 38: 423–34.

Hustvedt, S. (2013), 'Suicide and the Drama of Self-consciousness', *Suicidology Online*, 4: 105–13.

Koselka, E., L.C. Weidner, A. Minasov, M.G. Berman, W.R. Leonard, M.V. Santoso, J.N. de Brito, Z.C. Pope, M.A. Pereira, and T.H. Horton (2019), 'Walking Green: Developing an Evidence Base for Nature

Prescriptions', *International Journal of Environmental Research and Public Health*, 16 (22): 4338.

Libby, L.K., E.M. Shaeffer, R.P. Eibach, and J.A. Slemmer (2007), 'Picture Yourself at the Polls: Visual Perspective in Mental Imagery Affects Self-perception and Behavior', *Psychological Science*, 18 (3), 199–203.

Maier, S.F. and M.E. Seligman (1976), 'Learned Helplessness: Theory and Evidence', *Journal of Experimental Psychology: General*, 105 (1): 3–46.

Manley, J., A. Roy, and L. Froggett (2015), 'Researching Recovery From Substance Misuse Using Visual Methods', in L. Hardwick, R. Smith, and R. Worsley (eds), *Innovations in Social Work Research*, 191–211, London: Jessica Kingsley.

Matamala-Gomez, M., T. Donegan, S. Bottiroli, G. Sandrini , M.V. Sanchez-Vives, and C. Tassorelli (2019), 'Immersive Virtual Reality and Virtual Embodiment for Pain Relief', *Frontiers in Human Neuroscience*, 13: 279.

Moura, J.M., N. Barros, and P. Ferreira-Lopes (2021), 'Embodiment in Virtual Reality: The Body, Thought, Present, and Felt in the Space of Virtuality', *International Journal of Creative Interfaces and Computer Graphics*, 12 (1): 27–45.

Pham, L.B. and S.E. Taylor (1999), 'From Thought to Action: Effects of Process-Versus Outcome-Based Mental Simulations on Performance', *Personality and Social Psychology Bulletin*, 25 (2), 250–60.

Riley, J., K. Mok, M. Larsen, K. Boydell, H. Christensen and F. Shand (2020), 'Meeting the Needs of Those in Suicidal Crisis With new Models and Integrated Care', in Black Dog Institute (ed.), *What can be Done to Decrease Suicidal Behaviour in Australia? A Call to Action*, 1–14, Randwick, Sydney: Black Dog Institute.

Rizzo, A. and S. Bouchard, (eds) (2019), *Virtual Reality for Psychological and Neurocognitive Interventions*, Berlin: Springer.

Slofstra, C., M.C. Eisma, E.A. Holmes, C.L. Bockting, and M.H. Nauta (2017), 'Rethinking a Negative Event: The Affective Impact of Ruminative Versus Imagery-Based Processing of Aversive Autobiographical Memories', *Frontiers in Psychiatry*, 8: 1–12.

Stene-Larsen, K. and A. Reneflot (2019). 'Contact With Primary and Mental Health Care Prior to Suicide: A Systematic Review of the Literature From 2000 to 2017', *Scand J Public Health*, 47 (1): 9–17.

Wilson, F.C.L. and J.D. Gregory (2017), 'Overgeneral Autobiographical Memory and Depression in Older Adults: A Systematic Review', *Aging Mental Health*, 22: 575–86.

Part II

Culture and experience

CHAPTER 4

Knowing from the inside

Lynn Froggett and Noreen Giffney

Lynn: Your recent book, *The Culture-Breast in Psychoanalysis* (2021), takes up the question of cultural experience as frame, space and container for psychic life and the role of culture in public and private mental health. We share an interest in what it is to have a cultural experience and the conditions in which we can metabolize and reflect upon it. The book is directed at clinical practitioners, aiming to show that the question of how we are all 'fed' at the breast of culture is important inside the consulting room and beyond. You have long been working with this question in your pedagogic practice and in the cultural programmes you facilitate with a wider public. A similar question has informed my attempts to develop research methodologies that enable us to understand what cultural experience produces in people emotionally and aesthetically, rather than asking them their opinions about it.

Noreen: Working in gender studies, with women's and LGBT groups, I became interested in how theory could be used to facilitate people thinking about and from experience. I started using literature, art, film and music to help people engage, so that rather than coming between them and the object, the theory actually helped them see things in a way they couldn't have imagined before. I currently teach psychoanalytic and psychosocial theories at Ulster University, where a lot of health and social care professionals come to do their continuing professional development. I use cultural objects as a way of facilitating their having an experience – but I've also found that they are often feeling burnt out. A lot of trauma is communicated to them from their clients, and the cultural object is a way for them to have a safe experience where they can talk about trauma through the object.

Lynn: The cultural object occupies the position of 'intersubjective third' and is also an 'aesthetic third' (Froggett 2008), which for me is grounded in psychoanalytic theory where the third enters the psychic life of the child to overcome the dualism of self and (m)other. Colleagues in social pedagogy use the idea of the 'common third' as an intuitive understanding of the fact that – in any situation or encounter where there is potential for anxiety or conflict – generating a third opens out the mental space and therefore the capacity to think new thoughts. This is what's behind Winnicott's ([1971] 1991) insight that the pathway to creativity is discovering for oneself a world that is there to be found.

In social work education I find that students come with an immense amount of personal trauma from difficult life circumstances, and many of them are attempting to deal with their own issues vicariously through the course. Having a common cultural third introduced through an aesthetic object has been really helpful. They learn that we are not offering them a psychotherapy but that this shared cultural material makes it possible to talk about personal difficulties in a way that wouldn't otherwise have been possible and find a point of connection with others.

Noreen: I see my role as trying to help students develop their observation and analytical skills, as well as their self-awareness and self-reflectivity, which I see as capacities rather than skills. In skills teaching sometimes people show students how to do something and then get them to repeat it in a role-play or some other setting. The idea is that over time, through repetition, they become able to use it themselves. I don't think that is a particularly useful way to develop a capacity, because capacity is something that grows within. So, the idea is to enable people to have an experience and encounter with theory that is experiential.

I use what I term 'non-clinical vignettes', which I take from literature, art, film and music. I offer students an experience and invite them to creatively imagine this 'vignette' as a patient telling them their story, writing down any thoughts and feelings they might have about it while they're listening. What are they telling you? How does it feel to listen to it? This is not only about facilitating their becoming more aware of what they're feeling but also to convey that we think associatively, not linearly. Those stray thoughts they're having are important, linking back to something in their past. Through a sensory experience, they become aware they are having an emotional experience. I introduce the theoretical frame – but through the experience, so I'm inviting them to take it in and play around with it in their minds.

I also work with clinical practitioners in continuing professional development, and I run a lot of seminars and events with them. They may be from psychoanalytic, or from other therapeutic modalities, or other disciplines. They might include people who are from the arts or curatorship, academic disciplines, activists, members of the so-called general public – people who are interested in psychoanalysis, empathy or melancholia. I try to get away from the masterclass model where an expert gives a talk.

In order to grow capacity, it's not enough to be told something – that is knowledge from the outside. How do you facilitate somebody developing knowledge from the inside?

Lynn: I can see why the cultural event or object or process enables that, not only because of the safety it offers but because of the sense of vitality gained from 'performing' a new relationship to the object of knowledge, rather than simply expecting to be 'fed'. This brings me back to *The Culture-Breast in Psychoanalysis* (Giffney 2021) – it's the quality of thinking itself that is at issue. I like the way you put it: 'thinking from the inside'.

Noreen: It partly came out of thinking back to my own training after working as an academic for a number of years. In psychoanalytic training the experiential knowledge you gain is through your own analysis, through an infant observation and working with patients. There is also the group aspect, which sometimes feels like a group analysis. The question, then, is how to facilitate the integration of theory, experience and reflection. There was nothing that really provided an experiential context before going out to work with patients.

Lynn: Can you give me an example from the 'cultural encounters case study method', as you called it?

Noreen: This method brings together clinical concepts and cultural objects as creative sites for playing with ideas through encounter and experience. In opening up spaces for thinking and feeling, the method provides opportunities to work towards integrating theoretical knowledge with capacities and skills required for clinical practice. Photographer and psychoanalyst Mark Gerald has been taking photographic portraits of psychoanalysts in their offices since 2003, which are displayed on his website.[1] I show these photos to students and ask them what comes to mind. People can be quite anxious at the beginning, so it's about easing their way into an experience, into a relationship with me. I want them to understand that I'm not looking for the right answer, but I will make demands of them. Often a camaraderie will develop, because some react viscerally against particular images, while the response to others will be bland. I talk about how there's an enjoyment in omniscience – being able to see what others can't see – and that nobody is watching you while you're watching somebody else.

In fact, I'm also in the experience with them, as well as observing the experience, and trying to facilitate a movement from talking about what they've seen outside themselves (in the photo) to talking about what was happening inside themselves while they were seeing it. I'm trying to help them connect with that, and to think about how other people in the group are seeing the same thing in different ways. It's a way to begin thinking about *projection*: we partly see things for how they are, but also put our preconceptions, assumptions and biases onto things as if they belong to those things. I'm trying to facilitate their becoming aware of some of the ways in which they project. At the same time, I'm trying to help them see that the group itself facilitates their seeing things they haven't been able to see before. You talked about a relationship of discovery earlier, I like that phrase. The idea is to enable curiosity.

Lynn: I was talking about discovery in contrast to where material is merely offered and consumed. The colonial metaphor of discovery can get in the way because it is overlaid with the logic of appropriation and the attempt to re-make the world in one's own image. Winnicott's insight, of course, was that in the creative act of discovering the world we can make it our own, while at the same time respecting its integrity and its otherness. We find the same idea beautifully explored in C. Fred Alford's *Melanie Klein and Critical Social Theory* (1989) in his interpretation of the depressive position as epistemophilia driven by *Caritas* – by love. Curiosity in this vein comes of love of the world that lets its object be, while seeking to know it better. For Winnicott (1969) it's the difference between object relating through identification so that it exists 'for me', and object 'use' where I 'release' it so that it lives a life of its own – it can then act back on me with its own intrinsic properties. I think the point about the art object as aesthetic third is that it offers a greater resistance to appropriation, it incites curiosity, and so 'use' in Winnicott's sense. We can consider reading and engagement with theory in these terms. The point is to enable people to 'use' theory, rather than 'apply' it – to enjoy its suggestiveness and what it discloses about the world. This helps them get over fear of the theoretical concept – to see the concept as a container for experience.

Noreen: Thinking about discovery – I'm also trying to facilitate a relation to one's own experience. This aligns with psychoanalyst Wilfred Bion's idea that the point is for people not only to 'have' an experience but to be 'in relation' to their own experience; in a sense, therefore, to be inside and outside of it and observe it all at the same time.

Lynn: Let's reverse the lens now and ask what happens when you use clinical concepts in the field of cultural practice. These concepts have explanatory power, but they are not always readily accessible – and there is a justifiable push back when their meaning or relevance is not self-evident. As clinical practitioners move into the space of public well-being and mental health, how might they present the material they bring – which is often difficult to think about – in a form that can be digested or used?

Noreen: One issue is that artists have often had more exposure to Lacanian psychoanalysis. Lacanian psychoanalysis in Ireland is introduced as a perfect mode of thought to be admired, rather than something you can hold onto or bring 'inside'. My main influences are Klein (1997) and figures from the independent tradition – particularly Donald Winnicott (1984) and

Christopher Bollas (1987). People are often more open to object relations theory because it is based on the idea of experience and what we do within it. It helps us to be inside and outside of an experience and understand how what is happening in the present moment is linked to what may have happened earlier in our lives. This really illuminates what can happen when we go to an art exhibition, for instance.

When I lived in London and would go to the Tate Modern, I'd often hear babies crying or children acting out, distressed. There's a lot going on sensorially in these environments – too much! Children are acting out what they're feeling in behavioural terms. It's similar to IKEA, where you have to go round the whole store and by the time you come out you are wrecked and irritable from sheer over-stimulation. The first time I visited the Tate Modern I went with the intention of seeing Rothko's 'red squares', as I think of them. I saw the bookshop and got waylaid by other exhibitions. By the time I got to Rothko the only thing I could do was sit on the bench, because I couldn't take any more in. I got back to the hotel and had to lie down as if I'd eaten too much and felt sick.

An object relations perspective helps us become more aware of how we are experiencing an exhibition – what we are 'taking in'. It's all too easy to look at a work for five seconds, think 'it's crap' and move on. An artist might have spent five years on that work. Similarly, people often want to talk about a film immediately afterwards – instead of slowing down, thinking about what they've seen and digesting the experience. It's the difference between gratification and satisfaction. There is gratification from knowing you 'got it' (and someone else didn't). Satisfaction takes longer.

Lynn: The first time I went to see those Rothko paintings, I had an overwhelming desire to lie on that bench, rather sit on it. The effect of those paintings on a dark grey background gave me an experience I can only describe in terms of death – but a death that you could feel your way into, surrender to. I gave myself permission to be absorbed by that room. Satisfaction then comes when an experience unfolds beyond the immediate encounter.

Noreen: That's an interesting difference – it was only years later that I realized the significance of that surfeit. I was too much 'in' the experience, but I hung on to it and symbolized it later and learnt a lot from it in terms of how to engage with culture.

Lynn: Can you say more about how you run and curate reflective cultural events, and what it means to do so in Northern Ireland?

Noreen: In Northern Ireland a lot of historical experiences aren't talked about because they are seen as too sensitive. Ongoing tensions between people's affiliations have the added consequence that other things are not spoken about – anxiety, depression, unconscious trauma. If there is a role for the arts in mental health it may be to enable people to have an experience and reflect on it.

The first thing is to make sure an event feels welcoming, respectful and safe. We ran an event with Emilie Pine[2] around what we might we do with our vulnerability. Emilie's *Notes to Self* (2019) uses words to narrativize her life – something we all have to do in different ways, whoever we are, wherever we are from, whatever our experiences. We all need a story to make meaning of our lives and hold ourselves together in a psychological sense. This is particularly difficult in the context of Northern Ireland when so much cannot be articulated on account of trauma. We wanted to consider what happens with experiences which are unspeakable, unthinkable and projected into the next generation. We brought Emilie to Belfast for a carefully framed and curated conversation. The audience could pose questions on paper (presented to Emilie by a colleague), after which there was a break with scones, tea and coffee. What's offered in the break is important. The facilitator's role in any intervention is 'holding': holding is part of the experience. This is all underpinned by psychoanalytic theory – Bollas' 'evocative object' (1992) and 'transformational object' (1987), Winnicott's transitional object ([1971] 1991: 1–34), Bion's notion of 'learning from experience' and his theory of symbolization ([1962a] 1984, 1962b). However, I didn't mention any of those concepts. The feedback was that people felt satisfied: they had incorporated a 'good object'; they wanted more of it.

Lynn: If the experience is from the 'inside' and the 'outside' one can do something very valuable with it, yet this remains a neglected area in arts evaluation which is predominantly about the social or artistic impacts. That was why we developed the visual matrix methodology (Froggett, Manley & Roy 2015). People often struggle to talk of an aesthetic experience and are inhibited by not having an art critical language. However, they can dispense with specialist languages if they appreciate that their experiences are good enough. Fluency in expression comes from the sense that their observations belong to them. The visual matrix enables them to think associatively in a group – expressing experience from themselves as opposed to an ideational framework. They enjoy the permissiveness of being asked to follow their own thought processes and affective flows. But I sometimes wonder whether we make enough space for the critical tools that allow them to take distance from it again – that alternation between nearness and distance which is part of a creative thinking process.

Lynn: I'd like to talk more about art in public mental health, where shared experiences of trauma are at issue. The cultural sector is often sceptical of art for ameliorative social or health purposes. Partly, it's a long-standing unease about the instrumentalization of art; partly it's a scepticism about any proto-psychotherapeutic use of art – a diffidence about the ability to contain distress in public settings and a worry that we might lose sight of the distinctiveness of cultural experience.

Noreen: Since 2013 I've been running an event programme called 'Psychoanalysis +', which focusses on clinical, artistic and theoretical approaches to psychoanalysis. Numbers vary from twenty to one hundred participants, no more, so that everybody feels part of the event. Artists are generally interested because there is no particular agenda in terms of how their work should be understood. There is no *one* approach – a levelling effect.

'Melancholia' was a two-day, Psychoanalysis + event in 2014 convened with academic and clinical colleagues, one of whom worked in the arts and curatorship. Melancholia is often used to describe that intractable state where people can't shift out of depression but also the sublime. We held the event at the National Museum of Decorative Arts and History in Dublin in a beautifully ornate room with high ceilings and space for chairs in concentric circles, so people could leave the room if they needed to. It took place over two full days, which were intellectual but also affecting and emotional. The point was to think and feel as a group, even though we were individuals with very different views.

We started with an open discussion prefaced by 5-minute contributions from an academic, two clinicians (Lacanian and British Independent Tradition) and an artist. Five minutes stimulate ideas without overwhelming. The sessions were punctuated by breaks. We were careful to be welcoming and attentive, offering people refreshments, making sure we remembered their names. This is important for people to be able to feel they are in an experience rather than looking on, as if they don't matter. They need to feel that what they have to say is important, that there is no hierarchy; it is all part of holding the frame. We screened Lars Von Trier's *Melancholia* (2011), then we had lunch. People felt fed, minded and facilitated. If I saw anybody on their own, I'd talk to them. After lunch we had three longer papers to enable the critical thinking you were talking about, then a longer discussion.

The next morning we watched 'Melancholia', a 2005 video artwork by Cecily Brennan.[3] In this 11.5-minute video, a woman lies on a table in silence as black bile slowly seeps out of her. The work is deeply affecting, and it was a powerful experience to sit with the feelings evoked within us – this blackness that is seeping out but won't come out; it's torture. Then we had lunch, followed by a challenging art performance by Amanda Coogan titled 'Oh Chocolate' – again about melancholia.[4] Amanda starts by moving around the room in silence, offering everyone a chocolate. They thank her. She moves to the centre of the room and keeps eating, box after box, the chocolate oozing down her face. It's disturbing to watch and difficult to articulate; she's smiling broadly like Batman's 'Joker', with chocolate seeping through her teeth. She continues offering chocolate but people won't take it, won't look at her. Some are on their phone, some are laughing, chatting and becoming quite manic, managing the experience in different ways. Before the performance, Amanda had rubbed chocolate into the radiators, so we were smelling it as well. After a break, she returned for an open discussion about her practice, and our experience of being present during her performance.

The experience has to be quite compressed, quite intensive. The demand we made was that people attended both days of the event, and if they couldn't we returned their money. It's about layering experiences one on top of another. The emotion works through both the critical intellectual and visceral elements. Sometimes people want to come in and be sitting at the back so they can look at their mobile phone, but the frame has to be firmly held.

There is feedback throughout the event – but I prefer to write to people and try to communicate to them my sense of how they were and how they contributed to the event. Many wrote back to say the event was amazing, disturbing. People continue to approach me to say they've heard about it. People commented on the coffee and croissants in the morning – what they were saying was that they felt cared for.

Lynn: That takes me on to the uses of public art in situations of shared trauma. I'd like to invite you to think about this from the context of Northern Ireland.

Noreen: I started working at Ulster University in 2017, but before that I had only been to Northern Ireland twice. I knew very little about it – apart from the Troubles from the 1960s until the Good Friday Agreement in the 1990s. I feel nervous talking about it – nervous that I might say something that offends. I am aware that there are cultural sensitivities but not sure what they are. There are unspoken cultural codes expressed in very subtle ways, which during the Troubles were enacted in very concrete ways through a sustained campaign of violence. A mass traumatization has resulted from the violence that was acted out brutally by paramilitaries on the one hand and the state on the other hand. 'Trauma' is a small word for the enormity of an experience that cannot be symbolized or represented to oneself – so that when you're in that experience there is no distance from it, you're drowning in it. When I think about Northern Ireland, I think about a society that continues to live in that state.

I have become very aware of this experience of splitting, othering, projective identification among the population and between various groups. Some things are not spoken about. In some respects Northern Ireland is a society where I fit well, but because of my accent and because I come from the Republic of Ireland I'm aware that assumptions are made about me, projections. Sometimes I'm aware of a level of surveillance in the Foucauldian sense of people watching people, but also in that the trauma has been absorbed into the very institutions themselves. There is a lack of trust, a struggle to say clearly what one means, and constant talk about not disadvantaging people as if it were a given that people would be disadvantaged.

Nowadays, Northern Ireland has the highest level of mental health issues and suicides in the UK. More people have died by suicide in Northern Ireland than died during the Troubles (McDonald 2018). The undergraduates I teach are what are called the 'peace babies' – born after the Good Friday peace agreement. I also teach people who were alive during the Troubles. I see that state services are very underfunded and a lot of people give their time voluntarily to help those who have been traumatized. I feel I've talked round and round this issue but maybe that's the point. There's a Seamus Heaney (1975) poem: 'Whatever you say, say nothing.' That phrase is very dear to people and reflects some of the tensions that are under the surface all the time.

There are splits in political identifications but also more subtle splits that you see, for example, in work meetings. Temporality gets split. Decisions are made, and the next time there is a meeting it's as if it never happened. I've found it to be disconcerting and upsetting. You may think you know where you stand about something, but then it is as if you've never talked. Things can become contentious very quickly and need to be promptly de-escalated. Some people try to find commonalities in other aspects of life to repair the split.

Lynn: I wonder if that extends to the peace process itself. When I went to Belfast I was astonished at the intactness of the 'wall' that separated what were effectively Catholic and Protestant zones. It has not been actually or symbolically 'torn down' as in Berlin, leaving a sense of a very incomplete process. I was also very struck by the street art adorning walls in many parts of the city – mostly ideologically slanted towards conflict. Not only did the walls remain but they were still 'weaponized' – what does that say about the public state of mind?

Noreen: I think of the so-called 'peace walls' around Northern Ireland that separate – they're supposed to represent a coming-together, but they're locked at night. People are interested in hearing, learning and thinking about trauma, often at a very intellectual level because it's difficult to get their minds around it emotionally. The traumatization is not worked through and surfaces in other interactions.

Lynn: It's as if where there is a retention of walls, physical or mental, there is a concreteness of thinking. Traditions and rituals take on the aspect of a rigid carapace – a form of exo-skeleton that leaves you wondering what's going on inside and what will happen when the carapace fails to hold and cracks appear. Is that a point where artists and cultural practitioners can really do some work? I'm thinking of Bollas' notion of 'psychic genera' (1992) as the counterpart and antidote to trauma – a kind of procreativity of the mind that senses, elaborates and disseminates. Some of the mural art is very arresting and inventive, but nevertheless paranoid schizoid in terms of the state of mind it arouses. What would be the opportunities there? How are people working to symbolize and re-symbolize the state of Northern Ireland today, which has been thrown into turmoil again by Brexit?

Noreen: There are a lot of artists working in Northern Ireland, particularly performance artists, and there seem to be a lot of links between artists working in Northern Ireland and the Republic of Ireland. With some colleagues, I organized a series of online conversations on empathy. One of the people we invited was psychoanalytic psychotherapist and artist Geralyn Mulqueen who uses her art practice to enable people to reflect on and work through trauma. There are artists working in other parts of Northern Ireland in community settings who use art to help people reflect on mental health issues.

I've been running some events with colleagues in Belfast called 'Mental Health and the Arts'. I wanted to see how different art forms might help people think and talk about issues that are difficult to come at head on, how the arts could facilitate someone having an experience and also talking about something that is related to 'me' but at the same time 'not me'. We organized an event called 'The Long-term Impact of Childhood Trauma on Adult Mental and Physical Health'. I was particularly interested in how the effects of trauma have been projected from one generation into the next. There are a lot of people who weren't born during the Troubles, who carry the long-term fallout. It expresses itself as generalized or free-floating anxiety, and they might be experiencing severe personal anxiety.

We wanted to be able to think about that without naming it as such, so we showed a documentary about trauma in childhood and how it affects people throughout their lives. Afterwards we had five brief responses from people in professions dealing with the effects of trauma: a GP, a physiotherapist, a social worker, a counsellor and someone who worked in film – who was there to help us think about what got left out in the documentary, as films can sometimes present things in a neat and manipulative narrative form. Then we had a facilitated conversation with people about their own or their relatives' experiences with trauma and vicarious trauma. It was booked out, but afterwards somebody commented that if we hadn't held it at an East Belfast venue, more people would have attended. They were referring to the sensitivity of holding this event in a Unionist (Protestant) area. Space itself is partitioned, and what we are trying to do through art is to get people to think symbolically.

We put a number of frames around that screening: first, the documentary was set in North America – something that was happening 'over there'. However, some of these professionals were working in the Republic of Ireland and some in Northern Ireland, so it was very much a cross-border event. We had tea and coffee and a chance to talk to others, so people became aware of different ways of thinking about the film. Having short responses was important. The experience can be flattening with long papers, as if there's no room to think your own thoughts. By the time we came to the discussion, people were primed to say something. These layers – and the fact that people have time – helped facilitate the process of beginning to think, and that's where symbolization happens.

Cinema is an interesting medium in relation to trauma because it's a spectacle in itself. Trauma is a bit like that. In one sense you're inside of it, in another you're watching it going on; there's a dissociation at work. Ultimately I'm trying to create an atmosphere of curiosity, a feeling of thinking together while having one's own private thoughts, of being satisfied while wanting more. I'm trying to tread that line between desire and satisfaction over and over again. Participants need to feel that something has happened, even if it's a mystery.

Lynn: When I asked you to choose a single most influential text for you, you identified Bion's *Learning from Experience* ([1967] 1984).

Noreen: It's a very short book; I read it when I was doing my clinical training years ago. I'd been reading and teaching theory, especially poststructuralist theory. When I read it I felt put out to sea. I was disorientated, frustrated and kept losing the sense of what he was trying to say. I wondered what the big deal was about Bion because I'd been trying to understand the text intellectually. I was very familiar with the intellectual space – the feeling that I'd mastered something, gobbled it up, digested it and could then move onto the next one. This book demands that you slow down, and I realized that Bion is trying to evoke the experience that he's writing about in the reader. I'd never read anything that seemed to be written so plainly and yet had such an intense effect on the reader.

Over time we develop a pattern of experiencing and these patterns are how we make sense of our lives, but they can become concretized when we have experienced trauma so that we react to new experiences as if they were situations from the past. We repeat the experiences rather than learning from them. The experiences are different but we react as if they are the same. This is Freud's compulsion to repeat. What Bion asks is: How do we have an experience so that we can take it in, metabolize it, make meaning of it and so learn from it? If the reader can stay with the experience of reading it, the book facilitates us to become aware of a range of reactions in our minds and bodies that we weren't aware of before. It's related to Winnicott's ([1960] 1990) idea of 'holding'. When the mother holds the infant, in her mind she is living the experience with the infant but she is also the frame that is holding herself and the infant together – she is both in the experience and outside of it.

Lynn: I was thinking of Winnicott in *Playing and Reality* ([1971] 1991), where he is writing in different registers. There are parts that are theoretical and parts where he almost gives you bullet points, suggesting what you should be taking away with you. Then there are other passages where the writing is aphoristic, paradoxical and yet somehow disarmingly human. I see students enjoyably confounded by it, stopped in their tracks. It makes for a great discussion on the difference between conceptual/theoretical and experiential thinking.

Noreen: There's a book I did with Eve Watson called *Clinical Encounters and Sexuality* (2017). It was about trying to help clinical practitioners become more reflective about the transferences to sexuality that they bring in from culture unbeknownst to themselves, which they then enact with their patients. I wanted them to see that their clinical understanding of sexuality is awash with cultural and societal material. The front cover is an image of a 2011 Karla Black sculpture composed of ephemeral pink plastic bags, called 'There can be no arguments'. I show it to students and ask them what comes to mind. I tell them I don't have answers for them; I don't know what it means. I'm trying to get them to be curious about the way they think about it, to be tentative, to accept that no one really knows and that doesn't mean they haven't got something out of it. Remaining curious is key to the symbolization process, even if you're feeling bored – so that you're asking, what is it about the experience that is boring me? Often, they're not really bored – something else is making them disengage.

What I'm trying to get across is that experience is something ongoing from moment to moment. The psychoanalyst Betty Joseph (1989) spent about sixty-five years working on this – tracking the transitions in experience from moment to moment. Her work is distilled into a number of very short pieces which are to do with the capacity to remain in an experience. Thinking about going to a gallery – people often feel that they are going to see a certain artist's work, and that is the experience. That of course is only the manifest content, in psychoanalytic terms. There is also the latent content – the peripheral dimensions such as walking to the gallery, storing your things in the cloakroom, going to the toilet and passing the bookshop: all of that is part of your experience. It's like the importance in psychoanalysis of all the experiential bits around the consulting room, and how the analyst manages the gradual coming into awareness for the patient: the patient arriving at the front door, entering the building, making their way from the front door to the consulting room and across the room to the couch. Learning from experience is moment to moment and what happens in the spaces in-between.

Notes

1   See: https://www.markgeraldphoto.com/ (accessed 16 September 2021).

2   The event was 'What Can We Do with Our Vulnerability? Words to Make Meaning of Life's Experiences', at the Duncairn Centre for Culture and Arts, Belfast, 2019.

3 See: http://www.cecilybrennan.com/content/melancholia (accessed 16 September 2021).

4 See: http://www.amandacoogan.com/ (accessed 16 September 2021).

References

Alford, C.F. (1989), *Melanie Klein and Critical Social Theory: An Account of Politics, art, and Reason Based on her Psychoanalytic Theory*, New Haven: Yale University Press.

Bion, W. ([1962a] 1984), *Learning From Experience*, London: Karnac.

Bion, W. (1962b)_ The Psycho-Analytic Study of Thinking: a Theory of Thinking, *International Journal of Psychoanalysis* 43, 306–10.

Bollas, C. (1987), *The Shadow of the Object: Psychoanalysis of the Unthought Known*, London: Free Association Books.

Bollas, C. (1992), *Being a Character: Psychoanalysis and Self Experience*, London and New York: Routledge.

Froggett, L. (2008), 'Artistic Output as Intersubjective Third', in S. Clarke, H. Hahn, and P. Hoggett (eds), *Object Relations and Social Relations: Implications of the Relational Turn in Psychoanalysis*, 87–111, London: Karnac.

Froggett, L., J. Manley, and A. Roy (2015), 'The Visual Matrix Method: Imagery and Affect in a Group-based Research Setting', *Forum Qualitative Sozialforschung / Forum: Qualitative Social Research*, 16 (3): Art 6.

Giffney, N. (2021), *The Culture-Breast in Psychoanalysis: Cultural Experiences and the Clinic*, London and New York: Routledge.

Giffney, N. and E. Watson, eds (2017), *Clinical Encounters and Sexuality: Psychoanalytic Practice and Queer Theory*, Earth: Punctum.

Heaney, S. (1975), 'Whatever you say, say Nothing', in *North*, 60, London: Faber and Faber.

Joseph, B. (1989), *Psychic Equilibrium and Psychic Change: Selected Papers of Betty Joseph*, edited by M. Feldman and E. Bott Spillius, London and New York: Routledge.

Klein, M. (1997 [1975]), *Envy and Gratitude and Other Works 1946–1963*, London: Vintage.

McDonald, H. (2018), 'Northern Ireland Suicides Outstrip Troubles Death Toll', *The Guardian* 19 February 2018. Available online: https://www.theguardian.com/uk-news/2018/feb/20/northern-ireland-suicides-troubles-death-toll (accessed 21 September 2021).

Melancholia (2011), [Film], Dir: Lars von Trier, United States: Magnolia Pictures.

Pine, E. (2018), *Notes to Self*, Dublin: Tramp Press.

Resilience: The Biology of Stress & the Science of Hope, (2016), [Film], Dir. James Redford, Texas: KPJR.

Winnicott, D.W. ([1960] 1990), 'The Theory of the Parent-Infant Relationship', in *The Maturational Processes and the Facilitating Environment: Studies in the Theory of Emotional Development*, 37–55, London: Karnac.

Winnicott, D.W. (1969), 'The Use of an Object', *International Journal of Psychoanalysis*, 50: 711–16.
Winnicott, D.W. ([1971] 1991), *Playing and Reality*, London and New York: Routledge.
Winnicott, D.W. (1984), *Through Pediatrics to Psychoanalysis: Collected Papers*, London: Karnac.

CHAPTER 5

Radical creativity

Breaking the cycles of trauma

Marianne Wobcke with Jill Bennett

Marianne Wobcke has used her background as both a trained nurse and midwife, and a professional artist of Indigenous Australian and 'Stolen Generations' lineage, to develop an innovative programme of culturally connected birthing practices and trauma recovery. Grounded in radical creativity, her holistic approach to birthing and perinatal care aims to break the cycles of trauma that are the legacy of colonial violence. Informed by Aboriginal spirituality and cultural knowledge as well as understandings of intergenerational trauma and attachment, Marianne has established a practice called Perinatal Dreaming along with its own visual imagery. Perinatal Dreaming is a process for working with women, their babies and families to ensure that birth practices are culturally safe, using art as a tool for empowerment, agency and expression. Marianne is one of the 'Stolen Generations' of Aboriginal children, removed from their families at birth under the racist, assimilationist policies of successive Australian governments. Perinatal Dreaming re-establishes connection to a period of trauma and rupture, as well as to 'Country' and a culture that was taken from her and her family.

In this chapter, Marianne discusses the challenge of working with transgenerational trauma, bringing to bear diverse knowledge systems to understand the processes by which trauma is both transmitted and potentially met in a productive way. Through her own art practice, she has explored the imprint of trauma carried in the body – as well as the experience of good and bad birth practices. This extends to the 'good womb' – oceanic experiences of safety and containment – contrasted with a 'toxic womb'; and the 'good breast', relating to secure attachment. Such imagery, conceived within an Aboriginal cultural framework or 'dreaming', also evokes the psychoanalytic concepts of a container and 'good breast' or 'culture breast' (Giffney 2021; see Chapter 4).

Wobcke's focus on radical creativity and the generative role of art also resonates with the concept of 'aesthetic intelligence' (advanced by psychoanalyst Christopher Bollas) as a mode of knowing, grounded in the multisensory interactions that establish and shape emotional connection (Bennett & Froggett 2020; Bollas 1987). In this sense, aesthetic transactions are not associated exclusively with the production of art but are part of a continuum of sensory-affective, embodied experience. This broader notion of the aesthetic adds value to the role of the skilled artist, who for Wobcke plays a particular role in facilitating shared creativity. In Wobcke's integrated vision, art is something that is of pragmatic value rather than merely illustrative or expressive. Hence, Perinatal Dreaming images, such as the womblike environment of *Grandmother Dreaming* (Figure 5.1), evoke containment, security and connection to Country in a form that may support the development of an inner landscape.

As a midwife, Wobcke focuses on the importance of relationships and connections established in the pre, peri and postnatal period, combining insights from attachment theory with a new set of practices. The attachment relationship with caregivers in early life is known to be one of the mechanisms

FIGURE 5.1 *Left: Marianne Wobcke,* Grandmother Dreaming 2011; *Lino cut, 30 × 30 cm, edition 2/10. Photo courtesy of Jenny Sanzaro; Right: Marianne Wobcke,* Baby in a Cage – The Second Matrix – No Way Out, 2009. *Polystyrene, felt and wire sculpture. Photo courtesy of the artist.*

by which the effects of trauma are transgenerational (Milroy, Dudgeon & Walker 2005: xxi) – and hence is an important focus for interventions designed to break the cycle of trauma. But as Wobcke suggests, this cannot happen effectively within a purely medical model of care that reinforces power relations over people whose cultural expertise has been undermined by the legacy of colonialism – and where transgenerational trauma is itself the outcome of colonial violence (Atkinson 2002).

Marianne: Aboriginality is all about a personal, unique connection to our ancestors – something that was stolen through colonization (Wobcke 2009). I am from a stolen generation lineage, so when I envisage Songlines,[1] I see a continuous thread from my great, great grandmother and beyond, back 65,000 years; from the ancestors, through my pre and perinatal lineage and into biography. I also see a Songline that has become corrupted through trauma. I see five generations of the same story repeating, over and over again, in my family.

These effects are often compounded by birth trauma (for example, through unwanted and high-risk pregnancies or separation at birth), and inevitably by early childhood trauma. My work as a midwife and an artist is about identifying the patterns of intergenerational trauma and finding ways to break the cycle, drawing on a holistic, Indigenous well-being paradigm. Unlike the Western Disease Model, such a paradigm prioritizes collaboration, co-operation and creativity. It addresses something I find especially difficult about Western culture, which is the siloing of experience, the discontinuity and gaps.

In Aboriginal philosophy, art is understood as a process by which the individual accesses and integrates the spiritual and unconscious dimensions (Parker 1993). An individual's spirituality or *dreaming* is at once biographical and transpersonal, incorporating experiences prior to, during and after birth, and even prior to conception (Wobcke 2009). For me, the Aboriginal notion of the self as deeply connected to ancestry, culture and Country is therefore compatible with the Western psychoanalytic construction of the self as composed of the conscious and unconscious mind, wherein the unconscious mind is thought to contain repressed emotions from infancy and childhood. To understand and work with such connectivity, whether in terms of my personal experience or my work with mothers and babies, I not only prioritize 'Understanding Country' but also draw on fields such as attachment theory, which are informed by psychoanalysis, epigenetics and neurobiology.

Jill: This is an extremely interesting conjunction, which is a distinctive feature of your work. Attachment theory highlights the importance of forming a 'secure attachment' to a responsive carer in infancy – and the lasting consequences of 'insecure attachment', wherein a baby's needs are not met and distress is not alleviated (Bowlby 1999). Research has shown that stressed babies produce higher doses of cortisol which may cause neurotoxicity (Papapetrou et al. 2020) – so insecure attachment can impact on brain development, on the capacity to regulate emotion in later life as well as on lifelong mental health. And in fact, even before birth, cortisol imbalances in the mother during pregnancy can affect the baby (Papapetrou et al. 2020; Maté 2008).

Marianne: Trauma-induced brain pathways can be transcended – and new neural pathways configured, supported by a non-fear based hormonal ecology (including endorphins, oxytocin and prostaglandins). This requires habit building, based around positive, loving bonding experiences. As a midwife, my job is to support the building of connection, critical in the first three 'golden hours' following the birth, with the baby going straight to the mother and finding the breast (Thompson n.d.).

'Attachment' doesn't only start at birth, however. It is a continuum, both in terms of cultural connection and inherited experiences. Pre, peri and postnatal experiences have an impact (for example, it may be affected by whether or not the pregnancy is wanted, by how the mother bonds with the foetus during womb-time and how connected she feels to the foetus during the birth experience – are they a unit or does the mother feel disconnected from her baby?) As a midwife, my job is to support an ongoing connection.

Jill: This notion of continuity goes to the core of how we understand cultural connection and also the transmission of transgenerational trauma, which I think is perhaps harder to grasp from a Western individualistic outlook than it is from an Aboriginal perspective. Western thought places a premium on what is cognitively known and has far less grasp of the mechanisms by which embodied knowledge is transmitted. Attachment theory points to the importance of sensory transactions that occur before we consciously 'know' anything.

One of the most clarifying stories I've heard regarding the transmission of trauma is the author and physician, Gabor Maté's (2008) account of an event from his first months of life in a Jewish family in Budapest at the time of Nazi invasion. He relates how his mother calls a doctor because he, her baby, is in a state of constant distress. The doctor informs her that in fact all the Jewish babies in Budapest are distressed – the reason being that all the mothers were inevitably in a heightened state of anxiety or trauma. The story is so instructive as it underlines the fact that trauma compromises care, no matter how loving the parent is. A distressed parent cannot be expected to soothe a child and relieve that child's distress – but the effect of this omission is that the child does not then benefit from secure attachment and the sense of safety that enables emotional regulation and development.

Marianne: We talk a lot about *commission*, about the violence or whatever specifically occurs to cause trauma. When something happens to you, you can identify that as the source of trauma more often than not. When it's *omission*, it's far more difficult to deal with because that leaves a vacuum. I think what we've forgotten in Western culture is that with commission goes omission. So, we've not just got to fix the trauma, we've got to fill in the gap – and deal with the vacuum of what didn't happen for that individual from conception on, and transgenerationally too, for growth and transformation to occur.

Now one would think, because I was removed at birth, I wouldn't 'know' any of that history of separation and lost connection, but what shocked me is the intimate detail in which I've recreated this corrupted Songline, this pattern that was handed from one generation to another.

When I was working with the psychiatrist Dr Stan Grof, I started doing drawings relating to my own perinatal experiences (Grof 2006). These were images that I experienced as 'coming from inside'. I tried to transcribe these rather than thinking of myself as an artist composing work. When I look back at those drawings, they tell – sort of holographically – my entire perinatal story. As a researcher that absolutely fascinated me. Because I didn't 'know' the story, I couldn't describe the pain, but in one picture, I drew myself hanging in the womb by the umbilical cord with a dragon coming through the cervix to kill me. I found out later that my mother had an attempted abortion. So that image started to make sense. I discovered an 'intelligence' inside me, being able to bring forward an image like this, which could not only express that trauma but do so in a way that could be understood and, more importantly, processed.

With attachment theory, a lot of work has been done with early childhood, but it hasn't necessarily been done with midwives – or with this earlier period where the gap begins. Working as a midwife, I can see that lack of attachment often, when a mother tells me about a bad conception experience or when she says she was twelve weeks pregnant or more, before she knew it and so was drinking, taking drugs and smoking. You see those patterns amplified when you have those conversations with mothers, through a lens of continuity.

Jill: You have suggested that levels of trauma may be such that women who are told how to parent by the medical establishment will withdraw and reject advice – so rather than giving advice you promote creativity. That is to say creativity not only in terms of the act of making an artwork but of 'being' creative, so that childbirth itself can be experienced as generative and creative.

Marianne: This is what breaks the cycle. Well-meaning professionals can unconsciously perpetuate these chronic misperceptions, fuelling toxic patterns. Rather than being the expert and telling these young mothers what they should or shouldn't be doing, I'll first sit and start to unpack the story within her. Even the most traumatized young woman, I've found, will want to talk about their disconnection from Country, their feeling of not belonging, the feeling of aloneness and alienation.

I discovered early on (working at the Murri School, for the Aboriginal and Torres Strait Islander Community Health Service) that if I was sitting interviewing somebody or taking on the role of the expert, it was far more challenging to build that creative connection together. Working with young Indigenous people impacted by trauma, I'd offer them something to eat – or I'd ask if they wanted their hair brushed and do that, which immediately created bonds. That intimacy just invites a space where people feel safe to start talking. And then during community days with Indigenous mums, I would bring resources that ignited creativity.

Many young women would say they weren't 'creative' – but I'd put a variety of different art resources in front of them and let them choose, and through creative acts of making, whether scribbling on a page, doing some weaving or colouring-in, we would create that hormonal ecology where we could start to unpack a discussion on identity – who they were, where they were from – in a way that was very non-threatening. When you're sitting doing something creative like baking or colouring-in or weaving or doing someone's hair or makeup, any of these things, it creates a different landscape to start sharing what emerges from inside, whereas psychotherapy could be very threatening and often alienating.

Jill: Do you think it's because art or creative practice is literally a generative process; when you're doing it, there's a sense of agency and production. In Western culture, we tend to think of art-making as a hobby, or a distraction rather than a life-affirming force. But in fact, if you have lost connection or any sense of self-determination, it is a means to regenerate that connection. Of course, you can make and bake in a distracted disconnected way, but there's the potential to feel yourself to be actively generating something as opposed to having something done to you.

Marianne: You've nailed it perfectly. This is why it is important *not* to be an amateur, sitting with somebody doing a creative project, because if they don't create something of worth or value to them, then it may compound their trauma. It reinforces a story that they're not creative.

To sit with an art expert or a baking expert is transformative because the calling to create something from inside is supported through what I would describe as a very mothering sort of partnership, where that expertise can tease out something extraordinary. That's what would bring the song through, that feeling of excitement and positivity and self-efficacy that in fact you were (are) profoundly creative. It wasn't the artist's work because it was a partnership; they were helping you create something that was uniquely yours, but at a whole other level of efficacy. Your vision manifested through their skill. That's the beauty of partnership.

Jill: It's so interesting that you talk about partnership – because again, in the Western model, we focus on art as an individual expression rather than formative relationship. Also, of course, people generally don't want to be 'helped' by an expert in a way that reinforces a power dynamic. As you say, enabling people to partner, to be creative and do something with and for others is potentially much more empowering.

Marianne: Absolutely. And it nourishes something that's often been lost in early childhood development, which is turn-taking – that beautiful exchange that happens between parent (adult) and child, where a parent will do something and then the child takes their turn. So, it's building the development of all these childhood capacities that in families with compounded trauma doesn't occur. So, instead of you being the expert with the goal of fixing somebody, you're really creating that agency, true partnership and turn-taking and enabling people to develop their own proficiencies and skills, which brings forward such a sense of pride and self-worth, which was an omission in their childhood.

When you're with a therapist and there's a projection happening, you can fall in love with the therapist. Then there can be an endless need to be with the therapist to have a feeling of well-being – and as soon as you leave, it's gone again. It doesn't change that inner ecology. It doesn't change those neural pathways. You're still seeing yourself as the other, as not good enough.

Therapeutically, the breakthrough for me was a form of play therapy. I was working in the homes of some of our most traumatized mothers – teenagers with the most horrific histories – and we were usually allocated an hour to deliver relevant perinatal education. I remember once sitting on the floor with a young woman in a state of terror (under an ongoing threat of violence). We were debriefing about trauma and the awfulness of the situation, and although this was one way of supporting her, I wanted to create potential for change; to take it to another level, particularly for the baby who was sitting in this environment of terror. So, I introduced a little game that we could play together. And something really magical happened in that environment, in that experience where, almost immediately we transcended that trauma landscape and were somewhere quite different, sitting on the floor together. The baby was chuckling and laughing. Both mum and daughter were in this extraordinary state of bliss. That was a major shift in how I worked from that point on. My job, from the moment I met them for that day's connection, was to enable them to have an experience of joy. If I could guide them into an experience in their body where they weren't full of adrenaline and cortisol anymore, where we weren't talking constantly about potential dramas or dramas that had just happened. If we could, through breath and laughter and engagement, activate hormones such as endorphins and oxytocin and generate that beautiful ecology where we were sharing and exchanging love in its most authentic form, it didn't really matter whether I delivered specific programme content or not.

That's the 'Understanding Country' element – because irrespective of the Country on which we were standing, I was able to facilitate an engagement with their inner landscapes and allow that sense of well-being to emerge. In creating this environment, they became more receptive to learn through experience how to be a 'better mother'.

Jill: 'Playing is itself a therapy', as the psychoanalyst D. W. Winnicott famously said (1971: 67). Your understanding of the development of an 'inner landscape' resonates with psychoanalysis, as you have indicated – but particularly with Winnicott, who conceptualizes the mother in terms of a 'facilitating environment' transforming a baby's internal as well as external environment (Winnicott 1965; Bollas 1987).

I am interested in your focus on engagement, and on the environment and its affordances, which allow something to occur. In my work with Lynn Froggett and Lizzie Muller (discussed in Chapter 8) we have explored this in terms of using art to design the potential for experience – which is very different to defining or determining the experience itself. It's about facilitating growth and, as you say, the means to play.

Marianne: It's about empowering people to make changes that are deeply intuitive – not externally imposed. In this paradigm shift we're experiencing a shift in power – away from the hierarchy with medicine at the top, arts at the bottom. Health and the Arts need to combine in order for people to value their own experience.

These epic experiences: conception, womb-time, birth and the postnatal – by the time we've wrapped words around them, let alone Western science, we have completely distilled and homogenized the experience – and somebody else becomes the expert.

When a mother says to me, 'I'm not creative at all', I think, how can you say that when you've created a human being? There is no greater feat of creativity. If we can open up those internal channels – channels that can only be accessed through humility and surrender – if we can reimagine our stories, then every individual becomes an artist (Wobcke & Pa'apa'a 2021).

Jill: How do we create the environment – even in the midst of chaos as you describe? And how do we live these epic experiences rather than get lost in them?

Marianne: One way I've tried to do this in my installation work, which creates a structured environment for these experiences. I imagined a 'heroic journey' through the realms of conception, gestation, the birth process and early postnatal period constituted through nine rooms arranged in a matrix formation, so that one can experience in succession the good womb and the toxic womb, the good and the bad of labour and birth and the good and toxic breast. These are immersive landscapes created with lighting, sound, aromas and various art objects. The landscape of the good womb, for example, is the beginning of the individual's journey from conception into intrauterine existence. It is designed as an amniotic universe (including water elements) which represents not only genetic origins but also our connection to the Dreamtime.

I also designed a toxic birth landscape (where labour begins but the cervix is closed). This space was quite small, dominated by a large installation piece in a red spotlight, *Baby in a Cage* (Figure 5.1), with an umbilical cord, felted to look corrupted, around the neck of the baby. This environment encapsulates experiences of abandonment and rejection for mother and foetus. It realizes a space that imprints pain and trauma from generation to generation – an inherited 'dis-ease' that affects the biological functioning of the individual, and which psychologically and emotionally creates fertile ground for addictions and dependencies to flourish. A toxic womb and birth environment pollutes, corrupts and inevitably compounds perceptions that the world is hostile and harsh, requiring defensive strategies and persistent struggle. It extinguishes hope and imprints the misperception that there is no way out of this toxic experience and emotional landscape, fuelling anxiety and depression.

But in the multi-room installation there is literally a light at the end of a tunnel, which one passes through. The ultimate potential for every birth is a triumphant outcome, where the mother feels truly empowered. In traditional times, the mother would be reunited with her infant, resting supported in a sacred natural setting, connecting to Country. This is represented in the Good Breast environment, which is an alternative nourishing space that is full of light, aromas, seed pods and sounds of nature.

Leaving the installation space, the audience move outside to where there is nutritious, delicious food available and lots of support. We had yarning spaces, paper and pastels set out if people wanted to sit and draw and a number of qualified people to offer support for processing feelings, emotions and memories that had been triggered. There is potential here for a holistic hub of support with professionals from a range of disciplines including the arts to be available in the space. This was a temporary exhibition, but it is how I envisage care in a paradigm where arts and health are united.

It is important to recognize how shifts occur in these embodied, aesthetic encounters – shifts that don't happen if we simply try to deliver cognitive information, which the mind appreciates, but the body relates to experiences. We need to promote a maternal paradigm, where the hormonal ecology and attachment create an environment of profound relaxation and connectedness that is restorative and transformational. An organic falling in love that has no opposite, no struggle, just an infinite mutual exchange that is nourishing on every level. Here we become reinvested in organic sustenance, a delight in the mother's milk, an abundance of nourishment, individually oriented to create sustainable health and well-being.

This is critical to re-establish in the context of transgenerational trauma – and it has additional significance for those of us of Stolen Generations lineage. Growing up in a Western culture I never fitted in, and you'll hear this from a lot of Stolen Generations people. The contemporary Western religious and cultural 'maps' I was given didn't make any sense to me, and when I found out about my Aboriginality it was as if suddenly I was given a map which made sense, because everything – all I'd lost – connected up again.

Our perceptions of the world are reinforced by remembering our ancestral Dreamtime connection to the amniotic and oceanic space. Linear time collapses and we embrace the present moment. We consider our environment live-giving and enriching, our relationships are open and trusting. We see the world as a fundamentally abundant paradise, designed for our pleasure. We flow with life's experiences safe in the knowing we are deeply and profoundly loved and connected.

Understanding Country is fundamental to an appreciation of Perinatal Dreaming and a holistic Indigenous well-being paradigm. It creates the pragmatics and opportunities to heal Country, ecologically, biographically, biologically and spiritually in a contemporary context. This profoundly impacts our self-esteem and creates an environment where we can experience self-love and self-respect – the foundations of healing transgenerational, pre/peri/postnatal and biographical trauma. One day at a time . . . only small change is required . . . baby steps . . . .

Note

1   A Songline is 'a route through the landscape which is believed to have been travelled during the Dreamtime (or Alcheringa) and which features a series of landmarks thought to relate to events that happened during this time; a traditional song or story recording a journey made during the Dreamtime' (*OED* 2021).

References

Atkinson, J. (2002), *Trauma Trails, Recreating Song Lines: The Transgenerational Effects of Trauma in Indigenous Australia*, Melbourne: Spinifex Press.

Bennett, J. and Froggett, L. (2020), 'Aesthetic Intelligence', in Jill Bennett and Mary Zournazi (eds), *Thinking in the World: a Reader*, 223–37, Bloomsbury.

Bowlby, J. ([1982] 1999), *Attachment and Loss: Vol. 1. Attachment* (2nd ed.), New York: Basic Books.

Giffney, N. (2021), *The Culture-Breast in Psychoanalysis: Cultural Experiences and the Clinic*, London: Routledge.

Grof, S. (2006), 'When the Impossible Happens: Adventures in Non-Ordinary Realities', Part 3, *Revisiting History: Retrieving Memories of the Stolen Generations: The Story of Marianne*, 123, Louisville, Colorado: Sounds True.

Maté, G. (2008), *In the Realm of Hungry Ghosts: Close Encounters with Addiction*, Toronto: A.A. Knopf.

Milroy, H., P. Dudgeon, and R. Walker (2005), 'Community Life and Development Programs – Pathways to Healing', in P. Dudgeon, H. Milroy, and R. Walker (eds), *Working Together: Aboriginal and Torres Strait Islander Mental Health and Wellbeing Principles and Practice*, 419–35, Canberra: Australian Government Department of the Prime Minister and Cabinet.

Papapetrou, C., K. Panoulis, I. Mourouzis, and A. Kouzoupis (2020), 'Pregnancy and the Perinatal Period: The Impact of Attachment Theory', *Psychiatriki*, 31 (3): 257–70.

Parker, K.L. (1993), *Wise Women of the Dreamtime: Aboriginal Tales of the Ancestral Powers*, Rochester, VT: Inner Traditions International.

Thompson, R. (n.d.), 'The 3 Most Important Hours for a Mother and her Baby', *The Thompson Method*. Available online: https://www.thethompsonmethod.com/blog/the-3-golden-hours (accessed 28 July 2021).

Winnicott D.W. (1965), *Maturational Processes and the Facilitating Environment: Studies in the Theory of Emotional Development*, London: Hogarth Press.

Winnicott, D.W. (1971), *Playing and Reality*, London: Tavistock.

Wobcke, M. (2009), *Aboriginality, Art and the Perinatal*, Honours Research Paper, Griffith University, Brisbane. Extract available online: http://www.perinataldreaming.com.au/about.html (accessed 28 July 2021).

Wobcke, M. and L. Pa'apa'a (2021), 'Episode 1: Marianne Wobcke and Lia Pa'apa'a', *Ngamumu In Conversation Series*, 01 March 2021. Available online: https://www.ngamumu.com/inconversation (accessed 28 September 2021).

Part III

Dialogue and embodied encounters

CHAPTER 6

The Eradication of Schizophrenia in Western Lapland and Open Dialogue in the work of Ridiculusmus

David Woods and Jon Haynes

Aulanko, Finland, 2013

As co-artistic directors of the theatre company Ridiculusmus, we (David Woods and Jon Haynes) had been working on the play that would eventually become *The Eradication of Schizophrenia in Western Lapland* for twelve months before we had heard of the Open Dialogue approach in Western Lapland and what it had achieved. We called our evolving project 'the family play'; it drew on our personal backgrounds and was therefore littered with situations of family crisis due to mental illness. These backgrounds that we plundered with a fictionalized auto-ethnographic methodology had problematic outcomes, and we speculated whether the mental health system today would do any better for people in such situations. We met with systemic family therapists Dr Charlotte Burck and Gwyn Daniel at the Tavistock Centre, London, who were looking at the experiences of teenage carers of mentally ill parents. This was a role David had been in, but had never really reflected on. It was during this encouraging sharing of ideas that Charlotte urged us to look at what was happening in Finland.

It took another six months for us to be able to begin an exchange with anyone connected to Open Dialogue. The staff were all incredibly busy and in high demand as conference speakers, consulting with the pope and so on, and so we spent time attempting to understand something of the approach from published articles, Jaakko Seikkula and Tom Erik Arnkil's 2006 book and a 2012 documentary by Daniel Mackler: *Open Dialogue: An Alternative Finnish Approach to Healing Psychosis.*

Jaakko (Seikkula) encouraged us to attend the 2013 *Dialogic* conference at Aulanko in Finland, so that we could spend some time with him and his colleagues. Bartering the fees for a performance of our work in progress, and with the support of a Wellcome Trust grant, we set off on an ambitious field trip. On the way to the conference, we visited the Keropudas Hospital in Tornio where Open Dialogue had evolved, with the hope of broadening our knowledge about what these working methods actually looked like in practice. The hospital was in the midst of a demolition. We expressed sorrow, assuming this was a typical undesired reduction in bed capacity, but Timo Harrinen assured us the space wasn't needed anymore and it would make a pleasant park. The combobulation continued.

At the conference Jaakko asked if our characters from the play could take part in a staged treatment meeting for the benefit of the delegates.[1] This was an unexpected invitation given the packed schedule of the conference, but one to which we readily agreed. We already had extensive experience of improvising in role and felt it would be good for the development of the characters' back-stories as much as gaining first-hand experience of the approach.

FIGURE 6.1 The Eradication of Schizophrenia in Western Lapland *at Battersea Arts Centre, 2014. Left to right: Jon Haynes (patient), Patrizia Paolini (Mum, through window) and David Woods (doctor). Photograph by Richard Davenport.*

What took place that morning at Aulanko had a profound, transformative influence on the play and our practice in general. The effect it had on David personally remains a life-defining moment that he still doesn't fully understand.

Some background

We formed Ridiculusmus in London in 1992. *The Eradication of Schizophrenia in Western Lapland* is possibly the most ambitious of the twenty-three plays we have created, a body of work that has increasingly leaned towards socially engaged issues while staying true to our small-scale poor theatre aesthetic and its oxymoronic aim of creating seriously funny plays. It attempts to convey the experience of visual and auditory hallucination by simultaneously performing two plays about a family in crisis to two separate but adjoining auditoria. The audience in one space is able to hear, and occasionally see, what is happening in the other and vice versa. At half time the audiences swap sides to see what they had previously heard and to hear what they had previously seen. It is an ambitious and sometimes frustrating construct, but one that we felt gave some physical and experiential form to psychosis for a non-psychotic audience.

Our method of making work has evolved from a background of enthusiastic engagement with academic study of laboratory theatres, popular and obscure influences from post-war British upbringings and rigorous drama school training, through a cycle of enthusiastic failures on the small to mid-scale touring scene, fringe and underground, into a disarmingly simple arrangement of responses to circumstances and opportunities.

We meet in an empty room somewhere, improvise for a set period of time while recording everything, and then edit that material into a play. This affords space for material to develop but is also a structured situation where we feel safe to create, fail and create again. This initial phase highlights areas of interest that we then research. This research in turn informs a new phase of improvisation, which leads to specific discoveries about the material that expresses our concerns about the state of particular matters in an entertaining, engaging and stimulating way.

There was a sense of the uncanny when we discovered the Open Dialogue project. Like our own, Open Dialogue's working methodology had also emerged over a number of years, and used structured gatherings to explore issues of concern from the perspective of the people involved. Similarities were also evident in the modes of attention and receptivity required by both Open Dialogue practitioners and improvising actors. Sensitivity, listening, openness and playfulness are all aspects of Open Dialogue and of the Ridiculusmus creative process. As improvising actors, we challenge ourselves to respond 'in the moment' – tricking ourselves into believing an action is being taken for the first time by our characters. Similarly, Open Dialogue therapists need to leave any pre-conceived notions outside treatment meetings. Working from moment to moment, at the same time we also think dramaturgically about our contribution to the narrative, reflecting within our roles as we push the story along, enacting a sequence of actions that are pre-planned or that spontaneously arise. This process mirrors the use of reflecting processes that Norwegian therapist and academic Tom Anderson (1991) contributed to Open Dialogue, an element that involves live reflection within a treatment meeting between therapists, as the community in need of help listen in. Finally, tolerating uncertainty, a cornerstone of the Open Dialogue approach, is something Ridiculusmus embrace as a mode of being essential to the fragile industry that we inhabit.

Clearly there was an affinity between our own working methods and those of the therapeutic approach, but whether these discoveries might inform or be included in our evolving play remained to be seen. For reasons of confidentiality, actual exchanges from treatment meetings were scantily available. A 2002 paper by Jaakko Seikkula tracked moments in therapeutic treatment meetings that created the foundation for 'good outcomes' where the patient recovers, and 'poor outcomes' where they did not. But to us, at that early (pre-Aulanko) stage of research, the extracts from these transcriptions (Seikkula 2002: 269–70) were bafflingly simple and short:

> M: [son, the patient]: It was wrestling.
> TF: [female team member]: But did you mean it quite seriously?
> M: It was like pitting oneself against . . .
> TM: [male team member]: Which of you was wrestling?
> M: I think that he got furious.
> TM: Which of you was wrestling?
> M: Well, I took hold of his neck . . . I got a little bit frightened.
> TM: (*turning towards his team-mates*) . . . it is a kind of outrage when you realize your own child has . . .
> TF: Yes, but on the other hand, a father can be proud that his own son is so strong . . .

Seikkula (2002: 270) comments, 'The team take the discussion of wrestling seriously and normalize it.' In contrast, the following extract from a 'poor outcome case' shows the team ignoring comments that are offered by the client:

> P [father, the patient]: I slapped her. She ran out into the corridor and started screaming. I said that there is no need to scream . . . and then I calmed down. At that point I got the feeling . . . it is not allowed to hit anyone. But there are however situations . . .
> T1 [therapist 1]: Was that the point when you went into primary care? (Seikkula 2002: 270)

Jaakko (Seikkula 2002: 271) describes the phrase 'it is not allowed to hit anyone' as the 'origin of an inner dialogue to deal with what he had done', but the 'team did not respond to this', instead changing the subject and missing their opportunity to construct meaningful dialogue about the situation.

Reading these extracts didn't bode well for contributing magical moments to an exciting new play. The dialogical moments seemed so subtle as to be invisible and revolved around the 'un-dramatic'. Successful outcomes are moments where tension is dissolved. Theatre generally aspires to the opposite of this, creating tensions that are ratcheted to a high level and maintained for as long as bearable. Explorative contemporary drama might even be said to aspire to stage the unbearable. Waves of 'In-Yer-Face' theatre action, objectionable situations and characters commonly populate the main stages of the world, demanding an audience to pay attention amidst more palatable and less expensive alternatives.

Family drama has tended to opt for crudeness in the mechanics of its revelations – big things are communicated in big moments at big gatherings with great intensity. For example, the plays and films *Festen* (1998) or *August: Osage County* (Letts 2007) are both hugely successful family dramas, where accusations of neglect and abuse are aired at significant gatherings.

We considered this to be the stuff of cliché – there seemed to be no traumas left that we would be able to unveil that would generate surprise. So, while the prospect of finding something stunning in the Open Dialogue literature seemed unlikely, resorting to the conventions of family drama was equally unpromising.

We already had much of the dramatic tension of the work embodied in the staging, but on 'the public side' in the psychiatric hospital, the exchange between psychiatrist and patient was awash with unfulfilled potential. The patient character Richard (played by Jon) remained locked into his psychotic vision of events, and his psychiatrist (played by David) seemed uninterested and unable to help him. We struggled with the meta-theatrical conceit that the whole play was created by Richard, and that the psychiatrist and other patients were acting it out for him. However, the problem remained that there was no sign of hope for Richard's recovery; rather, there was a consolidation of his delusional thinking.

Meanwhile in Aulanko

After the opening speeches at Aulanko, we set up the conference hall into our double auditorium arrangement. It was awkward and strange, more for the venue than the delegates: a gathering of around 300 family therapists, psychologists and others, who seemed very prepared for adaptation and innovation. We presented a fifteen-minute extract and were met with a ponderous silence. We then cleared the wall and made a central circle of chairs for the staged treatment meeting that would follow. David changed into the character of Dad (not a costume change, but a subtle head shift from one thought pattern to another; a touch of physical transformation in the spine or face – a jigsaw of people from real life and elements of himself, glued together with imagination). Patrizia Paolini was in-character as Dad's new wife, Jade; and Jon and Richard Talbot as the two sons, Richard and Rupert. We took our places in the circle. What a circle it was: Peter Rober (Belgian academic, clinical psychologist, family therapist and family therapy trainer), Markku Sutela (chief psychologist at Keropudas Hospital) and Jaakko Seikkula (professor of psychotherapy at the University of Jyväskylä, co-author of *Dialogical Meetings in Social Networks* and worldwide presenter on Open Dialogue) – not that they were in any way intimidating! Markku wore toe sandals and socks, Jaakko a Hawaiian shirt and jam-jar thick glasses and Peter Rober – who had stayed on an extra day to be part of the fun – started by telling us how much he was missing his family.

The meeting skipped along, Jaakko heartily thanking us, the family, for coming along to the meeting. Richard had a problem with books, Mum had gone. Jaakko asked: 'What do you think Mum would say about the books? Shall we have a chair to represent Mum? Where should we place the chair? Next to Dad? Next to Richard? Away from Jade?'.

We seem to have talked about nothing, but after a few simple actions and exchanges Dad/David was bursting with hot emotion, swelling up with grief, but also relief. David was asked something and couldn't speak. Instead of words there was a torrent of pain. Jaakko and Markku also started to cry. We all mourned the absence of the fictional mother. Jon had done a lot of preparation for his role as the psychotic Richard, aware that, as Adam Phillips (2011) points out, acted madness 'has to make the repelling of attention as alluring, as intriguing, as the courting of attention'. In the session Richard/Jon is slightly frustrated that all his 'mad acting' and the delusional titbits he offers in-character appear to be met with indifference from the therapists. Only later does it sink in, with relief, that their attitude reflects the central Open Dialogue approach: the 'problem' is located in the situation and the social group, not in an individual.

It ended. We agreed to meet again the next day. This is what would usually be said at the end of a treatment meeting, but everyone agreed that we should actually stage the treatment meeting again the next day, the last day of the conference.

The second treatment meeting at Aulanko

The next morning, we gather in the main conference room again and get back into our roles. An extra chair has been put out. David, partially as

Dad, but still part David, moves the chair from the stage. It is cluttered enough and we don't need it. Pretty soon David realizes that it was intended to represent Mum again. The pain is acute. The chair is brought back. Here we go again, the wash from the feet up of tears welling, the voice draining away. Rupert has been to see Mum. Dad didn't know he'd been. Dad/David breaks down again – this time realizing that the feeling flushing through him is one permitted and welcomed in these circumstances, that there could be no safer place to melt down than surrounded by several hundred progressive and hugely empathetic family therapists.

The fictional problem has now been clearly aired. How can this family resolve what needs to be acknowledged or mourned, that they have lost their mother? They have unearthed this trauma and the play has found its big revelation, but doesn't know it yet. Still in a state of embarrassed confusion about what has been happening to him, David goes along with the idea that he was performing all of Dad's emotional responses. Inside, as someone who has cried less than five times in his whole adult life, he finds it all confusing.

We return from Finland surrounded by a *Ready Brek* glow. We haven't really comprehended what change has occurred for us, but we are back in the same room at Shoreditch Town Hall in London, with this still incomplete and unfulfilling work in progress. We are agreed that it cannot be a demonstration of the Open Dialogue approach. Such 'info theatre' is not to our taste. For us, it encourages laziness on the part of the audience that won't lead to genuine learning. There has to be an active step towards engaged thinking to fully comprehend and be able to put into practice what we are drawing attention to. To demonstrate Open Dialogue in this context we feel would be the theatrical equivalent of rote learning. It needs the tension of proximity to this work but must not be a demonstration of it. The characters must know of it but be unable to practice it. We insert some lines around this idea into the script:

Doctor: A colleague of mine – we did a training course together on a way of working that has practically eradicated schizophrenia in . . .
Richard: Western Lapland?
Doctor: You know it?
Richard: Very well, it's the name of the play that we're in.
Doctor: Play? Right. Well then, you'll have heard they think psychotic meaning making is meaning making – they don't want to medicate meaning making . . . anyway my friend, he got struck off.
Richard: Why?
Doctor: Well, he tried it and the CMD[2] claimed he was harming his patients by not prescribing the anti-psychotics that the pharmaceutical companies wanted him to.

A performance in Salford consolidates this direction. Mental health service users there tell us of the production line treatment meted out to them. We are alerted to two studies (Oedegaard et al., 2020; Morrison et al., 2014) that highlight the effectiveness of medication-free treatment. This seeds an idea that Richard might recover through improved psychosocial connection with his therapists when he is un-medicated, though he prefers to frame such a dialogical breakthrough internally: 'I've got my drug already. I've got my intellect.'

Brighton premiere, 2014

We open the play, still unfinished and unresolved, but into it we have created such chinks of light. Richard unlocks his traumatic memories through writing about them and he acknowledges that his writing is a way of coping or 'managing' these problems:

> Richard: The whole thing is kind of constructed to help me recover from these whatever-you-call-them that are going on. Have been going on, for some time, probably will continue to go on, these, um, problems.
> Doctor: So, the fictional realms help you manage your problems?
> Richard: Is that what I said?
> Doctor: Yes.
> Richard: I didn't say my problems. I said *these* problems.

Through this process Richard accepts that his mother is gone and will never come back.

> Richard: You don't need me anymore. Don't need me anymore. Don't need me anymore do you? Don't need me anymore. And I'd say, 'Oh thank you, Mum. Thank you very much. That's very nice of you. I'm very well. I wish you'd come back and do your cooking again, the quiches, the flans and all that, the Mediterranean vegetables, yes, would be nice to have that all back . . .'
> Doctor: That's her saying that it would be nice to be back or that's you saying . . .
> Richard: That's me saying it would be nice.
> Doctor: She's capable of coming back/home and doing that?
> Richard: No.
> Doctor: No?
> Richard: She won't be the same again.

Unravelling this tangled strand of possibility without sentimentality or over-written obviousness takes another six months or so for us to work out.

Six more months of thinking

During this time, we review some of the video footage of the show and a post-show talk with Markku and Mia Kurtti. They believe all psychoses are responses to traumatic events. The treatment meetings provide an opportunity to unlock the memory of these events and help defuse them. Defusing first the psychotic language and behaviour and, secondly, the trauma that has triggered it. From this come ideas about the structuring of the play we have been struggling to find since the premiere.

With this simple aim to communicate we are able to include subtly inserted changes that provide signposts to Richard's recovery. The acceptance of changed circumstances at home and of the loss of Mum remains incomplete, but their airing offers at least the possibility of resolution.

In the play we have developed this theme of the unearthing of traumatic memory to a point where Dad becomes visibly distressed by the memory of Mum. This is where David finds a place in the show for his personal meltdown in Aulanko, which he can now explore in every performance. While the therapist facilitates a self-generated therapeutic narrative and understanding for a client, we – in our minimalist articulation of therapeutic breakthrough – attempt to allow the audience to come to the work with their own narratives, perhaps with traumas that are unresolved for them. By underwriting the specifics of our staged family drama we allow the audience space to process their own experience. At Aulanko, while David's un-thought-out character creation engaged with the specifics of the fictional situation, his thinking dramaturgical self unearthed something in need of emotional release. He was unable to pinpoint exactly what it was – the feeling that the play had finally come to fruition? Grief for a childhood cut short by necessary adoption of the carer role? The fragility of his ongoing existence in an impoverished industry? Of leading? Or something encompassing all these things that recognized, in the empathetic safety net of a dialogical situation, that all of these things could be heard, understood and valued. The trauma is now something not only between the characters, rather than borne solely by the character Richard, but also between ourselves and our collective work, between us and our audiences. A resolution that, we hope, would be assessed by Jaakko Seikkula as a 'good outcome'.

Conclusion

Despite operating in very different spheres, theatre and therapy, Ridiculusmus' working method and output share a remarkable similarity to Open Dialogue. Paying close attention to the details of dialogical exchange, clarifying meaning and allowing time for empathetic reflection while concentrating on being 'in the moment' and 'soul-full' inform both practices. These qualities act as enablers of genuine communication and ultimately serve in both scenarios as building blocks for healthy societies.

The exciting implication for practitioners both in the arts and therapy is that there is an opportunity to improve both praxes through creative exchange, enhancing the therapeutic quality of performance, and the performative qualities and skills of therapy and therapists.

The Eradication of Schizophrenia in Western Lapland was premiered at SICK! Festival in Brighton in March 2014 and has since played seasons in London, Melbourne and Edinburgh and toured around the UK from Scarborough to Cornwall. It remains in the Ridiculusmus company's touring repertoire. The play has robustly managed cast changes, front-on stagings with a curtain down the middle of the stage, table performances and digital platforms. The circumstances that supported its creation look unlikely to align in a similar fashion for the foreseeable future, and so this play stands as a remarkable testament to the seizing of opportunity and circumstance to constructive ends.

Acknowledgements

The development of this play was supported by Wellcome Trust funding under the 'Large Arts Awards' scheme, awarded in 2016 for the project, 'Ridiculusmus Mental Health Trilogy: Dialogue as the Embodiment of Love'.

Notes

1 The staged treatment meeting at Aulanko is available online: https://vimeo.com /98305028 (accessed 16 June 2021).
2 The CMD is a fictional health/regulatory body created for the play.

References

Andersen, T. (1991), *The Reflecting Team: Dialogues and Dialogues About the Dialogues*, New York: Norton.
Festen (1998), [Film] Dir. Thomas Vinterberg, Denmark: Nimbus Film.
Letts, T. (2007), *August: Osage County*, New York: Theatre Communications Group.
Open Dialogue: An Alternative Finnish Approach to Healing Psychosis (2011), [Film] Dir. Daniel Mackler. Available online: https://youtu.be/HDVhZHJagfQ (accessed 16 June 2021).

Morrison, A.P., D. Turkington, M. Pyle, H. Spencer, A. Brabban, G. Dunn, T. Christodoulides, R. Dudley, N. Chapman, P. Callcott, T. Grace, V. Lumley, L. Drage, S. Tully, K. Irving, A. Cummings, R. Byrne, L.M. Davies, and P. Hutton (2014), 'Cognitive Therapy for People With Schizophrenia Spectrum Disorders not Taking Antipsychotic Drugs: A Single-Blind Randomised Controlled Trial', *Lancet*, 383 (9926): 1395–403.
Oedegaard, C.H., L. Davidson, B. Stige, M. Veseth, A. Blindheim, L. Garvik, J.-M. Sørensen, Ø Søraa, and I.M.S. Engebretsen (2020), '"It Means so Much for me to Have a Choice": A Qualitative Study Providing First-person Perspectives on Medication-free Treatment in Mental Health Care', *BMC Psychiatry*, 20: 399.
Phillips, A. (2011), 'Acting Madness: The Diary of a Madman, Macbeth, King Lear', *The Threepenny Review*, 126: 14–17.
Seikkula, J. (2002), 'Open Dialogues with Good and Poor Outcomes for Psychotic Crises: Examples from Families with Violence', *Journal of Marital and Family Therapy*, 28: 263–74.
Seikkula, J. and T.E. Arnil (2006), *Dialogical Meetings in Social Networks*, London: Routledge.
Woods, D. (2015), 'Breakthrough Moments: Open Dialogue in the Ridiculusmus Play: "The Eradication of Schizophrenia in Western Lapland"', *Context: The Magazine for Family Therapy and Systemic Practice*, 138: 36–8.
Woods, D. and J. Haynes (2014), *The Eradication of Schizophrenia in Western Lapland*. London: Oberon.

CHAPTER 7

The Visit

A collaborative confabulation

Gail Kenning, Jill Bennett and Volker Kuchelmeister

Viv stands at her kitchen bench, looking out of the window. There's a shed visible in the small backyard outside. Music is playing: the first movement of Peter Sculthorpe's *String quartet no. 16 with didjeridu,* titled 'Loneliness'. Viv turns, makes eye contact, walks towards me, gesturing towards the kitchen table positioned between us, and says, 'You're back, come and sit down where I can see you. We can have a chat.' I dither for a moment, and she urges me again to sit as she takes the seat opposite me at the table, 'Don't hover! You can stay for a bit, can't you? I don't get to see you that often. I've just made us a pot of tea. I'll get you something to eat in a while.' I sit and she takes up the conversation (Figure 7.1).

Viv is the sole digital character in *The Visit,* an immersive media artwork developed in collaboration with women living with dementia by our transdisciplinary research and creative team of artist-designers and psychologists.[1] Using a virtual reality (VR) headset or engaging with an interactive screen, the viewer – interpolated as Viv's 'visitor' – arrives in a virtual set (created from a scan of the kitchen and lounge of one of the women collaborators), where a teapot and two cups wait on the table. Via tracking sensors, Viv is 'aware' of the viewer's physical presence, and speaks as if she knows this visitor to whom she discloses freely. She also speaks sporadically to a child, seated in what appears to be an empty chair at the same table, in front of which Viv lays a plate of toast and jam. Joining this

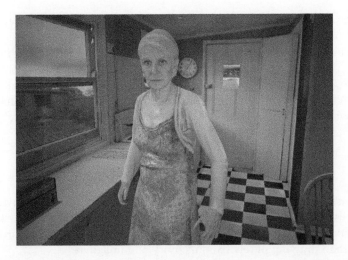

FIGURE 7.1 The Visit, *immersive media (still), 2019. Courtesy fEEL UNSW.*

FIGURE 7.2 The Visit, *3D LiDAR (Light Detection and Ranging) scan of a physical kitchen with props created using photogrammetry, 2019. Courtesy fEEL, UNSW.*

tableau, the visitor is met with warmth, drawn into Viv's conversation as a familiar friend or family member (Figure 7.2).

The Visit was derived from a series of open-ended interviews with five different women, who talked freely about their experiences of confusion, memory loss, auditory and visual hallucinations and life in general. From these we fashioned a single, composite character and a script voiced by Australian actor Heather Mitchell, also working with a motion capture actor to develop the digital character's embodied enactment of the script.

Part of a larger research project on the lived experience of dementia, the interviews preceded the conception of the artwork, the format of which is a response to a set of priorities emerging from the data and more specifically from lived experience. Much of our interview material explored the challenges of interpersonal and professional relationships after a dementia diagnosis – the 'very poignant moment of awakening to the lack of understanding and awareness' and to the anxiety that dementia promotes in others. Managed symptoms such as memory slips, momentary confusion or perceptual disturbances are often taken as a sign of global cognitive decline ('losing one's mind') (Cuddy & Fiske 2017); discomfort with neuropsychological change prompts attempts to fix and correct (Phillipson et al. 2015). This anxiety – as much as dementia itself – became the focus of the work, which combines the methods of both verbatim theatre and immersive media to explore the potential for attuning to another's experience.

Verbatim

In discussing the merits of verbatim theatre, English playwright David Hare describes the potential for surprise and revelation when a writer works with the 'found material' of recorded interviews to 'reveal the extraordinary', rather than drawing purely from memory and imagination:

> if you go out and collect evidence about people's way of life, things are revealed to you which are completely extraordinary and which you don't see coming. (National Theatre 2014: 01:03)

For Hare (2010), verbatim theatre has the revelatory impact – and the relationship to truth and lived experience – of good investigative journalism, but is less reductive: 'Journalism is life with the mystery taken out. Art is life with the mystery restored.'

Verbatim theatre, on this account, is grounded in a 'bottom-up' process of engagement rather than one of imposing ideas onto the subject matter. 'Things are revealed': that is to say, *noticed*, through an attentive reading, an active methodological attunement to the material of an interview (to what is said, to how and where it is said, to the affective valence and intensity of expression) (National Theatre 2014). If journalism summarizes, condenses and glosses, the verbatim writer/artist works with the texture of this communication, the performer with its rhythm, flow, prosody, sound, physical dimensions. While the verbatim method (depending on the practitioner) can allow greater or lesser degrees of editing, infill and elaboration, the commitment to the found text is its defining constraint, so that for actors, writers and directors the challenge is to attend to, amplify and accent what is *found* in the recording: a skill of deep listening and translation (National Theatre 2014: 04:49).

This close attention to all aspects of an interview resonates with phenomenological approaches, which 'bracket' top-down interpretation or categorical labelling in order to focus on experience – as well as with the procedures of relational psychotherapy or of the 'person-centred therapy' pioneered in the 1950s by Carl Rogers (1959). For us, the latter inspires not only a method of engaging with experiential narrative but the modelling of a virtual encounter that addresses the interpersonal dynamics and the affective entanglements that shape the experience of living with a condition such as dementia. Rogers' belief that a client's self-understanding – rather than expert interpretation – should be the focus of therapy, necessitated listening with (Freud's) evenly suspended attention rather than judgement, attuning to what is present and repeating back to the client what is heard without embellishment or opinion, avoiding the imposition of themes, constructs or interpretation.

Our starting point, as with verbatim theatre, was a commitment to retaining the integrity of the interview data – but in addition to this traditional 'objectivity' we wanted to examine the intersubjective potential of an art form. More specifically, the possibility for actively cultivating empathy – which, following Rogers (1959) we understand in terms of an attunement to – rather than appropriation of – the other's experience:

> The state of empathy, or being empathic, is to perceive the internal frame of reference of another with accuracy and with the emotional components and meanings which pertain thereto as if one were the person, but without ever losing the 'as if' condition. Thus, it means to sense the hurt or the pleasure of another as he senses it and to perceive the causes thereof as he perceives them, but without ever losing the recognition that it is as if I were hurt or pleased and so forth. If this 'as if' quality is lost, then the state is one of identification. (1959: 210–11)

We worked primarily with women diagnosed with vascular dementia who had in common a number of symptoms or experiences – notably auditory and visual hallucinations and a tendency towards confabulation. They each had significant insight into these symptoms and had evolved various strategies for managing their experiences (in *The Visit*, Viv talks about 'her' methods of reality-testing, such as the 'thirty-minute rule', which entails holding off on reporting an apparently missing object in the expectation that it may be perceivable in time). Working with this material presented an opportunity to examine the perceptual experience of dementia, elaborated from the subjective perspective of a complex character, encountered on her terms, in her environment.

The nature of the interview material (which often dwelt on day-to-day living and the experiences of an older person alone in a home environment) suggested the format of monologue in a relatively constrained home setting – a touchstone for which are the fictional worlds created by Alan Bennett in his BBC television series, *Talking Heads* (1988). Like Bennett's characters, Viv talks to both the notional visitor/viewer and to herself, becoming at times self-absorbed and reflective. This draws the listener into the character's world and stops the dialogue from becoming contrived or protracted (Jobert 2011: 47).

In contrast to a broadcast television play, however, the immersive media presentation is designed to create the illusion of a shared space, so that the diegetic space of the character's domestic environment extends to contain the viewer. The sense of dropping in on a character is more palpable. The visitor feels they are in the character's space and so the expectation of dialogue shifts from that of a self-contained play with its own internal momentum to that of ambient conversation arising within a domestic environment.

Conversational vignettes, drawn from the interview material, are organized within a loose formal structure provided by the sections of a musical soundtrack featuring Peter Sculthorpe's 2005 *String quartet no. 16 with didjeridu* (selected because one of the women admired and knew the composer, 'used to see him twice a year . . . and bring him boxes of marmalade'). The five movements of this piece (I. 'Loneliness', II. 'Anger', III. 'Yearning', IV. 'Trauma', V. 'Freedom') underline the shifting emotional tonality identified in the source material and amplify the transitions that often occurred in discussions.

The visitor's initial encounter with Viv finds her apparently alone in her kitchen, solicitous of company ('Loneliness'). She is, however, preoccupied with a child, served toast and jam, which goes uneaten. The visitor cannot see the child with whom Viv engages, and is drawn into a sequence of conversations, each with a subtle but compelling emotional valence. Viv talks of her carers with a mischievous affection, joy and playful flirtation giving rise to a wistful reflection on the absence of touch:

> I like Goran the best . . . he's very funny and I find [laughter] that I get so much support from people who are very funny. . . . He's got these great big hands! And is quite comfortable about giving me a hug every now and again, which none of the others have ever done. I quite like that, it's really nice. . . . It's really gentle, only a minute or two. . . . Just reassuring.

There is sudden irruption of 'Anger' and annoyance when Viv recounts the intrusion of another carer:

> I can't remember her name now. . . . She knocked very lightly once and just walked in. Didn't wait for me to come to the door or say 'come in' or 'just a moment!' I told her to get out. . . . I said if she had to come in, she had to knock and I had to answer . . . otherwise I'd report her.

Indignation gives way to a sense of self-satisfaction as agency is once again asserted:

> I actually called the person who controls the carers . . . and said I'd file a written report if she does anything like that again. I said, 'I want you to know that this is what happened'. So, she could take further action if she thought she needed to . . . . She was grateful that I'd told her . . .

> I think I handled that quite well. I don't think I've lost my temper with anyone else . . . just ignoring the basic courtesies . . . they have a responsibility to treat us all with respect.

'Trauma' is evoked with a potentially distressing hallucination (prompting a phone call to Viv's daughter, which is at first undermining but ultimately stabilizing). 'Yearning' is characterized in memories and hallucinations of people who are missed, although these bring comfort. Finally a sense of 'Freedom' is expressed as Viv recounts her travels, wanderings and future plans:

> I've been for my walk already. . . . I do about one kilometre there and one kilometre back from wherever which way I go. I used to swim a mile every morning before breakfast and a mile before five. I need to get some new swimmers. I'm planning to go to the indoor pool.

Immersion

What does it mean to 'see through the eyes of another' as opposed to simply seeing more? Michel Serres, in his book *Eyes*, imagines a museological project in which the world is seen as if through the eye of a fish; in other words, not only from a different vantage point but through a distinct perceptual apparatus (Serres, 2015). Laing notes: 'The only true voyage, as Proust once remarked, would be not to travel through a hundred different lands with the same pair of eyes but to see the same land through a hundred different pairs of eyes' (Laing 1969: 28).

VR is the 'ultimate empathy machine', claimed filmmaker Chris Milk (2015) in a much-quoted TED Talk. Generally understood as multidimensional, empathy entails emotional and cognitive components as well as the capacity for imaginative transposition or seeing as if through another's eyes.[2] VR achieves this direct translocation, potentially enabling a viewer to inhabit a virtual world from an unfamiliar embedded perspective. Shot or modelled in 360-degrees and from a first-person field perspective, VR generates the illusion of a 'through the eyes' viewpoint. The viewer thereby takes up the position of a girl in a refugee camp in Jordan (Arora & Ousman 2015), or a homeless person in the gamified, *Becoming Homeless* (Herrera et al. 2018), from Stanford University's Virtual Human Interaction Lab.

The obvious criticism of such virtual tourism is that while it may give a vivid impression of what a particular refugee camp looks like, the lived experience of being a refugee cannot be reduced to a visual-spatial experience of place. Virtually occupying the position of a person living on the streets may inspire consideration of the difficulties of such conditions but it usurps rather than acknowledges the experience of the actually homeless. To the extent that the intersubjective is ignored, VR risks appropriation, displacing those whose experience it purveys by substituting technological vision: it simply takes us to 'a hundred different lands with the same pair of eyes'.

The Visit is constructed as an immersive experience, accessed either in VR or in an installation version, comprising a large vertical screen, a seat identical to the one in Viv's kitchen and an ambisonic (spatialized) soundtrack played via headphones. Absorbed into this tableau, mediated entirely via Viv's monologue/dialogue (she is variously 'in conversation' with herself, the viewer, the unseen child at the table and her daughter, whom she calls on the phone as the visitor sits and waits), the visitor is an interloper, arriving in the confined space of Viv's kitchen, not so much to *become* her, but to *be with* her.

Within this space, different perceptual realities are accessed; 'reality' coheres in the process of making sense of what is seen and heard. The sound of an old mechanical typewriter clickety-clacks in a room 'upstairs' (the ambisonic soundtrack, delivered through personal headphones, immediately locates this somewhere above the listener's head). Hearing this, we are with Viv in her perceptual world. The sound appears to infuse the room. We assume the sound to be 'real' until it is interpreted by our host:

> He's upstairs typing again . . . you hear him? My father used the old Continental for his Herald job . . . [pause]. . . . Of course, those old clickety-clack typewriters don't exist anymore, do they?

The interactive immersive media system randomly selects different pathways, each offering a different scenario involving an auditory hallucination. In an alternate scenario, the visitor hears the sound of a swarm of bees immediately behind their head. This sometimes induces the visitors to turn around to investigate the source of the sound as Viv also moves to swat away the bees:

> Oh, not the bees again [looking around/ swatting]. . . . You better watch out . . . Dad kept bees . . . [pause]. . . . They wouldn't be inside, would they?

These sounds, revealed as auditory hallucinations, are, however, emotionally reassuring, rather than intrusive or disturbing. They emerge as sensory memories prompting reminiscence and a connection to people remembered:

> I was very close to my Dad. I still see him. Sometimes he's standing right there in the hallway. It doesn't bother me. It's quite comforting.

Many of the stories recounted in our interviews manifest emotional fluctuations and a 'working through' of confusion or difficulty. This is the case with both hallucination and confabulation. Conventionally regarded as unreliable, 'made up' explanations for phenomena that are no longer understandable (due to some piece of information being lost or unretrievable), confabulations may also be a productive form of *meaning making* (Orulv & Hyden 2006). Lisa Bortolotti (2018) suggests that 'ill-grounded explanations fill gaps in knowledge, and . . . make a contribution to people's sense of themselves as competent and largely coherent agents'. Thus, in the following story from Viv, stealing seems a plausible explanation for the absence of some jam, but the point of the story is to reaffirm a sense of self:

> That nurse used to steal my jam, you know? The one I was telling you about? I left the jam on the table and she just took it! I confronted her once. I said, 'Stealing is illegal, if you ever steal anything from me again, I'll call the police. Or a solicitor'. So that put her off stealing from me. She resented me because of the effective way I dealt with her. She really quite enjoyed stealing from me. She tried to steal my newspapers as well.

This new work on confabulation foregrounds the emotional dimensions of narrative, cautioning against the urge to 'fact-check' and correct in favour of attuning to neurodivergent storytelling. Artist David Clegg does likewise in *The Trebus Project*, for which he collected the stories of over 300 people with dementia in residential care in the UK. Clegg found that the elements of these stories remained largely consistent, even when some conflation of time periods was apparent (Clegg & Young-Mason 2014). Thus, he challenges the idea that a confabulating speaker is an 'unreliable' narrator. Clearly the stories told have an emotional drive and coherence. But more than this, *The Trebus Project* corpus has a particular experiential truth value, reflecting the fact that for some people with dementia the past and present coexist, and 'come together in a constellation like a flash of lightening' (Clegg & Young-Mason 2014; Capstick 2015).

When Viv tells us about her love for walking, time is compressed; the listener cannot know for certain if activities occur in the present, the past or will occur in future:

> I just loved going for walks. I used to walk to school, that's a mile to and back . . . until I could ride a bike. It clears my mind. I like to get outside the house. I sometimes walk to the library.

There is, in fact, a vast sweep to her poetic reverie that transcends the distinctions of temporality, in a continuous present tense:

> I travel. All the time. I'm always travelling . . .

She travels; we are not required to travel. All that is asked of the visitor is to remain in place, to be in the room, open and curious, to take in experience as it unfolds.

Notes

1 Full credits for *The Visit* by fEEL – along with video extracts – can be found at: https://www.thebiganxiety.org/ (accessed 17 September 2021).

2 A formal study with viewers *of The Visit* tested its impacts in terms of these key components of empathy. Results showed increased empathy and decreased emotional distance (Papadopoulos et al. 2021).

References

Arora, G. and B. Ousman [Writers] (2015), *Clouds Over Sidra*, in G. Arora, C. Fabian, C. Fabien, & S. Kakoulides [Producers], Virtual Reality Production Company.

Bortolotti, L. (2018), 'Stranger Than Fiction: Costs and Benefits of Everyday Confabulation', *Review of Philosophy and Psychology*, 9 (2): 227–49.

Capstick, A. (2015), 'Re-Walking the City: People with Dementia Remember', in T. Richardson (ed.), *Walking Inside out: Contemporary British Psychogeography*, 211–25, Lanham, MD: Rowman & Littlefield International.

Clegg, D. and J. Young-Mason (2014), 'Art, Body, and Soul, Part 2: A Conversation With David Clegg', *Clinical Nurse Specialist*, 28 (2): 121–5.

Cuddy, A.J.C. and S.T. Fiske (2017), 'Doddering but Dear: Process, Content and Function in Stereotyping of Older Persons', in T.D. Nelson (ed.), *Ageism: Stereotyping and Prejudice Against Older Persons* (2nd ed.), 3–26, Cambridge, MA: The MIT Press.

Hare, D. (2010), 'David Hare: Mere Fact, Mere Fiction', *The Guardian*, 17 April 2010. Available online: https://www.theguardian.com/culture/2010/apr/17/david-hare-theatre-fact-fiction (accessed 17 September 2021).

Herrera, F., J. Bailenson, E. Weisz, E. Ogle, and J. Zaki (2018), 'Building Long-term Empathy: A Large-scale Comparison of Traditional and Virtual Reality Perspective-taking', *PLoS ONE*, 13 (10): e0204494.

Jobert, M. (2011). '"Instant Contextualisation" and Readerly Involvement in Alan Bennett's "Bed Among the Lentils"', *Etudes de Stylistique Anglaise*, 3: 45–58.

Laing, R.D. (1969), *Self and Others* (2nd rev ed.), New York: Pantheon.

Milk, C. (2015), 'How Virtual Reality Can Create the Ultimate Empathy Machine', *TED: Ideas Worth Spreading* [Video], Available online: https://www.ted.com/talks/chris_milk_how_virtual_reality_can_create_the_ultimate_empathy_machine (accessed 17 September 2021).

National Theatre (2014), *An Introduction to Verbatim Theatre* [Video], UK: National Theatre. Available online: https://youtu.be/ui3k1wT2yeM (accessed 17 September 2021).

Orulv, L. and L.-C. Hyden (2006), 'Confabulation: Sense-making, Self-making and World-making in Dementia', *Discourse Studies*, 8 (5): 647–73.

Papadopoulos, C., G. Kenning, J. Bennett, V. Kuchelmeister, N. Ginnivan, and M. Neidorf (2021), 'A Visit with Viv: Empathising with a Digital Human

Character Embodying the Lived Experiences of Dementia', *Dementia* (London): 1471301221998888.

Phillipson, L., C. Magee, S. Jones, S. Reis, and E. Skaldzien (2015), 'Dementia Attitudes and Help-seeking Intentions: An Investigation of Responses to two Scenarios of an Experience of the Early Signs of Dementia', *Aging & Mental Health*, 19 (11): 968–77.

Rogers, C.R. (1959), 'A Theory of Therapy, Personality and Interpersonal Relationships as Developed in the Client-centered Framework', in S. Koch (ed.), *Psychology: A Study of a Science, Study 1, Volume 3: Formulations of the Person and the Social Context*, 184–256, New York: McGraw-Hill.

Serres, Michel (2015), *Eyes*, London: Bloomsbury Publishing

Talking Heads (1988), [TV programme], BBC, UK.

Part IV

Designing for experience

CHAPTER 8

Facilitating environments

An arts-based psychosocial design approach

Jill Bennett, Lynn Froggett
and Lizzie Muller

This two-part chapter examines the practice of arts-based psychosocial design in relation to the creation of a facilitating space. It focuses on two projects delivered as part of The Big Anxiety festival: *Awkward Conversations* (Sydney 2017, 2019; Queensland 2019, 2022), in which one-to-one conversations about mental health were offered in experimental aesthetic formats; and *Parragirls Past, Present* (Sydney 2017), a reparative project culminating in an immersive film production that explores the enduring effects of institutional abuse and the ways in which traumatic experiences can be re-figured to transform their emotional resonance and meaning. Bringing psychosocial theory into dialogue with an arts-based inquiry into lived experience, these two projects examine the imbrication of lived experience and social settings and the potential for evolving strategies for supporting mental health and emotional well-being.

The term 'psychosocial' describes a (psychoanalytically informed) field of research and practice, which seeks to overcome the abstraction of psychology from embodied, lived experience, situated within a social nexus. Arts-based psychosocial projects may be understood to work from and with lived experience, examining the subjective aspects of that experience in relation to social, material and institutional settings – but also providing a structure within which the dynamic complexity of experience may be processed. It is specifically the capacity to activate and transform a 'container-contained' relationship (Bion 1970) that defines this as a psychosocial inquiry. The container–contained relationship moderates unprocessed sense data and the anxiety it arouses so that it can be symbolized. The artwork, designed and conceived as containing process, performs a 'metabolizing' and transformative function in relation to material that may otherwise be hard to think of and hard to bear.

The projects we discuss offer a terrain on which to investigate – and navigate – the processes and effects of symbolic elaboration, and specifically of presentational symbolization, which Suzanne Langer (1942, 1953) describes as a process of finding form for feeling, characteristic of art and music. Kenneth Wright (2009: 116) points out that the notion of a presentational symbol implies a container–contained structure which 'shows forth' rather than denotes that which it contains: 'such a symbol evokes and resonates with the experience stored within it, and from this perspective the container–contained is a living structure consisting of inter-communicating elements.'

In this regard we are interested not only in how the arts accommodate and give expression to the vitality of lived experience but in how there might be a carrying forward of this experience through aesthetic/art practice. This enables us to develop art projects that make a practical contribution to mental health and well-being, though for reasons outlined throughout, we understand this contribution to reside in cultural practice rather than a health domain.

As practice-based researchers (Bennett is director of The Big Anxiety festival, responsible for the design of programmes; Froggett and Muller have been engaged in its formative evaluation) we investigate this 'living structure . . . of inter-communicating elements' not as a given but in terms of a field of affordances (Gibson 1979). Following J. J. Gibson, we understand affordances as the possibilities for action and experience that exist in the relationships between the participants and the environments designed and created within these projects. Designing with affordances in mind shifts the focus from the idea of shaping or crafting 'an experience' to creating the potential for a repertoire of active engagements. If affordances are perceived as opportunities for action, they are also *felt*. The concept of the affordance is derived from valence (Gibson 1979: 138), referring to the emotional value associated with a stimulus, which in turn may be linked to power relations. These affordances, which pertain to relational and sensory interactions, are, of course, a mixture of intentional, accidental and emergent as the creative process proceeds through cycles of action, evaluation and adjustment *in situ* (Muller & Langill 2016).

As Winnicott ([1951] 2000) pointed out, 'creativity can be destroyed by too great insistence that in acting one must know beforehand what one is doing'. We discuss in this chapter the practice of working with affordances to create generative and containing settings. These settings, which may also be understood as 'facilitating environments' (Winnicott [1965] 1990), offer the opportunity for an expanded range of interactions and therefore a potentially enriched lived experience. 'Containment' is envisaged as a guiding curatorial principle in presenting art relating to mental health (Bartlett & Muller 2017) and the facilitating environment that enables it to emerge through a practice-based process of development and testing on the ground.

Part one: *Awkward Conversations*

Our first example is a public engagement programme – *Awkward Conversations* – in which affordances were crafted to create the potential for exchanges which might help participants to articulate and process objects of hitherto inexpressible anxiety.

The *Awkward Conversations* programme creates opportunities for conversation in facilitating environments at public venues rather than in spaces that are coded as either art or health settings. Fundamentally, it aims to 'design away' the barriers to holding a conversation, attending to institutional positioning, affordances of place and to how a conversation that is awkward and anxiety-provoking becomes possible and potentially transformative as a two-person engagement beyond the realm of help-seeking. It was first staged in 2017 in Customs House, a multipurpose site in the tourist hub of Circular Quay, owned by City of Sydney, housing restaurants and a library and attracting a continual flow of visitors. The 'Awkward Conversations' programme was run from the front desk with volunteers acting as concierges taking visitors to one-to-one bookable conversations held throughout the building and forecourt.

The initial programme included twelve different types of conversation, generally one-to-one, each lasting around twenty minutes. They were hosted by artists and others with lived experiences of anxiety, neurodiversity and the mental health system. A conversation called 'The S-word' addressing suicidality ('for anyone who has ever thought about suicide – as well as those who haven't and feel they need to know more') was delivered in a corner of the public library by Alessandro, a host with lived experience. Autistic artist Dawn Joy Leong hosted conversations in purpose-built adjacent pods, designed to accommodate those not comfortable with close or face-to-face contact or the intrusive excesses of ordinary environmental stimulation. First Nations artist Amala Groom hosted a conversation about anxiety over a footbath using native medicinal plants. Other conversations were informally situated on comfortable chairs in the library foyer areas. Some made use of props (pens, paper, art materials), though the majority did not. Another conversation involved a walk around the Harbour with Debra Keenahan, an artist with achondroplasia dwarfism (Figure 8.1).

FIGURE 8.1 *Left:* Awkward Conversations *in Customs House; Right: Debra Keenahan's* Awkward Conversations *walk. The Big Anxiety, 2017; photographs by Gisella Vollmer, Skyline Productions.*

With the goal of engaging with the general public, including those who may require psychosocial support – the aesthetic focus of the project lay in creating conditions where host and visitor could enter into a respectful dialogue in which the lived experience of both might be introduced. Thus, there was an offer to connect through experience insofar as it felt possible within the parameters of the conversation, but no expectation that participants should disclose personal information. Hosts likewise do not necessarily place emphasis on telling their stories, but their self-styled introductions (along with advice about 'what to expect') signal an identification with lived experience, whether in diagnostic or other terms, as per these excerpts from the *Awkward Conversations* programme:

> Drawing on his own experience with self-injury and self-harm, Daniel Regan finds language in photography in the absence of words (and it helps).

> Bhenji dances as resistance, her body is her protest. Bhenji Ra is a trans woman of colour. She negotiates her identity at the intersection of body dysmorphia and gender dysphoria through dance, choreography, and her community practice hosting balls and performance events.

> Artist and self-described 'kook', Wart lives in extraordinary schizo-affective realities. She has 30 years hard experience navigating medications, community mental health programs, and private psychiatric encounters.

Advertised via the portal of an arts festival – such informal, sometimes whimsical descriptions recast conversations about mental health as playful and creative, rather than merely helpful. The generative, and also collaborative, nature of play has a particular potency in terms of establishing creative agency and enabling the reconfiguration of traumatic experience (as discussed in the following paragraphs, and by Marianne Wobcke in Chapter 5). More generally, however, this orientation shifts expectations towards an encounter that may be enjoyable, inspiring or stimulating. Under these conditions, visitors reported not only positive emotions but also perceived significant shifts and benefits:

> [The conversation] changed my experience/relationship to my mental health . . . provided a healing experience without having to do a 'therapeutic' intervention. (2019 visitor survey response)

Hosts were invited to identify and arrange the spaces (with or without props) in which conversations occurred, and attention was paid to the comfort of transition via the role of the volunteer 'concierges' who also served as 'minders' at a discrete distance from the conversation. The design of the overall programme and the individual conversations was thus shaped through attention to the *affordances* of the whole situation.

The settings of the *Awkward Conversations* were created through purposefully crafting relational possibilities between the people and elements that are felt emotionally (attending to temperature, noise level, visibility, physical comfort, proximity and so forth) in each situation, with the goal of engendering an easily accessible, public but relatively secure and semi-private facilitating environment (Winnicott [1965] 1990).

If the practice-based approach to creating this space builds on Gibson's work, our understanding of its operation owes more to the classic Winnicottian conception of a holding environment that is not just 'supportive' but able to secure or 'hold' the conditions in which a potential space can arise. Beyond its common-sense advantages for conversation, the value of constituting such an environment in an arts-based activation is to provide a temporary counterpoint to the relative lack of a secure holding in society at large. The *Awkward Conversation* settings had to create conditions where people had permission (and literally the guidance of concierges) to walk up and inquire about things they had wanted to know but had always been afraid to ask – or to seek some initial support for unmet needs, even though it was made clear that this was not a counselling service.

Capitalizing on the potential for mental health conversation beyond the health sector, we also sought to preserve and play with a sense of the awkwardness attached to conversations about mental health. One of the hosts encapsulated this in reporting that he felt able to be his 'awkward self', in contrast to working within a mental health setting where one is expected to be 'on message'. Participant feedback (via the festival survey) similarly reported: 'Feels very positive to be able to talk about difficult subject matter without having to filter or downplay.' Rather than disavowing or overcoming awkwardness, we sought to use its transformative potential as something that, under the right conditions, can impel rather than obstruct a conversation.

Recoding the locus of conversation as an aesthetic space enables a process of feeling into and articulating each conversational partner's aesthetic presence (described by Bollas as 'idiom', 1992). Each engagement in principle had to get to a point where it *felt good* as well as stimulating. This is not to distinguish the 'pleasure' of the arts from the functionality of therapy: 'aesthetic moments are not always beautiful or wonderful . . . many are ugly and terrifying but nonetheless profoundly moving because of the existential memory tapped' (Bollas 2011: 12). In this context a conversation that feels good is one in which apprehending the aesthetic presence of the other becomes possible because there is no compulsion to air-brush the awkwardness of the encounter. Accordingly, 2017 participants reported a range of emotions:

> Anxious at first. Proud once had actually spoken to someone.
> Overwhelmed but it felt like a necessary conversation.

They also ascribed positive sensation and emotion to the apprehension of the other:

> Embraced. The Conversations were really comforting, and the artists
>   were really giving.
> Fulfilled and liberated by the ability to engage in meaningful
>   conversations with strangers.
> Not awkward at all. It was the first time I had the opportunity to speak
>   to another person who had a similar express of mental illness to me.

In general, they reported feeling positive as a result of the encounter:

> Really engaged and stimulated.
> Open, confident, supported.
> Energized. Stimulated and engaged.
> More connected to other people.

Participants in the 2019 programme (held in the same location with different hosts) used noticeably similar vocabulary:

> Grounded. I came feeling burnt out, it gave me energy.
> Energized and liberated. Worthwhile.
> Glad to be alive. Energized. Loved it. Keen to talk more. Hopeful.

The people I conversed with were generous and open. It felt safe to
speak with them and it was a caring exchange.
More connected. More understood. Feel like I'm a little less alone.

Artist Debra Keenahan's walking conversation incorporated a further
dimension, co-opting ambient social interactions into the *Awkward
Conversation* experience to promote a level of empathic unsettlement
(LaCapra 2001), while nevertheless ensuring the supportive holding
environment of the one-to-one conversation. While many of the other hosts
had lived with anxiety associated with neurodiversity or mental health issues,
Keenahan identifies as disabled in respect of achondroplasia dwarfism and
for her, anxiety comes from a hostile and disabling environment. It is a
product of everyday social interaction, originating in the unease of others
and the intrusiveness of their gaze. In Keenahan's words, 'I will no longer be
disabled when I can walk down a street in peace.'

Her fifteen-minute walk brings into play the hostile environment through
which she and her companion move. The stares, comments, abuse and
photography that her presence elicits are, in effect, part of the material
fabric of the work. At one point in each conversation, Keenahan invites her
companion to stand still and watch what happens behind her back while she
proceeds alone for some 50 metres and then turns back towards them. Up to
this point the two have been walking side by side, but now the companion
becomes a spectator in a live tableau as subtle and not-so-subtle intrusions
unfold. Invariably, some passers-by turn to stare, others blatantly capture
photographs (volunteers sometimes had to intervene when people assumed
the right to photograph Debra after privacy was requested).

Keenahan (having psychology training) had studied the prevalence of
an avoidant/resistant response to the 'novel stimulus' of a body that is
unlike the subject's own. In her everyday experience, most people display
reticence: at best unconfident in how to approach or meet her eye, at worst
stigmatizing and avoidant, with those lacking impulse control more overt in
their response. Her expectation was that in facilitating an experience-near
(Geertz 1974) engagement, empathy could be engendered, not as a moral
ideal but as a stance cultivated through perspective-sharing and the act of
'being with'. Any detached expression of pity or moral indignation could be
undercut by the face-to-face encounter. Thus, the experience promotes what
La Capra (2001) calls 'empathic unsettlement', but of a kind that arises
from affective attunement (Stern 2004; Gobodo-Madikizela 2015: 1104).

Pumla Gobodo-Madikizela's Kleinian-informed approach to public
victim-perpetrator encounters during the South African Truth and
Reconciliation Commission (TRC) (Gobodo-Madikizela 2015) is
instructive here on the cultivation of empathy via face-to-face encounter.
Public settings that carefully constitute facilitating environments may,
argues Gobodo-Madikizela, serve as potential spaces facilitating the

'emergence of unexpected moments that might create connections' (Gobodo-Madikizela 2015: 1099). In other words, the experience-near encounter brokered within the facilitating environment can be the basis for imagining and feeling one's way into the other's perspective, experiencing and responding to their idiom and thus for humanizing them, and laying the basis for empathy.

Gobodo-Madikizela, herself a psychoanalytic psychologist, professes amazement at 'the idea that the imagination is necessary even to recognize the existence, the human beingness, of the other' (Gobodo-Madikizela 2015: 1111) (amazement was of course what was experienced in Keenahan's *Awkward Conversation* by stunned participants). Though 'extraordinary' this idea is borne out in the encounters that Gobodo-Madikizela brokered during and following the TRC, which lend support to Jessica Benjamin's conceptualization (1990, 1999, 2004) of 'mutual recognition' as the core of intersubjectivity through which 'the subject gradually becomes able to recognize the other person's subjectivity' (1990: 33; Gobodo-Madikizela 2015). Benjamin (2004: 5) describes 'a relation in which each person experiences the other as a "like subject", another mind who can be "felt with", yet as a distinct and separate centre of feeling and perception'. Gobodo-Madikizela suggests that

> The 'caring-for' element in empathy is the result of a deeper level of imagination and understanding of the other's experience. This deeper level of imagination takes 'feeling into' the mental state of the other to another level, and asks the question, What should I do about it?' (2015: 1112)

For Keenahan it was essential to reach this point of asking, 'What should I do about it?' In the event, Keenahan reported that three of her walking companions were shaken and moved to tears after witnessing the extent of this stigmatizing behaviour in a live enactment. For her, this emotional reaction was unplanned but not entirely surprising – and within the holding space formulated for the conversation, such well-intentioned, affectionate responses could be effectively supported, processed and discussed. Saying, 'I'm so sorry!' is not for Keenahan a useful response, particularly since it calls upon her to then take care of the participant/bystander whose own emotion becomes the focus. The potential for being with and feeling into is thus carefully brokered by Keenahan as a shifting perspective onto the environment; at the end of the walk the companion is literally 'drawn in close' to arrive not at a place of full identification or appropriation but at a point of asking, 'What are the options for action?'

From the intrusiveness, abuse and aggression of the public reactions to Debra we also have clues to the shame that may have been provoked in participants at their own unseemly or prurient curiosity, along with a desire to know more and also fear of causing harm. The maternal facilitating environment Winnicott had in mind was one in which the child may come to recognize and test the limits of their own fantasized destructiveness. Here it is not only the holding but the resilience of the 'surviving' mother that enables her to be recognized as a 'like subject' to be 'felt with'. Similarly, if a relatively unconstrained exchange was to occur in an *Awkward Conversation* it required confidence in the survival of the host who could moderate without retaliating any aggressive inquisitiveness on the part of the conversational partner. Keenahan's expressed confidence in her own resilience comes primarily from a lifetime of learning from experience (Bion 1970) where she has developed, as our example shows, the capacity to think in the face of continual adverse reactions – that Bion likened to 'thinking under fire'. Art practice here is guided by intuitive moves – which are in fact the mobilization of past experiences and reflection applied to a unique situation (Muller 2012), and can be understood as particular forms of aesthetic intelligence in action. Here these are sustained by the aesthetics of the encounter and the affordances of the total situation which included the volunteers and concierges, the framing and boundaries of the conversations and their material design.

If 'the role of design is to make affordances perceivable' (Dong & Burlamaqui 2015), a psychosocial design practice is one that enables not just good feeling but the full valence of lived experience to be shared, perceived and 'held'. To that end, we see a consistency in visitor responses, articulating depth of feeling from overwhelm and burn-out to the joy of being alive, activated and 'energized' in the encounter. Nik Rose and colleagues (2021) have recently invoked Gibson's theory of affordances to underpin their proposal for an expansive 'neuroecosocial' approach to mental health – a macro perspective that argues at the same time for greater attention to the ecological niches in which mental health is experienced and identified. They suggest that the 'causal architecture' or 'mechanisms' through which ecosocial experiences are embodied can only be grasped via an integrated understanding of how humans inhabit their 'ecological niches' – enfolding the micro-phenomenological detail of interactions across the field of affordances, which includes the actions of others, 'from their posture and gestures, to their facial expressions, to their behaviour more broadly' – all of which can 'afford' particular kinds of responses (2021). We have presented an approach that attends to the salience of these micro-interactions, a bottom-up approach to the design of mental health support that is experience-led (embodied, intuitive, guided by felt experience and relational contingencies) rather than programmatic; and attuned to negatively perceived as well as productive affordances, purposefully 'designing out' the barriers (physical, institutional, psychological, social) that must be negotiated in health systems. Such an approach, we would argue, is vital if we are to envisage psychosocial support within a framework that addresses the politics of lived experience.

Part two: *Parragirls Past, Present*

Our second example is a reparative project that engaged participants in exploring the enduring effects of institutional abuse in which affordances were (historically) systematically diminished and designed to oppress. The goal here was to promote conversation between survivors that not only expressed hard-to-articulate, traumatic experience but located this in the environment, bringing to visibility the emotional valence of interpersonal communications in the present, and the effects of micro-interactions in social and institutional settings.

'Parragirls' is the name adopted by former residents of the Parramatta Girls Home (PGH), a state-controlled child welfare institution, adjacent to the convict-era Parramatta Female Factory in Western Sydney, Australia. In 2017, five Parragirls – Bonney Djuric, Lynne Paskovski, Gypsie Hayes, Jenny McNally and Tony (Denise) Nicholas – collaborated with artists Lily Hibberd, Volker Kuchelmeister and Alex Davies on *Parragirls Past, Present*, an experimental 3D immersive film (twenty-three minutes long, screened in an immersive theatre or Virtual Reality headset). The film emerged from a longer-term community project with the women who had been committed to PGH as teenagers in the 1970s, having been deemed by the Children's Court to be neglected, uncontrollable or exposed to moral danger. The PGH regime was harshly punitive and girls were subjected to physical, emotional and sexual abuse. In 2017, the report of the Royal Commission into Institutional Responses to Child Sexual Abuse (RC) brought to public attention the scale of such abuse and a governmental apology followed in 2018. Produced at the time the women were testifying to the Commission, and with the buildings and grounds facing redevelopment, the film was conceived by the women to capture, document and imaginatively re-inhabit the site on new terms.

The women's aim was not to evoke the horrors of the past (they are averse to sensationalizing media coverage) but to take possession of the site and its representation in the present. Having lived for more than forty years with the institutional denial of their abuse, freighted with the authority of official descriptions, making peace now entails wresting back control of the site's contested meaning. For this primary reason the creative team of the Parragirls and collaborating artists undertook terrestrial and aerial surveys to capture the whole complex. Rather than simply making a narrative film, the goal was to recreate the site and the experience of moving through it. No figures appear on screen, but the voices of the women guide us into and through the immersive experience, beginning with a recollection of the brutality of entering remand as we pass inside the walled compound:

> When you go into any remand, you go for internal examinations. Now, you're virgins at this time. . . . I remember being held down by staff

members forcing internal . . . you're screaming and the police are standing there and they're not doing a thing. And you were really scared . . . after the brutal examination . . . you are thinking what the hell else is going to happen to ya?

Photorealistic imagery of a corridor and sandstone 'dungeon' area of a segregation room and a laundry – each sparking different recollections – are interspersed with point-cloud representations which, while topographically accurate, create an aesthetic of fragmentation as objects and surface textures appear to break into pixels: delicate luminescent points of colour that 'simultaneously generate the perception of authenticity and scientific accuracy while presenting a fragmented and broken world' (Kuchelmeister, Hibberd & Davies 2018). The project, however, is not simply about what is remembered but *how* it is remembered, encountered, shared in a context where the truth of the women's experience was systematically denied and undermined, often leaving them with only the defences of dissociation and self-harm.

Psychoanalytic trauma theorists have drawn attention to the impossibility of witnessing massive psychic trauma during its occurrence. The force of the event precludes its registration, such that it is 'a record that has yet to be made' (Laub 1992). Moreover, within a totalitarian architecture, 'the inherently incomprehensible and deceptive psychological structure of the event precludes its own witnessing' (Laub 1995: 65). As such, there were minimal but significant affordances enabling resistance in PGH; as the women's testimony to the RC affirms, 'at Parramatta Girls Home, there was nowhere for any of the girls to go to talk' (RC Case Study 7, exhibit 17:29), but in the film the women describe escape attempts, the practice of scratching graffiti into the sandstone (which Bonney calls a 'really remarkable act of defiance', given the punishment); the hiding of pins from the industrial sewing room under the skin; the practice of harming their own bodies as a means to register survival:

> My existence was my own damage. And that was my own bodily injuries. I chose that over the scratching because I was terrified of the consequence. And so, I marked myself and chose that way of seeing my own blood instead of seeing my name on a wall.

The film voiceover, created and spoken by the women, emerged through initial experiments in which they roamed the site in pairs, recording their conversations and comparing memories and perceptions. Thus, the voiceover is less a narration for an imagined audience than an emergent discussion. As with *Awkward Conversations,* the aesthetic technique was intended to promote a process of elaboration within a holding space – with the distinction that in this case, the facilitating environment had to be engendered within the walls of the Parramatta site. It is in this very profound sense that *Parragirls Past, Present* differs from objective (or sensationalizing) reports of the site's notorious past. The aim – and unique

FIGURE 8.2 Parragirls Past, Present, 2017 *(viewer in immersive 3D film). The Big Anxiety, 2017; photograph by Saeed Khan/AFP.*

capacity – of the immersive film as an arts-based psychosocial inquiry was to locate the continuing effects of trauma in present-day interactions. It is in this way that we come to understand the force of institutionalized discourse (Figure 8.2).

Jenny McNally relates two key examples, each located at particular sites:

> If we had muster, that's where they'd stand and that's why I was so offended when the FaCS [Family and Community Services] worker stood up there and started reciting the history of Parramatta Girls Home and getting it all wrong. And I just told her how I felt she was so flippant about the whole of Parramatta Girls Home. And how easy it fell; all this garbage fell out of her mouth that was so non-factual. And I just saw outrage. . . . Actually, it was very hard for me to bear. I just wanted to scream at her because she was lording over us. And the sad thing was she turned to me and said, 'And who are you?' And I went regimented and I said my name. What I should have told her was, 'Go f . . . go fuck yourself, love'. I said my name because she was standing on the step and I just transformed into an insignificant nothing and responded in the expectation that a superintendent would expect me to respond. And, oh, I was beside myself that that had happened. I was so angry that someone could turn me so quickly with, 'And who are you?'

Such paralysis – often described in terms of 'triggering' – may be understood as replaying originary trauma in a process that Freud (1991) characterizes as *Nachträglichkeit* or 'afterwardsness' whereby later memories, struggles and the partial work of healing vanish and the trauma is reconstructed retroactively – as if time and memory had not elapsed. The paralysis returns, unbidden and unanticipated in an unresolved repetition not only of the experience but of the relations of powerlessness associated with the silencing – a 'deferred obedience' (Freud & Breuer [1895] 2004) to an internalized and cruel authority.

In this retelling, the tables are turned on that authority. The audience is confronted not only with the painful legacy of abuse but with a sense of how authority is still assumed without question or insight within institutional settings in ways that re-enact coercive power relations. For the survivors themselves, the film – and filmmaking process – may be considered as a potential space that has the effect of expanding affordances for action. In this context the potential space enables the settled convention of authority to be re-figured and re-imagined so that agency now resides with the women themselves finding expression in an aesthetic object of their creation.

The 'paralysing' event recollected is not represented visually but is situated within the institutional architecture in a manner quite distinctive to immersive 3D film, which moves the viewer into and around the unpopulated grounds. Space in this experiential medium is not a backdrop but appears to open up and enclose; space, this time round, is made for the women's experience. At the point at which the violence of silencing was experienced 'internally' by Jenny, the film enables the registration of this experience: the space onscreen, depicting the vacated site of PGH, is momentarily stilled, so that it is envisaged as containing a felt response: a silent scream. It is a space where this can now be witnessed.

On a second occasion described by Jenny, a visitor's response is even more insensitive:

> Bonney was telling the history and one of the men turned around and said, 'If all of these rapes happened, where are all the pregnancies? Where are all the babies?' And I was nearly sick. I was nearly sick. And Bonney answered so well. She just said, 'They knew our cycle'. . . . I went outside and I was so explosive with that comment. . . . I did a silent scream. And I just stood there with my hands up thinking, 'How dare anyone speak like that in front of us?'

Towards the climax of the film, this account of a devastating interaction is given its own expansive space; the camera moves away and up from the building mentioned, opening up a *caesura* at the spot where Jenny remembers herself standing, 'hands up, thinking'. The camera surveys the scene from above so that the women's voices now speak to and of the site below. As the camera continues to pan out, encompassing the entire site, in an oblique aerial view, we hear on the soundtrack the women's plea that government authorities must be accountable so that nothing like this will happen again. This calling to account reflects the dual purpose of testimony; Laub (1995: 63) says of his work with Holocaust survivors that they 'did not only need to survive so that they could tell their stories; they also needed to tell their stories in order to survive'.

In the film Jenny talks about her dismay at being punished for nothing, describing her refusal to stay silent as a question of survival: 'I have never hurt anyone. I just had a mouth on me, you know. I could have shut up, but I felt if I'd ever shut up, I wouldn't be who I am today.' Jenny's published testimony (RC Case Study 7, exhibit 17) details a catastrophic failure of care, compounded at every level (family, school, church, welfare, government and judicial process). Throughout it, she describes how screaming was her only recourse, sometimes effective in the short term in warning off abusers, more often eliciting beatings: 'I was screaming out and nobody would listen. Nobody heard. But I was so noisy, I don't understand how nobody heard' (RC 7.17.40).

The truth is that many people – parents, teachers, pastors, police officers, mental health professionals, welfare workers, PGH staff – heard the noise; nobody listened. Even a psychiatrist professes herself unable to understand why Jenny would 'muck up'. Yet, as Winnicott (1958) argued, the apparent 'anti-social' tendency of children must be 'met' and understood as a reaction to environmental deprivation; that is to say, as a reaction to the lack of a facilitating or holding environment, notwithstanding 'the roof over your head' for which Jenny was told by child welfare to be grateful (RC 7. 17.14). If the Royal Commission was able to bring to light the truth of institutional abuse, *Parragirls Past, Present* played a different reparative role.

As Bollas (1992: 70) explains, 'the work of trauma is to sponsor symbolic repetition, not symbolic elaboration.' It is in the possibility of symbolic elaboration that we find the key to understanding the contribution of an artwork, especially one that brings memories of the past vividly into the present – not only as narrative re-enactment but also as 'lyric' creation, experienced immersively in the moment (Abbott 2007). For the Parragirls, the film – and associated aesthetic process – offered a container for re-symbolization, within which trauma could be transformed into psychic genera ('something that will link with and possibly elaborate the psychic material that is incubating into a new vision' (Bollas 1992: 79)). Such symbolic elaboration is an essential counterpart of the political re-positioning of the self as 'survivor'. Without it survivalism is brittle, subject to set-backs, and can collapse into the dynamics of 'doer' and 'done to' that characterize the sadomasochistic relationship (Benjamin 2004).

The conclusion of the RC and its wider reporting inevitably represented both welcome acknowledgement and a risk of disappointment and loss of control over the narrative, which the women sought to mitigate by generating their own project out of their recovery process. Most importantly, this was grounded in their aesthetic perception, felt experience and sensibility – to which no space had ever previously been given.

The film offered a context in which the women's memories could in some sense be objectified in the materiality of the setting. The challenge was to work with the affordances of the environment, transforming them through the site exploration and filmmaking so that, from a locus of oppression, the buildings and grounds of Paramatta Girls Home became an arena for the realization of a hard-won resilience. In contrast to the discursive space of media exposure that is opened up in stories of the 'scandal' of Parramatta, the artistic process enabled the women to access the potential spaces of creative imagination which found expression in the narrative and imagery of the film – not a documentary but an aesthetic rendering of a structure of feeling (Williams 1981) associated with the walkways and empty rooms of a place that now appeared less substantial through the shifting, breaking patterns of spectral point-cloud light.

The point of making an artwork of this experience is neither testimony nor representation. While the story is told in the voiceover, something of the quality of feeling aroused for the Parragirls is made experientially available to the audience – but through the aesthetic containment of the film. In this context there is a reparative aspect (felt and told) to the replaying of fragments of traumatic memory, now transformed, re-symbolized and overlaid with a narrative of survival. What is at stake here is believability. As Jenny articulates in a subsequent video interview:

> I think that's the most amazing thing. . . . That I was believed . . . to have my first-born son, who was taken from me through Parramatta say, 'Mum, this is stunning and now I understand your story, I understand who you are'. It gave me back my reality. (McNally 2017)

From a practice perspective we have highlighted the relational work of designing with affordances – felt opportunities for action that allow for an active empathic engagement that neither demands nor allows a participant to easily co-opt, normalize or resolve the experience of another.

An awkward conversation is therefore not only awkward by virtue of its subject matter – its affordances enable active work with the discomfort that arises in the conversational dyad rather than seeking to ameliorate or 'art-wash'. The facilitating environment favours an 'optimal graduated awkwardness' (to paraphrase Winnicott) which can moderate inquisitiveness, embarrassment or diffidence by supporting both the self-awareness of the participant and the resilience of the 'surviving' host. The aim is to create the conditions of mutual recognition in which the reality of another is not so much explained as revealed in the encounter – a learning from experience (Bion 1970) where it can be apprehended and thought about.

The knowledge acquired in the process substitutes neither for critique of medicalized mental health systems nor for therapeutic practice. Arts projects such as those described seek another route to shared understanding of mental distress which, following Alford's (1989) interpretation of Melanie Klein's (1930) account of epistemophilia, can be seen as a quest for empathic knowing which is rooted in *Caritas*, rather than *Eros* – where the desire for knowledge benefits the knower. Such a quest aims to achieve a compassionate knowing without impinging on or damaging the object: Love as *Caritas* 'lets its object be', rather than appropriating the other.

As interest grows in accounting for the mental health benefits of art, there is a risk that measurable dimensions extraneous to lived aesthetic experience are foregrounded. A theorization of art's transformative potential therefore becomes ever more necessary. This can be derived – as we have indicated – from Bollas' account of aesthetic transformation, which expands Winnicott's conception of the 'environment-mother' to include its aesthetic aspect:

> The mother's idiom of care and the infant's experience of this handling is one of the first, if not the earliest human aesthetic. [It] will predispose all future aesthetic experiences that place the person in subjective rapport with an object. (Bollas 1987: 32–3)

For Bollas (1987: 16) the expectation of being transformed by a process arises from the manner of the mother's tending through which she expresses her own distinctive idiom – 'never cognitively apprehended but existentially known', shaping in her child an aesthetic intelligence that will be elaborated throughout life. Creative practice is likewise intuitively concerned with creating the conditions – the facilitating environment – through which the transformative aesthetic moment can be realized. This entails a delicate negotiation between control (the drive towards a strong aesthetic outcome) and the potential space that 'lets the object be', or 'become', while holding the arena of engagement.

The Parragirls project was coextensive with a public reckoning alongside which a different need arose – for a holding situation – no longer the forensic knowing and exposing of what had happened. To the extent that the film engenders the feeling of containment, it is the registration of a process by which the women determined to create a vehicle that could hold their experience. Their impulse then was a reparative re-inhabiting of the site, finding in its imaginative re-creation an alternative set of affordances. Rather than the repetition of incommunicable trauma, working with the potential spaces in the immersive film offered an opportunity for symbolic elaboration. Such a generative process is vital to the refiguration of traumatic memory.

> The 'work' of trauma will be to collect disturbing experience into the network of a traumatic experience (now a memory and an unconscious idea) while the play work of genera will be to collect units of received

experience that interanimate towards a new way of perceiving things. (Bollas 1992: 78)

Parragirls Past, Present exemplifies aesthetic work in the case of complex trauma, itself marked by the systemic deprivation of a potential space that would enable a re-figuring of their relations to that trauma. It enables listening and hearing and opens the possibility of an empathic response. We have shown how such an approach can in practical ways enable the fundamental components of an empathic response, and how and why such a response must be actively enabled where inhospitable conditions exacerbate anxiety and trauma. Through greater aesthetic attunement we can provide options for action.

* * *

Both Debra Keenahan's walking conversation and the Parragirls' immersive environment recast and consciously expand the affordances of an environment in reparative ways. Perception *in action* is central to Gibson's concept of affordances: moving through the world, we relationally perceive the possibilities for action that different features and objects – including the other sentient beings – 'afford' us.

A psychosocial approach to affordances reveals the multivalent complexity of the material environment, shot through entirely with these 'interpersonal' affordances. The potentials for action in our environment are at once and indivisibly social and physical. Affordances are fundamentally relational qualities – they exist always in the relation between the perceiver and the perceived. These relations are physical, social, emotional, symbolic and internalized. If a psychosocial understanding of affordances emphasizes the social nature of the environment, and the environmental nature of our social relations, its application in design attends not only to the optimal facilitating environment but to the internalized, pre-reflective capacities which enable the actor to make sense of – and act on – an affordance in the first place.

In design practice there has been a great deal of emphasis on imagining the affordances available to differently abled people. While such practice has always included an awareness that affordances can be social, symbolic and cultural (Dong & Burlamaqui 2015) the focus has remained on redesigning environments or objects with improved affordances for all, rather than in designing environments that reveal the negative affordances produced by other social actors in and through environments. In our work on psychosocial arts and exhibition-making we have frequently described the value of 'containing environments' which support the conditions to experience and metabolize discomfort. There is a danger that this space of containment could be misperceived as a static 'safe' space, cut off from the world or bounded. Combining the idea of the containing environment with the concept of affordances demonstrates how a containing environment is mobilized. In both of the above examples the participant is invited to 'walk with' another human being through a process that reveals traumatic affordances that would otherwise be imperceptible to that participant. In this sense the 'containing environment' is the opposite of an enclosed 'safe space'. It is a way of perceiving through shared experience the limits and the violence embedded in environments that may otherwise *seem* safe.

The conscious expansion of our capacity to perceive affordances 'either for good or ill' (Gibson 1979: 127) is a pressing ethical requirement. Understanding the partiality of our own perception and how that is shaped by the affordances available to us is a crucial step towards 'feeling' the world in the way that others feel it.

References

Abbott, A. (2007), 'Against Narrative: A Preface to Lyrical Sociology', *Sociological Theory*, 25 (1): 67–99.

Alford, F. (1989), *Melanie Klein and Critical Social Theory: An Account of Politics, art and Reason Based on her Psychoanalytic Theory*, New Haven and London: Yale University Press.

Australia (2017), *Royal Commission Into Institutional Responses to Child Sexual Abuse: Case Study 7*. Available online: https://www.childabuseroyalcommission .gov.au/exhibits-case-study-7 (accessed 29 September 2021).

Bartlett, V. and L. Muller (2017), 'Curating/containing: Exhibiting Digital art About Mental Health', in: J. Arango, A. Bubarno, F. Londoño, and G.M. Mejía (eds), *ISEA2017 BIO-CREATION AND PEACE*, Manizales, Columbia, International Symposium on Electronic Arts.

Benjamin, J. (1990), 'An Outline of Intersubjectivity: The Development of Recognition', *Psychoanalytic Psychology*, 7 (Suppl): 33–46.

Benjamin, J. (1999) 'Recognition and Destruction: An Outline of Intersubjectivity', in S.A. Mitchell and L. Aron (eds), *Relational Psychoanalysis: The Emergence of a Tradition*, 181–200, Hillsdale, NJ: Analytic Press.

Benjamin, J. (2004), 'Beyond Doer and Done to: Recognition and the Intersubjective Third', *Psychoanalytic Quarterly*, 73: 5–46.

Bion, W. (1970), *Attention and Interpretation*, London: Karnac.

Bollas, C. (1987), *The Shadow of the Object: Psychoanalysis of the Unthought Known*, London: Free Association Books.

Bollas, C. (1992), *Being a Character: Psychoanalysis and Self-experience*, New York: Hill & Wang.

Bollas, C. (2011), 'Psychic Genera', in *The Christopher Bollas Reader*, 57–78, London: Routledge.

Dong, A. and L. Burlamaqui (2015), 'The use and Misuse of the Concept of Affordance', *Design Computing and Cognition DCC*, 14: 295–311.

Freud, S. (1991), *Case Histories II*, London: Penguin Books.

Freud, S. and J. Breuer ([1895] 2004), *Studies in Hysteria*, London: Penguin Classics.

Geertz, C. (1974), 'From the Native's Point of View: On the Nature of Anthropological Understanding', *Bulletin of the American Academy of Arts and Sciences*, 28 (1): 26–45.

Gibson, J.J. (1979), *The Ecological Approach to Visual Perception*, Boston: Houghton Mifflin.

Gobodo-Madikizela, P. (2015), 'Psychological Repair: The Intersubjective Dialogue of Remorse and Forgiveness in the Aftermath of Gross Human Rights Violations', *Journal of the American Psychoanalytic Association*, 63 (6): 1085–123.

Klein, M. (1930), 'The Importance of Symbol-formation in the Development of the ego', *The International Journal of Psychoanalysis*, 11: 24–39.

Kuchelmeister, V., L. Hibberd, and A. Davies (2018), 'Affect and Place Representation in Immersive Media: The Parragirls Past, Present Project', in J.P. Bowen, J. Weinel, G. Diprose, and N. Lambert (eds), *Electronic Visualisation and the Arts 2018*, 71–8, London: EVA.

LaCapra, D. (2001), *Writing History, Writing Trauma*, Baltimore, MD: Johns Hopkins University Press.

Langer, S. (1942), *Philosophy in a new key: A Study in the Symbolism of Reason, Rite, and art*, New York: NAL Mentor.

Langer, S. (1953), *Feeling and Form: A Theory of art*, New York: Scribner's.

Laub, D. (1992), 'Bearing Witness, or the Vicissitudes of Listening' in S. Felman and D. Laub (eds), *Testimony: Crises of Witnessing in Literature, Psychoanalysis and History*, 57–74, New York: Routledge.

Laub, D. (1995), 'Truth and Testimony: The Process and the Struggle', in C. Caruth (ed.), *Trauma: Explorations in Memory*, 61–75, Baltimore: Johns Hopkins.

McNally, J (2017), Jenny McNally Interview, Parramatta. Available online: https://www.youtube.com/watch?v=4hFS8-Fq-c8 (accessed 22 September 2021).

Muller, L. (2012), 'Learning from Experience: A Reflective Curatorial Practice', in L. Candy and E. Edmonds (eds), *Interacting: Art, Research and the Creative Practitioner*, 94–106, Oxfordshire, Libri Publishing.

Muller, L. and C. Langill (2016), 'Curating Lively Objects: Post-disciplinary Affordances for Media Art Exhibition', in D. England, T. Schiphorst and N. Bryan-Kinns (eds), *Curating the Digital: Space for art and Interaction, edn. Cultural Computing*, 31–49, Switzerland: Springer International Publishing.

Rose, N., R. Birk, and N. Manning (2021), 'Towards Neuroecosociality: Mental Health in Adversity', *Theory, Culture and Society*, January.

Stern, D. (2004), *The Present Moment in Psychotherapy and Everyday Life*, New York: Norton.

Williams, R. (1981), *The Sociology of Culture*, Chicago: University of Chicago Press.

Winnicott, D.W. ([1951] 2000), 'Critical Notice of "On not Being Able to Paint"', in L. Caldwell (ed.), *Art, Creativity, Living*, 117–19, London: Karnac.

Winnicott, D. (1958), 'The Antisocial Tendency', in *Collected Papers: Through Paediatrics to Psycho-analysis*, 306–15, London: Tavistock.

Winnicott, D. ([1965] 1990), *The Maturational Processes and the Facilitating Environment*, London: Karnac.

Wright, K. (2009), *Mirroring and Attunement: Self-realization in Psychoanalysis and art*, Hove: Routledge.

CHAPTER 9

I have a thing about tables

Lois Weaver with Laura Hunter Petree

I have a thing about tables
I thought I should just come right out and say that

I love a table
I love the lines, the angles, the sides
I love the legs.

I love how stable a table, how upright and firm, how ordinary.[1]

Growing up in the rural south of the United States in the 1950s, the only social outlet for a white working-class girl, too young to drive, was the church. There were always Bible studies, Sunday schools, ice-cream socials, potluck suppers, baby showers and June weddings. My father was the janitor or custodian, as he called himself, and one of my jobs, besides dusting off the pews and replacing the hymnals in the sanctuary, was setting up and breaking down the many two and a half by six-foot folding tables in preparation for these events. I began to associate dragging these tables out of their closet and into the church hall with the anticipation of occasion and contact, with homemade cake and tuna casseroles, with the chaos of children let loose in the safe confines of a church basement and the lingering conversations and enthusiastic recipe sharing between adults too tired and too reluctant to leave the company of the table. Perhaps this anticipation, activation and return lay the groundwork for my life as a touring performance artist. It's how I learned to gain satisfaction from arriving, unpacking, enacting, breaking down and packing up. I suspect it is also how I developed a love for the temporary and transformational. It is most certainly how I developed my fondness for tables, and more than sixty years later, the folding table is at the centre of my performance research and practice.

Folding means to bend, to mix ingredients gently or to rearrange; tables are the ubiquitous custodians of municipal, civic, social encounters and familial sustenance; and to table, of course, is to put forward or suggest. Since 2005 I have used folding tables, both real and conceptual, to bend and mix public space into something more familiar, accessible and conducive to conversation. I have set up folding tables end to end in the middle of a room to make a table long and equally accessible from all sides. I have set tables up in a circle on stage and invited the oldest people in the room to publicly state anxieties and address desires in the face of an uncertain future. I have dealt out conference papers like playing cards at tables of four and set up these same small tables in a café formation where the only thing on the menu is care. Things that fold tend to travel; they are transient and fluid. These tables have been unfolded in libraries, theatres, galleries, social clubs, city halls and town squares, unpacking and setting up topics of conversations on women's prisons in Rio de Janeiro, the effect of Brexit on individuals and organizations in the UK, and the future of queer theatre in NYC and lived experience and the state of the world at The Big Anxiety festival in Sydney.

In this chapter, I will keep to the realm of the domestic and offer brief descriptions of how these unfoldings have developed into usable *recipes* for public conversations, which I sometimes collect under the heading of Public Address Systems. I will describe the origin of these recipes and reflect on how they were situated in a consideration of arts and mental health at The Big Anxiety festival, which brought together artists, scientists and communities in September 2017 to examine the state of mental health in the twenty-first century. I will include basic open-source instructions for how to make your own Long Tables, Care Cafés and Porch Sittings. These recipes are like what you might find in a community cookbook, always an experiment and always open to the cook's creative interpretation. I extend an invitation to readers to use and abuse these for their own purposes by substituting ingredients and altering cooking times. I will also include some questions and suggestions for how to make it better the next time.

Long Table

The Long Table is the first and most widely used of the recipes for public conversation to date. It is based on the simple premise that everyone has expertise to share and deserves a place at the table. Participants are invited to gather in a comfortable setting around a difficult conversation, with the underlying objective to break down institutional barriers of knowledge and cultivate community. The format upends the conventional structure of a panel, which situates a few experts behind a table in front of a listening audience. Instead, the Long Table places the table in the middle of the room, inviting anyone to come to the table to speak, and letting the etiquette of sitting together moderate the discussion.

It was inspired by a scene from Marleen Gorris's film *Antonia's Line* (1995), in which a matriarch extends a dining table again and again to accommodate an ever-growing family of outsiders and eccentrics from the wider community. Ultimately, she moves the table outdoors so that it can continue to welcome newcomers. I wanted to build a space for this type of generosity, one in which our communities can come together in a familiar way without being family but perhaps functioning as one. What would happen, I wondered, if I dragged those folding tables out of the church closet and set them up in a town square, a lecture hall, a gallery? What would happen if I then invited people to come to both witness and participate in an easy familiar dinner table conversation on a difficult and unfamiliar topic? We may not necessarily get along, or have all of our issues figured out, but we could commit to sitting at the same table. My first terrifying experiment with this was a *Long Table on Women in Prison* in Rio de Janeiro in 2005 that invited artists, educators, government ministers, prison governors and women from the prisons to sit at the same table. In spite of having to navigate both English and Portuguese, this varied group accepted the terms of my experiment, and our memories of dinner table etiquette kicked in, allowing the group to speak about prison conditions and experience, criminal justice and human rights without an agenda. Just as I had hoped, the table became our moderator. So the Long Table was born as a way to gather, as a way to listen to more perspectives and to encourage voices less easily heard.

Bringing together a clear structure for conversation with a touch of theatricality, the Long Table creates a space that blends the domestic, through the frame of a dinner party, with the public, through an invitation to speak together about challenging topics that affect us all. Everyone in the room is given the power to shift the direction of the conversation, to mediate moments of tension and to make space for other voices. Extending the metaphor of the table, this dynamic seeks to create a horizontal structure, rather than a vertical one, which does away with the hierarchies we are used to, instead hoping that we can each hold and share an equal stake in the conversation at hand.

The first Long Table at The Big Anxiety was a *Long Table on Lived Experience*. That seemed like an appropriate place to start, since the premise of the Long Table itself is to privilege the expertise of lived experience. At a quick glance it seemed like an ideal Long Table: it was robust and energetic; participants eagerly came to take seats at the table and drew from life experience to share personal expertise; professional mental health workers insightfully contributed with their own questions and interjections. The speakers shared in a way that felt personal and heartfelt, while still being aware of the 'performance' of public speaking and that they were sharing beyond the table.

However, over a period of time the quality of the conversation shifted. It became more of a closed discussion, similar to the dynamics in a group session. I have seen this happen at other Long Tables that were occupied by groups who had knowledge of each or who shared particular conversational protocols, like students who were accustomed to speaking in seminar discussions. As this dynamic took hold, the conversation became more open and emotionally articulate, but those not sitting at the table seemed to be increasingly alienated and unlikely to chime in. It seemed as though those who may not have had experience with mental health issues or experience discussing them felt they didn't have the right to interject and were hesitant to participate. This aspect of an affinity group conversation can occur in Long Tables and can have the positive effect of giving voice and mutual support to marginalized communities, but it also has the potential for exclusion particularly along the lines of age, race and class. This led me to wonder how we might set up open and non-hierarchical democracies that still accommodate those who may sit outside for any reason, and how we can find ways to break with long-held traditions of conversational practices.

The second Long Table at The Big Anxiety was a *Long Table on The State of the World*, and it was open to anyone wanting to discuss the big issues of the day. A more diverse audience of artists, scholars, students, mental health practitioners and festival participants led to a productive conversation, which landed mostly on issues of institutionalized racism within the university system. Students of colour who were festival volunteers came to the table to express their concerns and highlight their experiences of racism and sexism as students and arts workers in predominantly white environments. The students spoke about how it was a relief to have an opportunity to express the things they were feeling in a public forum. One student volunteer used the opportunity to come out as LGBTQ to her friends, colleagues and the attending public in the room. It was a vigorous discussion on various forms of marginalization both in institutions and in peer groups which felt like a powerful and fitting use of the Long Table. This experience reinforced for me how the format can make room for more voices, particularly those who may typically feel disenfranchised by the institutions they exist within. It also highlighted how the performance aspects of this format inspire speakers to be more courageous in their expression than they might be in a more intimate setting. I left that conversation invigorated, mulling over how other institutions might use the Long Table for workers that might feel silenced because of institutional hierarchy. And beyond that, I was curious about how I could support the conversations and individuals who may have felt exposed during the Long Table beyond the public event.

Recipe

The Long Table is a dinner table structured by etiquette, where conversation is the only course. In this format a large table is set up with twelve chairs surrounding it and up to forty chairs at a distance from the table. The table is covered with a tablecloth and marking pens are provided so that participants can write comments or questions. Anyone can come to the table but you must come to the table to speak. To participate simply take an empty seat, and if the table is full you can request a seat. Participants can come and go, to and from the table throughout the predetermined time period which is usually one and a half to two hours.

Care Café

During the planning for The Big Anxiety festival, the Care Café was the event that I spent the most time thinking about and planning. It inspired a great deal of energy and intention, and I wondered if that somehow spoke to its relevance. The Care Café could provide a place for people to gather and process global events in an environment that would lend a sense of comfort and safety. These were difficult times and the context of a festival which was focused on themes of mental health seemed to call for extra support, which was certainly relevant to the Care Café's origin story.

In 2016 it felt like everything was coming to the surface. With the election of Donald Trump in the United States and the withdrawal of the United Kingdom from the European Union with Brexit, the racism and xenophobia that had always been present in the two countries where I have split my time over the last thirty years was brought to the surface. It appeared as though these countries were recommitting to the oppressive systems and painful dynamics which we lived in, and that left many of us feeling distraught and lost. It felt like there had been a death in the family or a tragedy in the community and everyone around me needed a place to gather, to breathe, to come together with comrades in action; a place that allowed for our grief, acknowledged our political activism and fury, and fostered our sense of, and capacity to care, for ourselves and our immediate community. Refocusing on care felt like a political act in itself.

Just prior to this, I had been working at a 'get out the vote' centre in New York City where people gathered to call or text potential voters in the US presidential election. These centres were disused banks and shoe stores that had been reclaimed temporarily and furnished with chairs and tables of various shapes and sizes. People of all ages, professions and persuasions showed up on lunch breaks or spent the afternoons sitting with strangers and engaging in casual conversation while concentrating on the singular purpose of getting people to commit to voting. What would happen, I thought, if we could replicate that informal sense of community and purpose now that the election was over, now when we needed each other the most?

Using the idea of a café as a community meeting place, I placed small tables and chairs in an empty room at La MaMa Experimental Theatre Club in NYC on a Sunday afternoon. I sent out a simple invitation to gather under the auspices of care, and about thirty anxious people showed up hopeful for companionship and possibly comradeship. Friends and strangers alike sat around tables within a loose framework of care, making homemade badges advocating for social justice and calling cards providing hotline numbers for survival, forging connections and acknowledging concern. This familiar social architecture coupled with cathartic hands-on activities helped to facilitate a gentle sharing of time and purpose for a community in need. After that, Care Cafés were set up in response to Brexit in the UK, as month-long safe spaces during several local arts and mental health festivals, and as facilitation formats for Boards of Directors of organizations looking to recalibrate their aims and objectives. Many Care Cafés include classic grassroots DIY actions like badge/sticker-making, writing letters to government representatives or sorting donations for charities. Sometimes they simply provide materials for doodling, cutting and pasting or colouring. Participants can interact however they choose, whether it's sitting alone quietly working on an activity or speaking with friends or strangers.

In my collaboration with The Big Anxiety to set up the Care Café we thought through how to locate the café in a public space in order to make this concept of care available to passers-by, while still managing to offer a quiet respite of care. We went through various iterations, focusing on how to secure not only the integrity of the space of care but also the security of those participating. One idea we lingered on was imagining how we might separate an area of a bustling street café and indicate to those entering that they were entering a space of care. In the end we settled on a public library as a potential site and began organizing the Care Café in collaboration with the State Library of New South Wales in Sydney.

Libraries are like tables to me. They hold a comfortable yet municipal attraction. While they are not exactly domestic spaces, they do often provide a more democratic use of space than other cultural institutions. They are both holders and dispensers of knowledge, but they are also places where anyone can sit in public without having to buy something or without being scurried off as a public nuisance. The collaboration with this library in particular was especially exciting because it held an archive of human rights and social justice activism. The librarians were keen to integrate this material and some of its spirit into the atmosphere of the café. This was not a usual practice for the Care Café, but a chance to experiment with ways to facilitate an environment of care by providing a visual and textual influence. Ultimately, we decided to hold the event inside the library building in a gallery space situated adjacent to the main library café. This allowed us to achieve our goal of generating curiosity and offering some exposure to a general public, while providing a quieter environment for care. The safe environment also allowed us to exhibit archival posters highlighting historical actions and protests relating to social justice. As an additional placemaking component, I designed 'placemats' that encouraged colouring and cutting activities around the subject of care and mental health awareness that would be specific to this event.

In retrospect, we may have reduced our potential audience by scheduling the Care Café on a Saturday in this governmental section of Sydney. We did, however, attract a combination of people who stumbled on the café while visiting the library, people who came out of interest in the festival and a sizeable group of festival organizers themselves.

One of the surprising outcomes from this combination of participants was that it allowed some of the festival organizers and volunteers a chance to sit together for two hours without an agenda. During the Care Café, they were afforded a period of selfcare in which they only had to engage with the activity at hand. Prior to this point, most of their time had been wrapped up in thinking about caring for others as preparation for the festival. I watched as they seemed to fully immerse themselves in the event, which is not something event organizers are typically able to do at their own functions. Witnessing this dynamic unfold brought into focus ways in which the Care Café might be used to dispense care for specific groups and left me wondering how we might create a Care Café specifically made for workers and carers. Thinking back to one of our original ideas to locate the Care Café in a busy local café, I was also interested in exploring further how a Care Café would function if it was placed in a busy public place.

Recipe

The premise of the Care Café is simply to inhabit a space where our need to give and receive care is acknowledged and valued. It can be adapted to a limitless range of contexts and communities. Care Cafés always include a small table activity of the facilitator's choosing, inspired by the domestic practice of women's craftwork or activists' making activities, which provides an easy entry point to conversation and community. Tables and chairs are arranged in clusters throughout the space to evoke the feeling of a café.

Porch Sitting

A porch is not a table – and yet there is something about the particular temporary community a porch creates and the way it situates us side by side, that yields a similar quality as a rectangular table. Like the table, porches and their equivalents – lanais, verandas, stoops – are comfortable, everyday places that seem to draw people together and provide a multitude of access points for connection.

Porch Sitting began as a natural progression from the Long Table and was influenced by the participatory research process for my performance project, *What Tammy Needs to Know about Getting Old and Having Sex*. The Long Table underscored the importance of creating domestic, horizontal space for new types of focused conversation, while my research into the experience of ageing and sex using my facilitating persona, Tammy WhyNot, highlighted the productive modes of conversation that arise out of simply sitting together for extended periods of time. In the guise of Tammy WhyNot, an ageing country Western singer-turned lesbian performance artist and researcher, I spent hours sitting with residents of care homes and elders at senior day centres. I let the conversation flow and the issues emerge until eventually we would get around to the subject of sex and intimacy and how that is affected by age. I began to think of this as a research methodology and called it Intense Porch Sitting. Developing this experience into a recipe for public conversation was as easy a transition as retiring to the porch after an evening meal.

Porch Sitting is perhaps the simplest of my protocols for public engagement. In it, participants are asked only to sit side by side facing in the same direction. By sitting side by side, participants are free to observe, dream or reflect upon our collective future. It is an informal discussion inspired by the notion of sitting on the porch, watching the world go by; it makes space for the things we wonder rather than providing a platform for the things we know. It attempts to foster an organic sense of communal contemplation, stepping back from the need to solidify ideas, stick to a logical order, explain or debate. On the porch, a shared moment is what is important.

The Porch Sitting for The Big Anxiety situated on the steps of the Customs House in Sydney was indeed an experiment in taking these conversational formats out and into the public. It was part of Awkward Conversations, a programme of experimental conversations that took place throughout the Customs House during the festival. Awkward Conversations aimed to give people an opportunity to engage intimately with subjects like anxiety and mental health. Advertised as one-to-one conversations that 'make no demands, have no expectations and require no social skills whatsoever', it seemed like the perfect context for a format like the Porch Sitting.

I chose a section of the steps that extended across the wide front of the building, allocating the top step as 'the porch'. On the porch, I set up six camping stools in a row, placed a fan imprinted with Porch Sitting instructions on each stool, and hung a sign indicating that anyone was welcome to come sit. Over the course of two days, I sat for three two-hour sessions and people joined me usually one at a time, and usually because they had come to take part in the festival activities. We chatted about a wide range of topics like the other conversations going on in the festival context; the behaviours of the many pigeons and the fashion choices of the many tourists trying to occupy the same territories; the dangers of sitting in the Australian sun. These exchanges of course also touched on deeper issues of isolation, mental health, urban precarity, global economics and climate change.

These were meaningful conversations, but because of the porch's location on the Customs House steps, the Porch Sitting had little impact on this public place. Sitting on the steps, side by side, facing the same direction and engaging in informal conversation was not an extraordinary occurrence for people who frequent a public square in front of a very public building. Looking around, it seemed that the entire front of the building was occupied by hundreds of Porch Sitters lost in their own world of lunch time or afternoon wonder.

Typically, Porch Sittings involve several rows of people committed to spending a good deal of time together, following one another's reflections and observations until several group discussions emerge. Because most of the conversations on this festival porch were one-to-one, it created an entirely different dynamic. That new dynamic made me wonder if there is actually a difference between an individual and a group Porch Sitting, and what instances might be better suited to one or the other. I was also curious about how I could facilitate group conversation in this type of public setting, which was already full of Porch Sitters.

Recipe

The Porch Sitting takes seriously the idea that conversation can happen side by side, taking inspiration from the domestic practice of sitting on a porch. In this format, participants are seated side by side, sometimes with a conversation prompt, and invited to engage in conversation as much or as little as they choose. Participants are encouraged to use phrases like 'I imagine . . . I wonder . . . I think . . . I feel'. Porch Sittings can happen in any setting with any number of people, and only require chairs set up side by side.

As an artist, teacher and even as an activist, I celebrate obsession as one of our most valuable material resources. What is the piece of music you keep replaying in your mind, what phrase or paragraph do you keep going back to, what injustice keeps interrupting your dreams? My obsession with the table and its everyday power to facilitate extraordinary communication continues. I keep refining and re-defining the dinner table, the café table, the porch. I keep setting up new tables. Lately, it's been tables in a Situation Room where elders are asked to mix their anxieties and their desires in a solution that might remedy our everyday problems. It's been tables triangulated to bring together a triumvirate of social need, creative skill and public know-how in a Public Studio. I even chose the table as a place to dance when it felt like I could no longer reach the floor. And like my father, who preferred the title of custodian over janitor, I hope to be a custodian of egalitarian public conversation, so I try to get there ahead of time and set up the tables.

Tables are everywhere,
Nesting, siding, accentuating, ending,

Always ready for the dining and the meeting
And the dressing, praying and playing,
The drafting, picnicking, even dancing.[2]

Notes

1 From the monologue, *How to Set a Table in an Emergency* from the Split Britches video, *Last Gasp WFH* (2020).
2 Weaver & Shaw (2020).

References

Antonia's Line (1995), [Film] Dir. Marleen Gorris, Netherlands: European Co-production Fund.
Weaver, L. and P. Shaw (2020), *Last Gasp WFH*, NYC: La MaMa Experimental Theatre Club.

Part V

Resistance, racism and decolonization

Narratives of resistance from indefinite detention

Manus Prison Theory and Nauru Imprisoned Exiles Collective

Omid Tofighian, Behrouz Boochani,
Mira* and Elahe Zivardar

This chapter brings together four voices and interventions emerging from two key theoretical frameworks and forms of resistance to border violence: Manus Prison Theory (via Omid Tofighian and Behrouz Boochani) and the Nauru Imprisoned Exiles Collective (via Elahe Zivardar and Mira in collaboration with Omid).

Manus Prison Theory emerged organically through years of collaboration, sharing and consultation between Behrouz – who was incarcerated in the Australian-run Manus Island immigration detention centre from 2013 to 2019 – and Omid, who supported and translated for him on the outside, communicating via WhatsApp. Manus Prison Theory explores the racial imaginary driving border regimes, the colonial logic underlying them and the debordering work necessary to dismantle them. The Nauru Imprisoned Exiles Collective addresses similar concerns with a specific focus on gendered violence from the lived experience of women locked up in the Australian-run Nauru immigration detention centre. Both movements work to disrupt and dismantle the material and epistemic conditions, the symbolic aesthetic and social imaginary underpinning systemic attacks against displaced and exiled people. Both centre joy, hope, celebration, love and pride within their intellectual, creative and political perspectives in radically challenging and generative ways. These interventions are introduced as embodied knowledges, deeply ingrained in different antiracist, anticolonial and feminist struggles. This work is transgenerational and aims to be transnational.

Manus Prison Theory and Nauru Imprisoned Exiles Collective are deconstructive and iconoclastic interventions into debates about forced migration and border violence. Our work does not play off distinctions between creative praxis, intellectual and theoretical efforts, political activism and cultural heritage. Examples include Behrouz's journalism, his co-directed film *Chauka, Please Tell Us the Time* (2017) and book *No Friend but the Mountains* (2018) – towards which Omid contributed through translation, collaboration and supplementary essays; Elahe's co-created film *Searching for Aramsayesh Gah* (2022), 3D interactive model of the Nauru detention centre, and painting collection *Border-Industrial Complex*; Mira's critical research and writing on psychology and mental health in the context of indefinite detention; Omid's scholarship on carceral-border phenomena alongside his work with Behrouz, Elahe, Mira and others, and with Arash Kamali Sarvestani (2020) on another film project about Manus Island.

The chapter explores some of the narrative works emerging from Manus Prison Theory and Nauru Imprisoned Exiles Collective through a discussion of their artistic features, characters and literary techniques, as well as the networks involved in their production. Central to this analysis is a sense of how theory and intellectual vision emerges from resistance and art, and how lived experience is best communicated through a combination of activism and creativity.

Omid and Behrouz

Omid: I think we are dealing with three interconnected pandemics. One is contemporary: Covid-19. The other two are much older: the pandemics of colonialism and of racial capitalism, which in fact created the conditions for the Covid-19 pandemic. Australia – the most powerful nation state in the Oceania region – is a product of colonialism; a result of British imperialism and the project to create an offshore prison. That prison has since morphed and multiplied into other prisons, so that now we have an archipelago of prisons in the Pacific and in Indonesia. But we also have an archipelago of resistance through letters, through the writing and art made by people in detention centres (Galbraith et al. 2021). In this, we can see the possibilities for new kinds of resistance from below, new decolonial interventions.

Behrouz: I think people who create these works of resistance and those assisting them are impacting the discourse, making history. These efforts are creating the kind of knowledge that we need; knowledge that comes from real people and real stories. With Omid, I have been addressing the issue of colonialism and the systems and mentality associated with it. We believe the policy towards refugees in Australia, both offshore and onshore, is founded upon a colonial mentality and the history of colonialism in Australia. This is very clear to us. We work hard to introduce our critical analysis to Australia and beyond.

Resistance, I think, is a key point in the context of the Manus and Nauru refugees and the policy towards refugees in Australia. Resistance is also a significant part of my background as a Kurd. Kurdistan has been colonized by different countries in the Middle East, which created a history and culture of resistance. When I arrived in Australia and they banished me to Manus Island I faced another colonial system; I was in another colony. Omid analyses this very well in his essays in *No Friend but the Mountains* (Tofighian 2018b), where he juxtaposes the images of these two islands – the small Manus Island and the bigger island of Australia, each with complex relationships to imprisonment and detention, and to each other. We can understand this relationship through the resistance of the refugees on Manus Island. This resistance is not only about me but about all refugees, a resistance with a long history. In February 2014 the refugees were involved in an uprising. In 2015 we participated in a hunger strike involving 700 people. In 2017 we resisted when they wanted to relocate us to new prisons. This resistance manifested not only through hunger strikes or similar kinds of protest; it impacted upon Australian political culture through our artistic works. Many refugees have been writing and creating art and music, which are acts of resistance. Writing is a weapon that challenges and exposes the system, and also presents refugees as human. It is a way to find freedom, to create hope. We can see this resistance in every aspect of the work created by different refugees, including our collaborative work. In Manus Island and in Nauru this resistance is a remarkable part of the story.

As a journalist I was writing for many years, publishing internationally, but mostly in Australia. Through that work I realized the language of journalism was not strong enough to challenge or expose the system. Literature, on the other hand, is a powerful language that can describe the meaning of systematic torture. Literature can take the readers into the prison camp, experience and witness the lives of the detainees. This is why I criticize the current language of journalism, and why I keep a distance from journalism in my book. This is why I wrote a literary work, a piece of art, even if it retains traces of journalistic language. Journalism is, of course, important, but its problem is that it tries to make people aware, which is not enough. Most people in Australia are aware of what has been happening in Manus Island and Nauru, and also in Indonesia. The problem is that awareness does not give rise to action; action does not happen through journalism. Journalism is also allied to the official language, the language used and created by the government, created by extant power structures. Literature and art allow us to challenge the images of refugees, to challenge perspectives towards refugees.

Omid: Regarding translation as resistance, I think it is really important to see both Behrouz's work and my translation as decolonial interventions. There were two forces, two wills coming together and joining with a team of people, consultants and confidants who all contributed to the translation process. That process was a testament to the power of collective activism, or collective struggle. In this respect it is important to understand how the translation took shape. I worked with Behrouz for a long time before he proposed the book project. He was already sending messages to his first translator, Moones Mansoubi, who was collecting these messages and assembling them into chapters on Behrouz's instructions. By the time I took on the project Behrouz had written about 30 per cent of the book. I'm not a trained translator, but had felt comfortable translating journalistic writing. When Behrouz asked if I would translate his book, I became anxious; translating journalism is one thing, but literature is another task altogether. However, I could already see how important and powerful Behrouz's work was, and the impact that it was having. I could already see the possibilities for the future.

Behrouz's book first appeared as a compilation of text messages that needed editing, but after the third page I realized it was going to be a masterpiece. I saw in his book a decolonial intervention, and wanted the translation process to also be decolonial and very deconstructive. We were creating new ways of engaging, new ways of resisting through the translation process. My own background of displacement and exile was important for understanding what Behrouz was going through and what he was trying to do. My experience in and understanding of Australia, particularly with respect to its colonial history and systemic racism, were also important in translating the book. I had a strong interest in studying and unpacking different forms of colonialism in different parts of the world. As well as drawing on my own experience and scholarship, I undertook a great deal of research to understand Behrouz's references to Kurdistan and Kurdish intellectual, artistic and political history.

Behrouz's book is an anti-genre, containing elements of journalism, philosophical ruminations, psychoanalytic examination, political commentary, testimony, more formal accounts of what was taking place and also myth, folklore, epic and poetry. A kind of magic happened when all of these elements came together and, of course, all the different contributions that people were making to the translation process as well. Our team was trying to imagine how best to convey what Behrouz was doing, because what he was writing and what we were translating was something completely new. It needed a new imagination, a new way of thinking, new terminology. In some cases, we created new words to represent ideas Behrouz was introducing. Behrouz also introduced new ideas, new concepts, new terms. We created a new way of conceiving and practising translation.

After the success of the book, Behrouz developed an excellent critique of celebrity culture, especially the fascination connected with the experience of displacement and exile. It is important to understand that border regimes are multifaceted. There is an ideology, there is a political economy – politicians and policies – and there are images, as Behrouz pointed out. This system is extremely complex and ever-changing; in Farsi, Behrouz creates the term '*system-e hākem*' to refer to it. In the book I translated it as the '*kyriarchal system*', a term I created and derived from the feminist philosophical concept of kyriarchy (Schüssler Fiorenza 1992, 2001 and 2020), which refers to an interconnected social system built around domination, oppression and submission. One aspect of this kyriarchal system is the refugee industry, which spans the whole spectrum of politics: supporters of refugees, those who are against refugees and everything in between. This industry is constituted by a range of things including academics researching refugees, art projects, films, books, forms of activism.

It appears that the majority of people benefiting from the refugee industry are those with citizen privilege. It is not refugees who become empowered, gain freedom, create opportunities or make use of resources from this particular industry. And what is dangerous about this industry is that it reinforces particular kinds of tropes, particular kinds of stereotypes – many of which are associated with a kind of liberal humanitarianism. What I love about Behrouz's work, and that many other people have not done or failed to do, is that he does not appeal to liberal humanitarianism. He refuses to explain why he left Iran, refuses to talk about his backstory and refuses to justify himself or try to humanize himself in the eyes of people with citizen privilege. He does not talk about what he has gone through to evoke sympathy; instead, he tells his audience that they should treat him as a human being without conditions. Behrouz says no to the political construction of the acceptable refugee and the criteria that help justify this image, his book highlights the problems with liberal democracies. He says you need to deal with your own problems and ask yourselves why you treat people seeking asylum and other marginalized and system-impacted people the way you do. He says you need to confront the violence that is part of your culture, your systems, your leaders, your background, your history. He says, I'm not going to play according to your rules. I'm not going to give you what you expect. He holds a mirror to the kyriarchal system.

One of the other important interventions coming from displaced and exiled writers and artists is the way they challenge the narrative and create a new narrative. This approach is radical because statistics, figures, data – all of these rational approaches to combatting the system – do not get to the heart of the problem. Using logic alone does not work, it can be manipulated and misinterpreted and exploited in different ways, and taken in unintended directions. But what art does, what creativity does, is create a rupture. It creates a new way of imagining. I think that is what *No Friend but the Mountains* (Boochani 2018; Tofighian 2018a and 2018b) achieves.

Behrouz: What Omid says about the refugee industry is very important. It is very simple: stories about refugees should come from refugees themselves, and be controlled by them. This is true not only for refugees but for all minoritized people, Indigenous people and marginalized people. These people should write their own stories, tell their own stories and control their own stories. The duty of people working with refugees is simply to create a space for them, to make sure their voices are heard.

The way Omid is working is a kind of decolonization of activism, practising better ways to work with refugees and offering an important example from which we can learn. In Western countries most people look at refugees as voiceless, but refugees have a voice. Sometimes refugees are accepted only because of their weaknesses, but they should not be reduced to an image of weakness. Refugees must be part of the main discourse, must own the discourse, they should not be marginalized within it. Writers and artists are particularly important in reclaiming this discourse, because they share their stories and so much about their lives through their work. And it is not only life experience they are sharing; they are also producing knowledge through their analyses or their own critical understanding. That is what Omid means by challenging and changing narratives about and images of refugees, creating a new language and perspective towards the refugees. Art and writing allow refugees to take control of the stories and discourses that belong to them.

In my film *Chauka, Please Tell Us the Time* (2017) the Indigenous dimensions of the story were important, and video offered a different, visual way to express this. For example, there is a sequence where the local people gather to celebrate their National Day and raise the flag of Papua New Guinea – an act that is both surreal and ridiculous given that the Australian government was using the land as a place of exile while the locals were celebrating independence and national sovereignty. The key concept in the movie is time, and how time is used as torture within the detention system. Waiting. Wasted lives in that system. In prison, violence is experienced through silence. Torture is not only about guards inflicting physical injury on refugees; torture happens through silence, which is why most sequences in the film are long and almost soundless. Perhaps people find these long film sequences boring, but that is the torturous nature of life inside the prison camp (Figure 10.1).

FIGURE 10.1 *Film still of Behrouz, Manus Island (left) and poster (right),* Chauka, Please Tell Us the Time *(2017), Sarvin Productions 2019.*

Mira

Omid: I was introduced to Mira's writing, research and resistance through Elahe Zivardar. What I found significant and empowering about her work was how she introduced new ways of knowing and challenging border violence through a deep analysis of trauma, stress, narrative and identity. Mira draws on her experience, the individual experiences of others in the Nauru detention centre and in other examples of collective struggles to find ways to heal and grow. Her aim is not only to expose and resist but also to find creative and radical ways of recovering, collective knowledge production and creating networks of support for displaced and exiled people. Narrative is key in this respect, as Mira will explain.

Mira: I'm currently researching a book about mental health in refugees held in indefinite detention, drawing on my experience in Nauru. Indefinite detention has a devastating effect on the psyche of children, women and men. Warehousing in mouldy tents and hazardous conditions, the lack of privacy and the fact that there is no oversight and plan for resettlement (among many other violations) all negatively affect this vulnerable group. The long-term effects of stress – both physical and psychological – are well-documented. Prolonged stress can change the structure of the brain – affecting one's thinking and logic, numbing one's emotions. Living under the stress of indefinite detention can lead to anxiety disorders, and untreated trauma can increase the likelihood of self-harm (from detention pressures) or suicidal thoughts. Refugees in detention centres are confronted with staff who are unfamiliar with their past and present situations, and whose racism or insensitivity can add to their trauma. These incidents trigger more anger, including towards themselves; self-harm becomes a way for injured refugees to punish themselves for negative feelings that arise. In turn, suicide attempts and self-mutilation can create new traumas in those who witness these acts of self-harm.

For those outside detention centres, learning about self-harm, suicide, hunger strikes and other forms of protest in refugee camps, these issues can trigger not only concern and distress but also confusion about why such things are happening. Public opinion holds that detained refugees are provided with essential needs like shelter and food. Other human needs – like the need to belong, the need for peace and respect – are, however, just as vital. Further, the withholding of these needs is used as a weapon to deter people from seeking asylum.

The journey towards freedom and protection is not over when refugees leave the camp; the trauma of detention can accompany them for a long time. Damaged self-esteem, grief over the loss of sentimental possessions, rejection by the new environment and lack of a sense of belonging in a new country and culture leads to depression and post-traumatic stress in many after detention. Refugees can face a crisis of identity in coming to terms with a narrative of the self that includes traumatic elements of past and present experiences.

An important step in the process of post-traumatic growth (PTG) is developing a new narrative; seeing your own story in a different way. It is possible to see yourself as both vulnerable and strong; to take time to process what is happening. Through this, you find ways to understand and critically analyse the oppression, to resist the new limitations to your life, to grasp the profound structural reasons behind what has happened to you. You find ways to keep going within changed and undesirable circumstances. Reaching this stage not only involves considerable difficulty and hardship but it also gives you a different perspective on life. You recognize your own strength. You are not a victim, but the author of your own new path. You are choosing a new narrative, creating a new, empowering story.

I found reading autobiographies and biographies extremely helpful. Through them, I learned about how people coped with and recovered from issues similar to my own. Reading others' stories allowed me to see the world through their eyes. In their narrative vision, I could track a process of transformation, locate ideas, structures and techniques that could be applied to my own story. In this sense storytelling is a form of social support and PTG, and I see my own writing, research and resistance as part of this collective movement.

We are social beings; we learn from others, grow with others, heal and cope with difficulties through the relationships we have with family, friends and community. We receive and offer strength and care for each other. Empathy assists us and emotional support makes it easier to handle difficult situations. The presence of a social support group and feelings of safety, intimacy, of being accepted and understood, all positively affect our mental health.[1]

I recall how other refugees survived during those six years in the detention centre, the progress was clear. We were about 1,000 refugees from different backgrounds, religions, cultures, ethnic groups, levels of education and socio-economic status. We had different forms of trauma: some escaped war, abuse, rape, torture; some almost drowned in the ocean during the boat journey from Indonesia and were rescued. At first, most of us found it difficult to live together in the detention centre, particularly since we were kept in such close quarters. Our own traumas left us stressed and vulnerable, and conflict was common between refugees. Some suffered from PTSD, anxiety and depression. The tension was high. Little by little, we changed.

I reflect on when and how PTG began for us. At first the conversation between refugees centred on the question of '*why?*' Why had this happened to me? Slowly, we made friends and listened to each other's stories; we shared experiences. It was like group therapy as we opened up with one another and exchanged opinions. We made strong relationships during that time, reinforced by the sharing of life perspectives, and conversations about God, religion, culture, humanity and immigration policy. We had disagreements, but debates left us with new ideas and thoughts, sometimes even changed core beliefs. Eventually, it was clear how the relationships between us transcended religion and race. We did not regard one another as *Other*, but as fellow human beings.

Our compassion towards one another – the care, strength and support we showed to each other – not only was helpful in the process of PTG but also made some situations harder. The powerful compassion between refugees meant that when *one* person suffered or self-harmed or received distressing news, it impacted *everyone*. Long-term exposure to traumatized peoples can affect mental health – as is the case for therapists, nurses, psychologists and social workers. Living in conditions of shared trauma is harmful in many ways.

During our incarceration some refugees lost loved ones back home, their pain made worse by the fact that they could not physically be there to grieve. We worried this might also happen to us and treasured time spent on the phone talking to distant family and friends. We learned to be grateful for those who were around us. We took joy in gathering together, simple acts like sharing a cup of tea. Despite cultural and ethnic differences among refugees in the detention centre, we built strong friendships; we considered ourselves family.

We learned to comfort each other, cope and find new paths. Some distracted themselves by reading, painting or writing about their own journey; some exercised to keep their mind busy. It wasn't easy. We noticed how people changed and how many were paradoxically both vulnerable and strong. Helping others with difficulties was part of our PTG process. I recall a young Syrian refugee (Ali) who was a minor while in detention, now a student of international relations. I saw Ali on the news, speaking about how the hard times motivated him to study and help others experiencing similar stressors:

> My journey was tough and I went through a lot, but when I look back at my story, I can see how it affected me. It gave me a different perspective on life. My recovery began when I tried to see my story in a different way. I didn't want to see myself as a victim, I decided to see myself as a warrior who came back from the battle with pride. I decided to see what I had gained from this journey, what had made me a different person.

Elahe

Omid: From 2001 to 2008 Australia began imprisoning women, unaccompanied minors and families in the Republic of Nauru, an island nation in the Pacific (men travelling alone were sent to Manus Island in Papua New Guinea). The Australian policy of exiling people seeking asylum by boat to privately operated offshore island prisons was referred to as the 'Pacific Solution'. In 2012 'Pacific Solution 2' was initiated, and in 2013 it was further militarized and officially named 'Operation Sovereign Borders'. Throughout all these years many have died, people have been living in constant danger and uncertainty. There are still refugees being held on Nauru.

I learned about Elahe's work while she was still held in the Nauru detention centre (using the pseudonym Ellie Shakiba). I was introduced to her by Janet Galbraith from the Writing Through Fences group while we were working on a special issue of the *Southerly* journal (Galbraith et al. 2021) to which Elahe contributed both writing and art (her painting *Concealed Borders* appears on the journal's cover, a work that is part of her Border-Industrial Complex series). We began collaborating further, particularly on her film project *Searching for Aramsayesh Gah* (2022) and the 3D model of the detention centre which features in the film. The model, as explained in the film, is interactive and uses audio and visual material and documents from Elahe's archive, which she compiled over more than six years when incarcerated in Nauru. I have been working with Elahe to examine the ways architecture is used to torture through an attack on the psychological, emotional and spiritual (and physical) state of detained refugees (Zivardar and Tofighian 2021). In *Searching for Aramsayesh Gah* we see how Elahe's skills and training, together with her creative resistance inside the prison camp, work together to develop new forms of storytelling and collective struggle (Figure 10.2).

REGIONAL PROCESSING CENTRE

ELAHE
ZIVARDAR
DOB: 06/06/1985
IRAN
Farsi

IVL057

FIGURE 10.2 *Left: Render image of a 3D model of the Nauru detention centre created by Elahe Zivardar for the film* Searching for Aramsayesh Gah *(2022); Right: 'What am I?/ Nothing. A number? Maybe. The number of a boat/IVL-57', Elahe's ID card. Both images courtesy Elahe Zivardar.*

Elahe: After being forced to flee Iran and undertaking a dangerous boat journey from Indonesia, the happiest day was when the Australian boat found us. Finally, I thought we would be safe. I was wrong. My name is Elahe Zivardar, also known as Ellie Shakiba. I do not know how to introduce myself; a serious identity crisis means I am no longer sure who I am. An Iranian woman who is a graduate in engineering and architecture. An artist and journalist. And then, suddenly, just a number: IVL 57. A detained refugee – an imprisoned exile – in an Australian offshore detention centre on Nauru.

When I arrived on Nauru, they took away my camera. I traded cigarettes for another camera and hid it from the prison guards. I wanted the world to know what the Australian government was doing to us. It felt as if they had designed this place to torture us; a cruel and clandestine architecture whose features were intended to inflict trauma.

As an architectural engineering student in Iran, I developed a prototype for a radically utopian space of healing I call *Aramsayesh Gah*. This name is a combination of three Persian words: *Aramesh* means 'peace' (from *aram*, meaning calm); *asayesh* means 'comfort'; and *gah* means 'place of'. It was suggested by renowned contemporary Iranian writer Abbas Maroufi, and translates as 'abode for serenity'. *Aramsayesh Gah* is an architectural prototype for the provision of mental health services to the general public, which aims to shift societal perspectives about mental health. *Aramsayesh Gah* is a purpose-built facility that can be tailored to the specific needs of different populations according to their own demographics, cultural traditions and aesthetic preferences. It is not a hospital or prescribing facility for those with acute mental challenges, nor is it a summer camp or recreation site. A collaboration between architecture, art and psychology, *Aramsayesh*

Gah is an architectural intervention to assist vulnerable people, those with anxiety or depression, or those who feel the need for rest and empowerment. A space for those working through a process of post-traumatic growth.

The film *Searching for Aramsayesh Gah* (2022) documents my efforts to expose the brutal architecture and conditions of the Nauru detention centre, and to highlight the site's direct contradiction with the architectural and social principles of *Aramsayesh Gah*. This film is a first-person narrative, a story of resistance. An exposé of secrets featuring photorealistic 3D modelling and the largest archive of never-before-seen footage from inside the Australian-run prison in Nauru. And a historical document that features powerful testimonies from former detainees, including from two children traumatized by the many deaths on Nauru, in particular, that of Fariborz Karami (a refugee who was driven to take his own life in a tent on Nauru; the children were friends with his younger brother). After Fariborz' death, the IHMS (International Health and Medical Services) kept the body in a freezer for a month. The children were fully aware of this; whenever they visited the doctor they could see the freezer that held Fariborz:

> **Excerpt 1** [*an Ahvazi Arab boy from Iran, imprisoned in the Nauru facility with his mother, father and his baby brother who had spent his entire life in the detention centre*]: We haven't got anything. We are bored and we are living in tents, and it's full of mud. And when it rains the tent fills up with water. And you can't sleep at night. They tell us if you go outside, they're gonna kill you.

> **Excerpt 2** [*An Iraqi girl imprisoned on the Nauru facility with her mother and father*]: I feel sad because I didn't have a childhood. I mean every child deserves to have a childhood, to have happiness in their life, but I didn't have happiness in my life. Nauru's a miserable place for a child.[2]

During my incarceration on Nauru I suffered repeated nightmares. I began creating artworks as an attempt at self-treatment. Inside this prison, I could distract myself during the day by focusing on positive tasks: helping other refugees with translation; teaching English; making short-term goals. But at night, the stress, anxiety and depression that dwelled deep down would manifest as deeply traumatic and recurring nightmares. I experienced different versions of the same nightmare every night on Nauru. It began with me running down the street towards my childhood home, chased by unknown government officials. I would reach home, but couldn't find my keys as the men chasing me got closer. At this point I would wake from the nightmare – heart pounding, struggling for breath. While the core story was always the same, the details shifted: for instance, I would find the key and enter, but my father would be shot at the entrance of our house. This hadn't happened in 'real' life. My father passed away when I was in Nauru prison; his heart stopped while he slept. I knew this recurring nightmare narrative was my psyche reminding me of all the traumas I had been through.

Having tried to incorporate practices from art therapy and mindfulness into my *Aramsayesh Gah* prototype, I started using these practices in the detention centre. My painting *19th of July* was the first artwork I created to confront the pain of this nightmare. I also tried different mindfulness techniques against the nightmares; these processes were difficult and emotionally painful, but effective. However, there were always new problems and traumas occurring in Nauru, stoking new anxieties. I would move on from one nightmare only to experience a new one – borne from this endlessly cruel environment and the equally cruel and mercurial Australian policies being used to torture us. Having recovered from the recurring dream of my father's death, I learned of the Australian policy concerning abortion and the incarceration of pregnant women. New nightmares began in which I found myself pregnant, fuelling a new, traumatizing fear of giving birth inside that prison. This experience inspired my painting *Nameless*, the second in my Border-Industrial Complex painting series.

Each painting in this series tells a story of my nightmares while incarcerated on Nauru. Art was my way of healing; my weapon to fight and survive the evil designs of my torturers: the Australian government; the soulless ghouls at the Department of Home Affairs. In my paintings, these figures are represented as monsters – those who targeted vulnerable refugees, those responsible for our ongoing mental and physical torture, those who drove us towards hopelessness and even death, and those who inflicted indescribable pain and suffering on me and others. Ironically, this trauma fuelled my artistic drive. I converted negative energies into artworks that not only helped me overcome personal trauma but empowered me to stand up and fight back.

> **Saba:** Do you remember the TV show *Lost*?
> **Elahe:** I remember exactly.
> **Saba:** The characters didn't know whether they were dead or alive. I would ask: What if we're dead and we just think we're alive?
> **Elahe:** Saba, you're not alone. I know many who experienced the same feeling.
> **Saba:** I would always ask: Could it be that we're all dead and we just think we're alive and struggling to leave here, and this place is actually our Hell?[3]

* Pseudonym.

Notes

1 From an interview with Maryam: "The most positive thing about those days in the camp was how we supported each other. When one of the girls lost her father, we tried to comfort her – bringing phone cards and food, making sure

she was not alone. This support was the most beautiful thing; everyone was responsible for everyone else, something I haven't experienced after detention."

2   English dialogue excerpted from *Searching for Aramsayesh Gah* (2022).

3   Dialogue excerpted from the film *Searching for Aramsayesh* Gah (2022); trans. Omid Tofighian.

References

Boochani, B. (2018), *No Friend but the Mountains: Writing From Manus Prison*, translated by O. Tofighian, Sydney: Picador Australia.

Chauka, Please Tell Us the Time (2017), [Film] Dir. A. Kamali Sarvestani and B. Boochani.

Galbraith, J., H. Abdile, O. Tofighian, and B. Boochani, eds (2021), *Writing Through Fences: Archipelago of Letters*, special issue *Southerly Journal*, 79 (2).

Searching for Aramsayesh Gah (2022), [Film] Dir. J.R. Gosselin, co-director E. Zivardar, produced by This Machine Media.

Schüssler Fiorenza, E. (1992), *But she Said: Feminist Practices of Biblical Interpretation*, Boston, MA: Beacon Press.

Schüssler Fiorenza, E. (2001), 'Glossary', in *Wisdom Ways: Introducing Feminist Biblical Interpretation*, 207, New York: Orbis Books.

Schüssler Fiorenza, E. (2020), 'Biblical Interpretation and Kyriachal Globalization', in S. Scholz (ed.), *The Oxford Handbook of Feminist Approaches to the Hebrew Bible*, 1–20, Oxford: Oxford University Press.

Tall Fences, Taller Trees (2020), [Film] Dir. A. Kamali Sarvestani.

Tofighian, O. (2018a), 'Translator's Tale: A Window to the Mountains', in B. Boochani, *No Friend but the Mountains: Writing from Manus Prison*, translated by O. Tofighian, Sydney: Picador Australia.

Tofighian, O. (2018b), 'No Friend but the Mountains: Translator's Reflections', in B. Boochani, *No Friend but the Mountains: Writing From Manus Prison*, translated by O. Tofighian, Sydney: Picador Australia.

Zivardar, E. and O. Tofighian (2021), 'The Torture of Australia's Offshore Immigration Detention System', *Open Democracy*, 16 March 2021. Available online: https://www.opendemocracy.net/en/beyond-trafficking-and-slavery/the-torture-of-australias-offshore-immigration-detention-system/ (accessed 14 September 2021).

CHAPTER 11

Poetic solidarities

Claudia Rankine with Evelyn Araluen

Evelyn: It's important in my own practice to think about where people are and where they're placed. Today I'm on the Kulin nations. Some of my family came to this Country in the last century when they left the reserve 400 kilometres north of here. This place has a very proud history, and recognizing the Kulin people's sovereignty and continued custodianship is part of the work I'm trying to do today in speaking with you.

Claudia: What you said about being cognizant about place is really important in terms of my work. America has such a deep colonial history that it's hard not to address all of the immigrants, refugees and First Nations, even as my focus is anti-Blackness in this country. In any country where a history of colonizing begins or hosts the history of nation, then you need an intersectionality around your subjects, because each public is both separate and overlapping in its commitments and its degradations, in its needs. The work has a focus: anti-Blackness, but the concerns are global. I can't imagine a country where the wounds and abuses are not played out with some segment of the society.

Evelyn: I can see that through works I'm most familiar with – the two *American Lyric* collections (Rankine 2014, Rankine 2004) and *Just Us* (Rankine 2020) – but also some of the film work you've done with your husband John Lucas. I hate the language of humanitarianism and the flattening logics behind it, but I think there is a strong emphasis on empathy and dignity in your work – and where dignity is denied from so many different vulnerable and marginalized communities. There is a compassion visible in your writing that is like a form of solidarity. You've also written about the language of racism being a kind of hyper-visualization, a hypervisibility. From my own experience of reading your work in an Australian context, I think making visible the psychic damage of institutionalized and structural racism is itself a solidarity: as colonialism operates globally, so too must that empathy.

Claudia: Exactly, but before even empathy I am committed to recognition. We live in societies. I'll speak for myself; I live in a society where rampant misinformation has framed people's education from the get-go. The initial desire was to take education away from Black people, to deny them that, and the ultimate place we've landed is one where education is being taken from everyone. We have just moved from a president who wilfully and constantly lied to the American public and called those lies facts. And now he has people in the Congress continuing those lies, misinformation. The struggle with the work is to keep the reality present and the effects of that reality on actual people present – the long-term effects of legislation, systemic racism. The idea that whiteness is benevolent has led people to feel that these injustices are idiosyncratic; they belong only to a moment or to a person. And you really have to be able to see the entire picture to understand the entire, full-on devastation that has been visited on whole segments of society.

Evelyn: We also have these same issues of the denial of education. My parents were the first in their families to have access to completing school, and my grandparents could not access education beyond the third grade. The impact of the denial of education is multigenerational. We are denied the inheritance of the knowings, and the fluency and capacity to empower young people. One of the many results of that is the mass over-incarceration of Aboriginal children. In the Northern Territory, 100 per cent of all children in detention are Aboriginal, some as young as eight or nine years old. We have a huge crisis of deaths in custody and mass over-incarceration.

Your work is directed towards dehumanizing the violent crimes of the American settler colonial military industrial complex. You're also very interested in language that is used to obscure, aestheticize or exploit these injustices – whether for political rhetoric of inciting further violence, performance of solidarity, or a much more paternalistic kind of care and control. Watching from afar, there seems to be an increasing public rhetoric around institutional racism and systemic injustice in the United States which is being met by a whole other spectrum of further oppression and disempowerment: from tokenistic performances of inclusivity to outright state violence, and silencing of the consequences of that violence. You hear of riots breaking out at protests and never hear of that protest again. How do you, as a poet conscious of linguistic harm, respond to these conflicting rhetorics and gestures of false solidarity? When thinking of this question, I thought specifically of Nancy Pelosi giving thanks to George Floyd for sacrificing his life in the pursuit of justice. I'm sure that statement was received horrifically by many people such as yourself.

Claudia: This has been the problem on the left from the get-go. The reality and experiences of white people have crippled their ability to actually know what they know. So you get Nancy Pelosi on the right side of many things, doing many good things, and then saying something like that. The statement becomes a window into the deep lack of understanding of what is actually going on. What is so wrong with saying, *the murder victim*, which is the case? The difficulty, I think, has been to get the left to take on accurate language to describe institutions, like the murderous activity of the police. I'm not trying to exaggerate; you have dead people and you have the people who killed them. So I really feel like my own writing is really an attempt, to quote myself, *to pull the lyric back to its realities*, to bring language back to its stated reality. And that's it. I am not trying to dramatize or over-sentimentalize. I am trying to state what I see, and what I know to be true.

Then there are other people who have different approaches. There are Black Lives Matter activists, some of them have decided to run for office and work within the system. Others are out in the street. There are many approaches to the corrective measure, knowing that how things are being spoken about or framed is incorrect. And you cannot just let it stand, you must get in there and state it as it is. This is one of the great things about now, with social media. We are no longer relying only on mainstream television or newspapers. Now *you* know, *Evelyn* can tell us, *I* can tell you, *people with cameras* can show you, and we have as much access to that as we do to the *Washington Post* or *CNN*.

Evelyn: Do you feel this capacity for counter-surveillance of violence – this witnessing of different acts of injustice – is actually protecting Black people, or do you think it's making them vulnerable to further harm? If you pull out your phone to witness or document what's happening, it seems to increase the potential for further harm.

Claudia: But that's assuming the harm is not always there. So, it's not the idea that, *oh, if you did nothing, nothing would happen*. It's happening, it has been happening. The guy who filmed the attack on Rodney King by LAPD police in 1991 was a white guy. We go back to 1993, 1994 – nothing happened. People saw the Rodney King video, and that's what led to the 1992 riots. Now, without the video showing George Floyd's murder, Derek Chauvin would not have been put in jail. And why not? Because the police filed a report that said Floyd died in hospital, that he died of his own illness. That would have stood as the official record. There's always some risk just speaking up. In my own life I've gotten threatening letters, phone calls, all kinds of things. I'm sure you probably get your share. You just decide what you can live with and what you can't. It's not about preventing more violence. Violence will happen; it has happened and happened and happened. We are now in a position where we can at least say – even if it continues happening, even if there's retribution – *we have evidence*. Evidence might not change behaviour, but at least you're not crazy. I've had it with people who say, 'Well, you don't really know. How do you know, you weren't there? That policemen could've been attacked.' And you say, 'But how, if the victim of police violence was shot in the back? How did the attack occur?' I hear what you're saying, but I think it's a kind of false logic to think anything will stop.

Evelyn: It's less about a question of, 'Will that prevent further harm?', and more an active state of terror. I watch these videos, and when the police turn around to whoever is filming, you hear that person asserting themselves: 'Listen, I have a right to film. I have a right to film.' In so many of these videos people are grabbed, choked, thrown on the ground, simply for the act of witnessing. We have an over-policing problem in Australia. In the United States you have an over-policing problem and then you've got everyone holding guns, which makes the situation so much more terrifying. I wonder how the act of witnessing is itself becoming criminalized through further police brutality. I cannot imagine the fear everyone must have in that moment – knowing not only the power of the witness but also the potential for criminalization of that witnessing.

Claudia: When I see people filming, I feel I'm seeing incredible acts of courage. Those people more than anybody understand what they are coming up against. Armed policemen are right there. It's an act of agency, it's an act of defiance, it's an act of citizenry. It's an incredible civic moment for these people and they know it. What you say is true in terms of the pushback, but they know about the pushback. We all know it, but what are you going to do? Just not say anything? Not do anything? We have all kinds of examples of people being silent while the worst is going on in front of them.

Evelyn: That kind of global circularity of footage has a really powerful impact on other racialized or over-criminalized communities. In Australia we had an inquest into violence against Aboriginal children in juvenile detention and juvenile custody, which revealed that eleven-year-old children were being beaten up, forced to wear spit hoods and literally tortured. I think that inquest was largely motivated by footage from inside these facilities. There's additional momentum because the same question is coinciding with a global recognition of the Black Lives Matter movement. We were able to force these benevolent white people to acknowledge that police violence and institutional racism is not only an American problem, it is also an Australian problem. Racialization operates quite differently in Australia. It's not simply skin-based, you can be criminalized for having an Aboriginal surname. In the United States, I think there's a much more visual aspect to the way racism operates, and also linguistic.

Claudia: And that's why Jews changed their names, many people changed their names. It's a long history in this country that feathers out before Caucasians lived under the umbrella of whiteness.

Evelyn: Yes. But it was enormously mobilizing for us here to have that public rhetoric and focus, even if it enabled a different struggle.

Claudia: And the same struggle. That's the thing, different but also the same. Kimberlé Crenshaw has an organization, *Say Her Name*. One of the important things about Kimberlé's work is that Black women and women of colour are often left out of the discussion around police violence, because those women are often killed in their homes. There isn't the same documenting of the kill; you don't have the videos, so they drop out of the public conversation. Not Breonna Taylor – now people are very actively bringing these names forward, but initially you noticed that it was just men, boys who were listed. It was because it was happening in public – the videos of men and boys – and then it gradually changed. Much to Kimberlé's credit, I would say.

Evelyn: We've had a lot of conversations about this in terms of Indigenous organizing, where it's not simply about who gets a spot on TV. It's about who is handing out flyers, who is organizing childcare, who is looking after the Elders and organizing rallies and protests. And they might not be the people getting up there speaking, but they're usually women.

Claudia: Exactly. We certainly saw that in Georgia during the elections, with Stacey Abrams and the kind of work that sat on the ground.

Evelyn: I'd like to focus back on mental health. In a lot of your work, you speak quite openly about your own experiences with psychiatry, therapy and the mental health system, as well as the experiences of your friends and other racialized people. For many colonized and racialized people Western psychiatry is an extension of other oppressive structures like the medical and industrial prison complex. Many Aboriginal people like me and my family struggle to find mental health professionals that don't insist on pathologizing our relationships with Country or culture, or on seeking languages of treatment for untreatable wounds of dispossession.

I understand this in a framework of what Eve Tuck and K. Wayne Yang (2012: 11) call 'a settler move to innocence'. Another attempt to emphasize, as you say, white benevolence, or an attempt to reconcile what has been done to us – to make *us* reconcile and be at peace with it. And if we fail at that reconciliation – if we cannot be healed or if our generational trauma leads us to other forms of illness – at the very best we're gaslit into nationalistic and secular structures of what healing might look like, or at worst medically criminalized, and in many instances killed by the police who are called instead of social workers. In your work, psychiatry and mental health structures can be a space of institutional racism, but there seems to be at least a kind of – I'm not sure if the word is 'trust'. Can you talk about how you came to a place of understanding or acceptance within these mental health structures?

Claudia: I really believe in therapy. I do. It's something that has been very useful to me in my own life. Part of recognizing the long-term effects of trauma on a community is also recognizing what is needed to address that trauma. Up until now, I think the Black church has worked as a place of healing, and certainly has its place. But I really believe that a kind of dedicated attention needs to be given to victims of trauma. I'm not the only one, Richard Wright worked with psychiatrists in the 1940s and 1950s to open something called the Lafargue Mental Hygiene Clinic in Harlem. It was a clinic where therapists across New York volunteered their time specifically to Black people in that community to address the social stresses without racializing the treatment. You got the same treatment, but it was open to the social issues that were affecting that community. Ralph Ellison (1964) wrote a piece called *Harlem Is Nowhere* in which he talks about the clinic.

It's necessary to understand that we need institutional transformation, but while that's happening, there are individuals with real trauma that needs to be addressed – not pathologized, as you say, but addressed. I think as a country we need to start thinking about how to prioritize that. There are certain things you cannot fix by throwing money at them. They take time, they take care, they take somebody who can rebuild what has been taken away internally. How does a person rebuild agency? How does a person understand how they can get access in a world that has told them they're incompetent, not worthy, inherently criminal? How do you put that aside and keep going in order to take care of yourself and your family? You cannot legislate that. You must express it. And that's what I'm really interested in: institutions that are dedicated to addressing trauma.

Evelyn: Decolonization requires lifetimes of work in deconstruction and rebuilding. We should hold a place for triaging other kinds of assistance. I've balanced experiences in social justice organizing and in academia with an attempt to reconcile what we must attend to with the structures and resources that are available now. People focus on decolonization, complete social transformation and revolution, and not on the fact that there are people to feed, that there's healing that must be done before any of that is attainable. It's very frustrating to be stuttered by that.

Claudia: I also think that we don't need to choose. The people who want to address radical institutional change, let them do what they want to do. And then those of us who are working person by person, let us do what we want to do. There's a book I recommend by Sarah Schulman (2021) called *Let the Record Show*. She talks about the ways in which the AIDS crisis in the United States allowed everyone to approach the problem of getting help and care to that community in whatever way they wanted. One of the reasons they were so successful is that while one person was in the insurance companies trying to get new drugs insured, another person was in the church throwing themselves on the ground, but nobody said, 'You can't go to the insurance company' or, 'You can't go to the church'.

Everybody just decided, 'I'm in this group'. And that's what they did. I say that we don't have to make those choices. We just have to *do*. Poets and writers, we share that. We understand the emotional life of people. That's part of the act of writing. That's what the lyric demands in a sense. And that understanding comes with the responsibility of the trauma that's inside that life. I get what you're saying, but as somebody who is old, I think, let's all just do what we can. That's all we can do.

Evelyn: Following on from that, there's a passage in *Don't Let Me Be Lonely* that I'm obsessed with. You write:

> Though Myung Mi Kim did say that the poem is a responsibility to everyone in a social space. She did say it was okay to cramp, to clog, to fold over at the gut, to have to put hand to flesh, to have to hold the pain, and then to translate it here. She did say, in so many words, that what alerts, alters. (Rankine 2004: 57)

Your work resonates with powerful and perhaps even idealistic notions of poetry as a form of radical responsibility to everyone in a social space, but it also seems to be cautious about utopias. Particularly, utopias that necessitate Black exhaustion, or the exhaustion of people of colour, or of colonized, racialized, marginalized peoples. This resonates with me – as an Indigenous woman educated in a tradition in which storytelling teaches us how to be responsible to our world. Do you see or encounter the limits of poetic responsibility in your practice today? Do you feel empowered by the fact that your work has touched so many people, or are you at times frustrated by the potential limit of that work, if there is a limit?

Claudia: I have spent all of my adult life in pedagogy in one way or another. I don't consider writing pedagogy, but certainly I have taught, and the reason I teach is because I have learned so much from the people I read, from the poets that have nourished me. I don't know what my books do when they leave me, but I know what other people's books do for me. They arrive in my world. I trust that. I believe in that. I honour that. The power of language, of an articulated moment, in the right light. I've been listening to you read your poems, and they're beautiful (Araluen 2019, 2020). You move through space really well. I get that movement.

I get frustrated, but I get frustrated *in* the act of writing, not afterwards. How do I get this thing to do the thing I want it to do? How do I get the language? How do I find the right word? How do I get the syntax to work in the right way? But that's the extent of the frustration. Once it leaves me, I don't know what will happen. I don't know. I just trust it will find its people, whoever that is. It could be you! Apparently, it was you. I don't really think beyond that. I move on, I try not to invest either in the criticism or the praise, because it goes both ways. If I'm going to be pulled one way or the other, then it's harder to go forward.

Evelyn: I think your work attests to the central idea of what responsibility is from an Indigenous perspective, because that's always grounded in sustainability. You have to honour who's come before you, or whose struggles might be aligned with yours – as so much of the anecdotal witnessing work that *Citizen* (Rankine 2014) in particular does – at the same time as continuously making space for who's going to come next. You're constantly holding obligation to your ancestors and to your descendants. I think your work embodies that responsibility, that double time of representation. *Citizen* is one of my favourite texts to introduce to people who need that work. My students are drawn to your work structurally, formally, politically. It's thrilling to be able to introduce them to something that makes what they wanted to say possible in ways that were perhaps not previously possible. Making space, I think, is the highest form of responsibility in a poetic sense. I can express on their behalf as well as mine a deep gratitude for that.

Claudia: Thank you. But some of that comes with making the work do what it needs to do, rather than falling into what is perceived to be the safe way of moving forward. It goes back to the other question of, 'Why witness, why photograph?' Because it does make a kind of space. The way I often think about my work is that it will make somebody else's work possible. So, your use of the word 'space' is gratifying, because it has always been my feeling that my work is possible because I read James Baldwin, because I read Paul Celan – and Rainer Maria Rilke and Sonia Sanchez and Nikki Giovanni and César Vallejo – they all come together, and then we have Claudia! And hopefully for somebody else that will then open out other possibilities. We're constantly building towards something that we couldn't do by ourselves. I can't do what you do. Then somebody else will do what we do together, but better. It's exciting to read new work like *Whereas*, Layli Long Soldier's (2017) work. It was one of those moments for me where I felt like, wow, this is a move forward in our poetic landscape. A necessary and needed move, and not something I could have done myself.

Evelyn: I definitely think you've opened up a lot for other writers, and I have a lot of love for that. There's a decent chance that the mark of your work is on *Whereas*, in its citational practice. I spoke with Billy-Ray Belcourt last week, who I think is very much marked by your work, not just around race and colonization but also formally. As Indigenous peoples we interpret citational structures as practices of honouring. I know that there are more complex linguistic formations going on than just reverence, particularly with Celan and Rilke and what they do with lyrical subjectivity. It makes sense to see your work on the lyric responding to them.

Historically the lyric's subject position is involved in hierarchies of transparency and capacity. You adopt the framework of the deliberately American lyric, but seek to ironize or problematize this idea by applying it to sites of interrupted or fragmented sovereignty, such as the ill, the Other, the incarcerated. To what extent do you think this kind of overarching national form can be made witness to a nation of silenced others?

Claudia: Formally, the addition of *American* (to the books' subtitles) (Rankine 2004, 2014) was probably the most aggressive act I've participated in in my writing. I'm interested in this notion that the lyric had centralized a certain kind of voice and experience that – without saying it – was excluding many people. There was no way to open up the field of interrogation of the poem without stating that that field had been closed down by an American sensibility, a power: patriarchy, whiteness, all of that. It was an insistence – at this point it's hard to say necessary or not necessary, because it is part of the way those books were formed. The shift to *American Conversation* (Rankine 2020) was an attempt to open out the landscape to include white people. To say, if the first two books were about giving voice to the Other, now let's all get in the room and see what we can do together. Knowing that the violence came from over there, what are we going to say? What can we say to each other, how can we move forward at this point? That shift – in both the book's form and subtitle – was necessary for the kind of conversation that we clearly need to have right now.

Evelyn: There's an incredible patience and restraint in your work. I've heard it when you've been interviewed by people who perhaps were not quite responding to the political stakes of your work. You're so restrained about the capacity of your work. I read that shift away from the lyric and the emphasis on witnessing in *Just Us: An American Conversation* (Rankine 2020) almost like a command. Or a threat. To me it says, 'Oh no, I've been watching, I've been observing, and now we're going to talk.' Like, this is *now*. Now you have to sit at the table and actually be responsive. It's no longer the absorption or consumption of your subjectivity through the lyric, which is itself a privilege for readers to access. I think it's a privilege to be able to sit down with your work, particularly with these descriptions of encounters that many white people will never hear about in any other way, or that they wish not to hear, or to have any part in witnessing.

Claudia: They're participating. Those conversations are had by everyone. And yet people think there's racism without racists. That's the problem. When we only concentrate on the grief, we forget there's a source. How do you switch the camera so we can see where the violence is coming from? People are not just moaning. Somebody is shooting them. Somebody is refusing to hire them. Somebody is slamming the door in their face. Somebody is doing all of that.

Evelyn: There seems to be a very clear presence of traumatic repetition in the movement from poem to poem in your work, or essay to essay or image to essay, or whatever that transition might be. A circling of motifs and gestures. In *Citizen* you write, 'If this were a domestic tragedy, and it might well be, this would be your fatal flaw – your memory, vessel of your feelings' (Rankine 2014: 7). As you explore in great detail throughout your writing, memory for the racialized, colonized, institutionalized, Othered subject is often a site of trauma. I feel like there are conflicting impulses in your work. I can't tell whether you feel, as Belcourt (2018) describes it, 'beholden to a project of lessening the trauma of description' through your poetry, or if you feel an imperative to use language to refocus the site of injustice, the site of trauma, as part of your representation of witnessing and of consciencism.

Claudia: That's a great question, and the quick answer is yes, they're conflicting impulses because there are multiple audiences. If one were only writing to Black people then maybe one thing would be done, and if one were writing only to white people another thing might be done. But if you're writing to a public, then the way I think about it, I'm circling a subject, and in circling it different modes are being activated at different moments. Sometimes you want to show the thing, but you don't want to re-traumatize people. Those are some of the kind of craft questions that come up in making videos and in writing poems and essays. How to put us back in the place without retraumatizing? How to make it clear what is happening so that the players are clear? How much do you pull back? How close do you get there?

There's no right answer. I think as poets, we have some formal ways of dealing with that. There's the ellipsis, there's the power of the unsaid, the place of metaphor. But at a certain point you just want to say, 'This is what it looked like'. It's an active question because it's an active field. It's a troubling one because I don't want to re-traumatize people, I don't want to be traumatized. It was hard to watch the Derek Chauvin trial, because it broke my heart to hear the prosecution telling people they couldn't be trusted in describing what they saw, because they were angry at the police.

One guy said, 'I was just trying to stay in my body'. Another woman said, 'I was upset'. Yes. Because watching somebody die is upsetting, so don't tell me I shouldn't be upset. This is the question of the moment. You have people saying, 'I don't want to see that anymore', and yet you talk about it without seeing it. How do you prevent it from happening again without saying, 'This is what it looks like'?

I wrote *Citizen* between 2010 and 2013, and it was published in 2014. What I would say then and what I feel I need to say now are very different. We've seen and seen and seen and seen. *Just Us* (Rankine 2020) didn't need to show many of those things. We were on the same page by then. Now, I feel like we know what happened. We can, in our minds, call up what happened to George Floyd, even though *Just Us* was finished before he was murdered. It's really a different moment now, a different time.

Evelyn: And one in which it should be more than acceptable to say, 'No, I don't need to perform this trauma for you to be able to have this conversation, because you've seen it. And if you haven't seen it, you're deliberately choosing not to see it.'

Claudia: Exactly. And we're having things happen in the culture that never happened before. Steve McQueen's *Small Axe* (2020) series, for example, showed historical moments in Britain of extreme anti-Blackness. Those films were a gift to the British culture. For years the Brits have been saying, 'We don't have racism here.' Then Steve McQueen put out those films, and you say, 'What? That happened?' You knew already. We are in a different moment.

Evelyn: It's incredible to see this movement of much more radical storytelling. In Australia, I've encountered publishers or festivals or literary organizers who want to take credit for that. To say, 'We opened the door and now you're in.' I love cheekiness in this space. I love snark in this space, completely divesting of the respectability politics around having access to major studios and major resources. I love people who take the money and run. I think that's what we need to do now as much as possible.

Claudia: But I also like it when people say, 'Look, we open the door and there you are.' Because the inverse to me is to admit that they had the door closed. And that is correct. I am glad we both understand that. Now, I'm glad that it's being said. Because it's the reality.

Evelyn: That resonates with what you said earlier – when I asked about the potential for more harm that witnessing opens up, and you responded that harm is going to happen anyway. Now we have a record of it. This is the kind of clarity of thinking and perspective that I really admire in your work. I know that comes from experience, from a real patience and dedication. That way of thinking is opening up other rhetorics of resistance and resilience, which are much needed in young people. And not just in young people, but older people who are emerging in their writing practice, or their forms of political resistance.

Claudia: I've had students who have spoken out against something and it didn't change, and they say, 'We did all this and nothing happened.' And I sit back and ask, 'But who said it's over?' It's not over until it's over you. If you say it's not over, it's not over.

References

Araluen, E. (2019), 'Interior Anxious', *The Big Anxiety*, 25 September 2019. Available online: https://youtu.be/ha0XfkEeldk (accessed 28 September 2021).
Araluen, E. (2020), *Dropbear*, Brisbane: University of Queensland Press.
Belcourt, B.-R. (2018), 'Fatal Naming Rituals', *Hazlitt*, 19 July 2018. Available online: https://hazlitt.net/feature/fatal-naming-rituals (accessed 01 September 2021).
Ellison, R. (1964), 'Harlem is Nowhere', *Harper's Magazine,* August.
Rankine, C. (2004), *Don't Let Me Be Lonely: An American Lyric*, Minneapolis: Graywolf Press.
Rankine, C. (2014), Citizen: An American Lyric, Minneapolis: Graywolf Press,
Rankine, C. (2020), *Just Us: An American Conversation*, London: Allen Lane.
Small Axe (2020), [Film series], Dir. Steve McQueen, UK: Turbine Studios and Lammas Park.
Soldier, L.L. (2017), 'Whereas', *Poetry*, January 2017. Available online: https://www.poetryfoundation.org/poetrymagazine/poems/91697/from-whereas (accessed 01 September 2021).
Tuck, E. and K.W. Wang (2012), 'Decolonization is not a Metaphor', *Decolonization: Indigeneity, Education & Society*, 1 (1): 1–40.

Part VI

Reparative action

CHAPTER 12

Designing reparations

Creative process as reparative practice

Andrea Durbach, Jill Bennett and
Pumla Gobodo-Madikizela

Reparation should start internally rather than . . . in monetary
terms. This is because the brokenness and the destructiveness
. . . happens at a deeply internal level and that's the work that
needs to happen.

(SOLMS & GOBODO-MADIKIZELA 2016)

Actually what you see in a lot of us is the shell, and I believe as
an Aboriginal person that everything is inside of me to heal me if I
know how . . . to maintain it, if I know how to bring out and use it.
But sometimes the past is just too hard to look at.

(HUMAN RIGHTS AND EQUAL OPPORTUNITY COMMISSION 1997, CONFIDENTIAL
EVIDENCE 284, SOUTH AUSTRALIA)

In 2019, leading First Nations trauma expert, Judy Atkinson collaborated
with artist r e a and colleagues on a project that activated the principles of

'deep listening' (*Dadirri*) – the ritual process that Atkinson (2002) describes
as the 'Aboriginal gift to the nation'. The work, *Listen_Up*, created for the
Empathy Clinic exhibition at The Big Anxiety, was fashioned as an 'aural
campfire', a 'creative learning and teaching space where elders pass on 'their'
knowledge and stories to listeners young and old; Judy is our story-teller'.[1]
The audio-track builds on a poem written by Atkinson in 2003 about her
own experience of sexual violence – and of the cultural inheritance of a
nation where 'sexual violence [was] a tool of colonization':

> I am without hope . . . and without a future because there is located in the
> most private part of me a pain so deep that my soul vibrates in the agony
> of the shame of what I am . . . what you have made me. I am . . . hope . . .
> and the future is in my hands. (Atkinson et al. 2019)

The same exhibition featured Uti Kulintjaku, a group of artists and
ngangkari (healers) from the Central Desert of Australia who use art to
address the cycles of trauma. They collaborated on *Wau-mananyi*, an
Anangu-led response to the experiences of constraint, entrapment and
depression through the traditional story (or *tjukurpa*) of 'The Man in the
Log' (see Chapter 15). The work is designed as a first-person visual reality
experience of being trapped in the log, bereft and disconnected from the
people searching, glimpsed through cracks in the bark. Eventually the
wasted and dehydrated man is found and released from the tree, fed and
tended by his community. He is weak but the agony of trapped trauma is
somewhat relieved.

An expression of the existential emptiness of trauma as an individual
experience, the two works are also cultural enactments designed to hold
the experience, placing it in a context where it is not only shared but
also envisaged as a complex inheritance: 'the collective emotional and
psychological injury both over the life span and across generations' (Muid
2006: 36).

These are gallery works but not exclusively; the primary purpose of *Wau-
mananyi* was for *ngangkari* to use the piece for mental health support work
with younger *Anangu* in remote desert communities. They are not simply
representations of trauma but an expression of a cultural process that
does not abstract pain and mental ill health from its social and historical
conditions. To borrow a line from Atkinson (2017) in the *We Al Li* trauma
workbook, 'This isn't "art therapy". The art process is healing in itself.'

In the same year, we gathered in South Africa to develop *Designing
Reparations* in collaboration with Studies in Historical Trauma and
Transformation at Stellenbosch University led by historical trauma expert
Pumla Gobodo-Madikizela. The project is designed to identify and test
the value of art processes as reparative practice within the framework of
transitional justice (TJ) strategies that seek to come to terms with violent
histories and their traumatic repercussions. We shared the Australian First

Nations artworks by Atkinson/r e a and Uti Kulintjaku, along with the documentary *A Common Purpose*, made with political trial lawyer Andrea Durbach and the community at the centre of an infamous South African death penalty trial (1986–91) to examine the ways in which such creative works address and seek to mitigate historical trauma – that is, trauma which is not only event-based but compounded by long-term systemic violence and human rights abuses, and which may also be transmitted intergenerationally. Candice Mama and Siyah Mgoduka, whose fathers were murdered by the South African security police, also discussed their collaboration with artist Sue Williamson on the video installation, *It's a Pleasure to Meet You* (2016) – a work exploring the legacy of trauma experienced by the now-adult children of those killed during apartheid.

Drawing on the objectives of and responses to the South African Truth and Reconciliation Commission (TRC) and the Australian Bringing them Home (BTH) inquiry, our interest was to explore the therapeutic benefit – Atkinson's 'art process is healing in itself' – of integrating the use of art practice within national processes directed at redressing historical harm and rebuilding post-conflict societies.

Specifically, we are concerned with the potential for building an enduring creative agency through art processes, which may in the first instance support the articulation of trauma at the point of its manifestation within a formal framework, such as a truth commission or national inquiry. In psychosocial terms, reparative work may be understood as a longer-term 'therapeutic' endeavour, addressing the internalized effects of both particular harms and of power relations that compromise agency. As such, we consider the artistic process not only as an expressive, communicative practice but as a means to re-establish the creative capacities and agency to move beyond the debilitating dynamic of 'doer and done to' (Benjamin 2004).

Truth-telling

Central to commissions and inquiries that have examined historical political violence in pursuit of TJ is the invitation to victims of state harm to bear witness. The design of these fora was predicated upon the aspiration that those who bore witness would be heard or listened to by those in attendance at public hearings and by perpetrators and executioners of harm, potentially enabling the victim 'to reassert the veracity of the past and to build anew its linkage to, and assimilation into present-day life' (Laub in Felman & Laub 1992: 76). In return, it was anticipated that perpetrators, or agents of the state, might verify or validate the victim's subjective experience, potentially offering remorse, a confession or apology. Underlying the rationale 'to reveal, to unveil, and to make known the true horrors of a conflict or an injustice' (James-Lomax 2005: 1) is the objective of preventing the future recurrence of violence expressed in the '"never again" mantra of many Latin American truth commissions and other official investigations' (Ross 2003: 327).

At the core of this envisaged reciprocal exchange were two objectives: first, that truth-telling would aid the healing or repair of individual victims; second, that a negotiated forfeiture of the model of retributive justice would encourage a peaceful settlement and reconciliation, potentially avoiding 'a return to violence' (Moon 2009: 72) for the re-modelled nation or post-conflict state. In the South African example, the dialogue of truth (South Africa 1999: 115) envisioned between individual victim and perpetrator offered a context in which victims 'break their silence in front of a national audience' and perpetrators give full public disclosure and confess politically motivated criminal conduct, often in exchange for amnesty (Gobodo-Madikizela 2016a). The affirmation of victims' experiences by a sympathetic audience – what Hartman (2002: 136) refers to as an 'affective community' – and the validation of these experiences for the historical record was fundamental to the objectives of the TRC. The TRC Final Report refers to the outcome of this interactive dialogue as 'social truth' (South Africa 1999: 113–14). Although the TRC had the power to grant amnesty to perpetrators in exchange for their truth-telling, their allegiance to the requirement of full disclosure of the circumstances surrounding their crimes often gave way to a desire that listeners simply serve as bystanders to their crimes (Herman 2015: 7).

While there are, as Cole (2010: 659) argues, 'good reasons to be cautiously optimistic about the therapeutic possibilities of narrative in many cases', these may have been 'idealized' (Young 2004: 151) and overstated, particularly where the consequences of historic injustice 'are still actively *evolving*' in contemporary social, political and cultural settings (Felman & Laub 1992: xiv).

The 'multiple and profoundly disabling' (Human Rights and Equal Opportunity Commission 1997: 199) consequences suffered by Aboriginal and Torres Strait Islander children forcibly removed from their families by the Australian state (1910–70) was the subject of the BTH inquiry (Human Rights and Equal Opportunity Commission 1997: 199). The majority of witnesses who testified before the inquiry spoke of the 'compounding effects' of the government's assimilationist policies and the long-term impact of the forced removal of children from families, many of whom were placed in institutions, on church missions or in foster homes and subjected to physical, psychological and sexual abuse, and loss of identity and culture. The resultant cycles of psychological and emotional damage – from which it was 'difficult to escape unaided' – 'render(ed) many people less able to learn social . . . and survival skills', impairing their 'ability to operate successfully in the world' (Human Rights and Equal Opportunity Commission 1997: 11). Consequent unemployment and poverty would in turn cause emotional distress 'leading some to perpetrate violence, self-harm, substance abuse or anti-social behaviour' (Human Rights and Equal Opportunity Commission 1997: 12).

The impact of forced removal policies extended beyond the children removed, 'leaving a powerful residue of unrecognised and unresolved grief that [has] pathological effects on Indigenous communities' (Koolmatrie & Williams 2000: 163). Similarly in South Africa, the systematic implementation of apartheid spawned 'the deepest social crisis' (Machel 2012). Despite the aspirations of the TRC, the 'psychological and emotional damage inflicted on men and women' (Machel 2012) by decades of racial injustice endures. Almost two decades after the end of apartheid rule, Graca Machel, wife of President Nelson Mandela, declared in response to post-apartheid violence that '(w)e are harming one another because we cannot control our pain' (Machel 2012).

Notwithstanding their therapeutic ambitions for individual and national healing, the design of TJ institutions, in particular their mandate and term, may limit opportunities and resources for 'deep listening' (Atkinson 2002) and sustained engagement central to the dialogic model of truth-telling. Indeed, Karstedt (2015: 53) maintains that the 'emotional reactivation of harm and trauma' in TJ contexts 'may elicit negative emotions in participants' which require alternative or transformative modes of reciprocal recognition, acknowledgement and redress. Cole reinforces this view in her case study of Yazir Henry's public testimony before the TRC, urging a 'more circumspect accounting of the power of narrative – [and] its power to heal and to harm' (Cole 2010: 659). In Henry's case, the subsequent mis- or re-representation of the testimony to the political and psychological detriment of the testifier signalled that 'participation in such proceedings may be less therapeutic than commonly assumed' (Kagee 2006: 20).

Reparations

While public testimony can render constructive psychosocial effect (Young 2004: 152), it is not 'sufficient simply to open old wounds and then sit back and wait for the light of exposure to do the cleansing' (South Africa 1999: 115). Critical to the long-term accomplishments of TJ is the extent to which the objectives of truth-telling and transformation are reinforced by the provision of parallel reparative measures.

Reparations made available to victims following their testimony may serve to enhance the therapeutic value of that experience and can be decisive for emotional healing; conversely, the lack of appropriate reparations following the truth-telling process may significantly undermine or suspend its therapeutic value, especially where the testimony of victims fails to elicit individual validation by perpetrators or the requisite structural transformation of the state (Martin-Beristain et al. 2010). As Moffett argues, '[w]e need a more articulated and complex vision of how reparations for conflict-related . . . violence can be delivered' (Moffett 2019).

Reparations provided within the TJ framework have customarily taken the form of acknowledgement (apology), monetary compensation, restitution (e.g. of land, language), rehabilitation (medical and psychological) and guarantees against repetition of human rights violations. Symbolic reparations, which often signal a plea against repetition of harm, may assume a public or collective form (e.g. memorials or museums) and include 'more performative or ephemeral gestures of recognition (of harm) and atonement, such as public apologies, annual ceremonies and rituals or performances' (Greeley et al. 2020: 166). Within our framework, artistic process is not confined to the symbolic but may also enact a process of rehabilitation; thus, rehabilitation as reparation is understood as a cultural and psychosocial process.

In the twenty years since the release of the BTH Report and the Final Report of the TRC, the Australian and South African government responses to calls for reparations have been erratic and piecemeal. In both countries, measures of reparation have failed to address the long-term impact of historical harm and the extent to which past practices permeate post-conflict societies and perpetuate systemic harm (Durbach 2019). Yael Danieli (2014: 18-19) observes that 'the complex nature of trauma requires an equally complex understanding of justice', highlighting that the process undertaken by victims (truth-telling) and the outcome (reparations) are both crucial elements to ensuring that 'their total experience of justice is healing'. Minimal or insufficient measures of reparation coupled with an absence of justice in the form of the prosecution of perpetrators and state accountability, risk generating cycles of expectation and disappointment which may act as barriers to emotional recovery (Martin-Beristain et al. 2010), reinforcing a collective disillusion with TJ processes and possibilities.

Feelings of justice

Giving 'value and meaning to the enterprise of transitional justice' (Rush and Simić, 2013: vii) necessarily entails attending to felt experience:

> [T]ransitional justice, precisely in acknowledging itself as a process inseparable from feelings of justice, is literally unthinkable without the lessons of literature and art. (McNamee 2013: 22)

In 2007, Nomarussia Bonase – National Coordinator of the Khulumani Support Group established to address the 'unfinished business' of transformational justice after the closure of the South African TRC (Seidman & Bonase 2015) – and artist Judy Seidman held a series of 'Art and Memory Workshops' for group members. The workshops sought to employ art-making as an alternative means of collating unrecorded accounts of the systematic use of sexual and gender-based violence (Seidman & Bonase 2016) perpetrated primarily against Black women by the agents of apartheid. Their rationale was to 'access memory through drawn images' and enable victims of apartheid who had not participated in the TRC hearings to share individual and collective 'recollections and ideas outside of the preconceptions and limitations' (Seidman & Bonase 2016) imposed by a TRC framework – in many cases, an expression of harm where 'experiences [were] so searing that they [could] not be reduced to words' (Le Barron & Sarra 2018: 22). For Seidman and Bonase, art-making was an 'activist approach' which encouraged participants to tell their stories and find solutions with 'each [woman] sa[ying] they felt stronger, affirmed, by the telling' (Seidman & Bonase 2016).

The Khulumani workshops created a safe space for women to speak about political violence unencumbered by form-filling and schedules or the formal requirements for the presentation of testimony before the TRC. Rather than focusing on a representational outcome (the narration of trauma and harm), the creative process functioned primarily to register and hold the emotion of participants in a supportive environment that envisaged, and often accomplished, a therapeutic and reparative outcome that the TRC had 'effectively failed' to secure for women (Seidman & Bonase 2016). As a consequence of these workshops, Khulumani negotiated with the South African Department of Justice to provide survivors with financial compensation to address medical, psychological and accommodation needs and develop commemoration initiatives (Khulumani Support Group 2010). Their negotiations for reparations included a request to incorporate psychosocial healing processes, such as the art-making process, *Art and Memory*.

Despite its therapeutic benefits, art practice is rarely conceptualized as material to the reparations process. In 2018, however, the Extraordinary Chambers in the Courts of Cambodia (ECCC), established in 2001 to try serious crimes committed by the Khmer Rouge (1975–9), determined that a dance production, *Phka Sla Krom Angkar* (*Phka Sla*), be recognized as a reparations project following the conviction of former Khmer Rouge officials. The ECCC mandate stipulated that reparations were limited to collective and moral measures directed at redressing emotional or social harms as distinct from material reparations (e.g. monetary compensation) devised to address physical damage to persons or property.

In Case 002/02, the ECCC found that the forced marriage of Cambodian men and women and the rape of women within such marriages constituted a crime against humanity which had led to the 'erosion of … psycho-emotional, familial, cultural … infrastructures', social exclusion and intergenerational stigma and discrimination (Balta 2018). Proposed as a form of redress by the lawyers for the civil parties (who gave evidence on the impact of forced marriage) and with funding from UN Women Cambodia and support from the ECCC Victims Support Section, the *Phka Sla* project had been developed a few years earlier in consultation with 150 civil parties through workshops led by the Transcultural Psychosocial Organization with other civil society organizations.

Based on the testimonies of women and men who had experienced forced marriage and who agreed to their accounts being 'performed as a dance' that might 'invite dialogue and healing', *Phka Sla* invoked a classical Cambodian dance style, an artform suppressed under the reign of the Khmer Rouge (Grey, Sotheary & Somaly 2019: 3). The collaboration of victims and survivors in the creation of *Phka Sla* saw their experiences reflected and validated by the dance, allowing them agency in the execution of the process. Primarily intended as a form of 'psychological compensation' for survivors of forced marriage (Sonyka 2017), the dance was performed by an all-female cast and designed to 'transform the understanding of gender-based violence and gender equality through the artistic memorialization of shared experience' (Heinrich-Boll Stiftung 2017) and to educate future generations about forced marriage. To this end, it was accompanied by a mobile exhibition on forced marriage, 'on-stage panel discussion between the now-elderly civil parties and the young dancers . . . and a documentary about the dance and its creative process' (Grey, Sotheary & Somaly 2019: 4). Yim Sotheary, a psychotherapist involved in *Phka Sla* project, reports the response of a survivor: the 'beautiful mix of movement, expression of emotions, narration, and echoing live music invited my tears [and] made me feel very connected to . . . all of the suffering I experienced under the Khmer Rouge'. Re-engaging with trauma through dance left her feeling 'much better now, because I was not alone. . . . I also feel special that our stories are being told to the students, with whom I had thought I could never share those stories' (Grey, Sotheary & Somaly 2019: 9).

The practice of art as repair and reparation

Justice is more readily experienced (as Laura Zlotowski observes in relation to the Rwandan genocide) 'where dialogue, forgiveness, and honest recitations of the harmful events occur on the survivor's own terms – rather than emanating from a formal national process where a third party is . . . the final arbiter of another person's truth' (Zlotowski 2014).

It is against the backdrop of increasing scepticism about the therapeutic assumptions associated with the TJ model (Mendoloff 2009; Doak 2011; Karstedt 2015; Niezen 2020) that this chapter seeks to explore how the 'salient features' of truth-telling and reparation (Karstedt 2015: 50) – agency, participation, transparency, reciprocity – may be preserved or extended through creative processes.

As Chapter 8 notes, recounting trauma risks reinscribing rather than moving beyond the dynamics of 'doer and done to' unless it can establish conditions under which a 'third' position can be instantiated (Benjamin

2004). Hence, it may be important for therapeutic work to focus not on the task of uncovering and 'symbolizing what is re-lived' but on 'creating the conditions for having a new experience' (Reis 2020: 105). Following Bollas, we suggest that this distinction illuminates the (therapeutic) register of art, which, rather than simply revealing or representing trauma, allows for its transformation through a reconfiguration of experience ('the play work of genera' is 'to collect units of received experience that interanimate towards a new way of perceiving things' (Bollas 1993: 78)). Within trauma-informed arts practice, this generative process is enabled through the affordances of a facilitating environment in which power relations or the assignations of 'doer and done to' are themselves reconfigured, and also by the cultivation of agency and control – not only in the generation of imagery, symbolism and narrative but in the sharing and dissemination of the work (Chapter 8 discusses the example of the Parragirls who sought to keep control of their trauma narrative in order to guard against the re-traumatization reported in the case of Yazir Henry).

At the core of our proposition is that *artistic processes* – as opposed to the employment of *art as representation* of harm (the dominant conception of art as symbolic reparation within existing TJ literature) – can both serve to enable truth-telling and inform or constitute reparative outcomes. Typically, the role of art in supporting the reparative objectives of TJ has been invoked primarily in the context of symbolic reparations as a representation of 'public acknowledgement and recognition that crimes have happened' (Simić 2014: 55). In developing guidelines for the creation of symbolic reparations that speak both to the repair of victims and 'aspirations toward a more moral and just society', Greeley et al. (2020: 191, 189) observed that symbolic reparations such as memorials, monuments and commemorative practices are often perceived as 'top-down affairs', positioning 'audiences – including victims – as passive recipients of a preconstructed meaning, rather than as active participants in creating meaning'. Artworks of memorialization have also been utilized to provide a '"creative pathway" to reconciliation' (Kerr 2017: 3; Garnsey 2016; Shefik 2018), opening up possibilities to foster communication across often antagonistic groups or factions in a political conflict. If created in a genuine, conscious collaboration with victims, symbolic reparations can also serve to articulate an experience-led connection between victims, the state and civil society, potentially generating steps towards post-conflict transformation (Greeley et al. 2020: 192).

Common to both the symbolic representation of historical injustice and the 'dialogic potential' of art to create channels for reconciliation is the capacity of art to convey the 'extent of trauma and the depth of emotions that [victims] and survivors experience' (Kerr 2017: 3). From the victim's perspective, the therapeutic rationale underlying the form of dialogic or relational encounter espoused by the TJ model has parallels with the ideas underlying 'transformative art practices' (LeBarron & Sarra 2018) applied in post-conflict environments. As with the promise of truth-telling, the development of certain transformative art practices has been promoted as enabling the participation of individuals in their own recovery and healing by 'catalyz(ing) shifts in previously frozen or violent relations and creat(ing) openings for new relational geographies' (LeBarron & Sarra 2018: 35).

Moving beyond conventional understandings of art as a mode of representation, the integration of an artistic practice within a TJ framework builds on contemporary research in participatory arts that emphasizes the relational and psychosocial dimensions of creative process (see Chapter 8). Within such a framework, art is not only a means of expressing or making known the lived experience of trauma. Conceived and facilitated as reparation and reparative process, it directly and continuously supports internal and interpersonal processing of trauma within a framework that builds creative capacity, bolstering the agency of survivors and attending to the ongoing dynamics of public engagement. Thus, the focus is not only on self-expression and representation but on co-designing and brokering engagements that promote the desired effects of such representation, such as public acknowledgement and 'being believed'. As such, art practice and associated public representation is not simply instrumental or directed towards some external material goal or outcome. Rather, the practice is in itself reparative, supporting a broader, ongoing, psychosocial process of repair, which anticipates the despair, re-traumatization and the seepage of trauma into the lives of subsequent generations (Gobodo-Madikizela 2016b: 3) that the TJ process alone is ill-equipped to remedy.

Acknowledgements

We acknowledge the contribution of Eliza Garnsey, who undertook initial research on the *Art and Memory Workshops* and *Phka Sla* projects.

Note

1   See The Big Anxiety festival website: https://www.thebiganxiety.org/events/r-e-a -and-judy-atkinson/ (accessed 11 September 2021).

References

Atkinson, J. (2002), *Trauma Trails, Recreating Songlines: The Transgenerational Effects of Trauma in Indigenous Australia*, Melbourne: Spinifex Press.

Atkinson, J. (2017), *We Al Li: Educaring – a Trauma Informed Approach to Healing Generational Trauma for Aboriginal Australians*. Available online: https://www.oics.wa.gov.au/wp-content/uploads/2017/07/Judy-Atkinson -Healing-From-Generational-Trauma-Workbook-We-Al-li.pdf (accessed 10 September 2021).

Atkinson, J., N. Simpson, M.M. Pesa, and A. Belletty (2019), 'Listen_UP', in *The Big Anxiety Festival*, Sydney: UNSW Galleries. Available online: https://www .thebiganxiety.org/events/r-e-a-and-judy-atkinson/ (accessed 17 September 2021).

Balta, A. (2018), 'Extraordinary Chambers in the Courts of Cambodia, Regulation of Marriage, and Reparations: Judgment in Case 002/02 Under Review', *OpinioJuris*, Available online: http://opiniojuris.org/2018/11/20/extraordinary -chambers-in-the-courts-of-cambodia-regulation-of-marriage-and-reparations -judgment-in-case-002-02-under-review/ (accessed 10 September 2021).

Benjamin, J. (2004), 'Beyond Doer and Done To: An Intersubjective View of Thirdness', *The Psychoanalytic Quarterly*, 73 (1): 5–46.

Bollas, C (1993), *Being a Character: Psychoanalysis and Self Experience*, London: Routledge.

Cole, C.E. (2010), 'Problematizing Therapeutic Assumptions About Narratives: A Case Study of Storytelling Events in a Post-Conflict Context', *Health Communication*, 25 (8): 650–60.

Danieli, Y. (2014), 'Healing Aspects of Reparations and Reparative Justice for Victims of Crimes Against Humanity', in J. Wemmers (ed.), *Reparations for Victims of Crimes Against Humanity*, 7–21, New York: Routledge.

Doak, J. (2011), 'The Therapeutic Dimension of Transitional Justice: Emotional Repair and Victim Satisfaction in International Trials and Truth Commissions', *International Criminal Law Review*, 11: 263–98.

Durbach, A. (2019), 'Keeping Justice at Bay: Institutional Harms and the Damaging Cycle of Reparative Failure', *Australian Journal of Human Rights*, 25 (2): 200–16.

Felman, S. and D. Laub (eds) (1992), *Testimony: Crises of Witnessing in Literature, Psychoanalysis and History*, New York: Routledge.

Field, S. (2006), 'Beyond 'healing': Trauma, Oral History, and Regeneration', *Oral History*, 34: 31–42.

Garnsey, E. (2016), 'Rewinding and Unwinding: Art and Justice in Times of Political Transition', *International Journal of Transitional Justice* 10 (3), 471–91.

Gobodo-Madikizela, P. (2016a), *What Does it Mean to be Human in the Aftermath of Trauma? Re-envisioning The Sunflower and why Hannah Arendt was Wrong*, Uppsala: The Nordic Africa Institute and Uppsala University.

Gobodo-Madikizela, P. (2016b), 'Breaking Intergenerational Cycles of Repetition' in P. Gobodo-Madikizela (ed.), *Breaking Intergenerational Cycles of Repetition: A Global Dialogue on Historical Trauma and Memory*, 1–11, Opladen: Barbara Budrich.

Greeley, R.A., M.R. Orwicz, J.L. Falconi, A.M. Reyes, F.J. Rosenberg, and L. J Laplante (2020), 'Repairing Symbolic Reparations: Assessing the Effectiveness of Memorialization in the Inter-American System of Human Rights', *International Journal of Transitional Justice*, 2 (14): 165–92.

Grey, R, Y. Sotheary, and K. Somaly (2019), 'The Khmer Rouge Tribunal's First Reparation for Gender-based Crimes', *Australian Journal of Human Rights*, 25 (3): 488–97.

Hartman, G.H. (2002), *The Longest Shadow: In the Aftermath of the Holocaust*. New York: Palgrave Macmillan.

Herman, J.L. (2015), *Trauma and Recovery: The Aftermath of Violence - From Domestic Abuse to Political Terror*, New York: Basic Books.

Heinrich Boll Stiftung (2017), 'Victims Support Section (ECCC): Wide Ranging Support for Reparation', *Press Release*, 17 March 2017. Available online: https://kh.boell.org/en/2017/03/17/press-release-victims-support-section-wide -ranging-support-reparation (accessed 16 September 2021).

Human Rights and Equal Opportunity Commission. 1997. *Bringing Them Home: National Inquiry Into the Separation of Aboriginal and Torres Strait Islander Children From Their Families*. Sydney: Commonwealth of Australia.

James-Lomax, A. (2005), *The Truth Must Dazzle Gradually: The Truth and Reconciliation Commission and the Ongoing Practice of Ignorance in South Africa*, M.A. Diss, Department of Political Science, University of Victoria, Canada.

Kagee, A. (2006), 'The Relationship Between Statement Giving at the South African Truth and Reconciliation Commission and Psychological Distress Among Former Political Detainees', *South African Journal of Psychology*, 36 (1): 10–24.

Karstedt, S. (2015), 'The Emotion Dynamics of Transitional Justice: An Emotion Sharing Perspective', *Emotion Review*, 8 (1): 50.

Kerr, R. (2017). 'The "Art" of Reconciliation', *FICHL Policy Brief Series*, 78.

Khulumani Support Group (2010), *Proposals for Reparations for Victims of Apartheid Gross Human Rights Violations*. Available online: https://static.pmg .org.za/170524Khulumani.pdf (accessed 10 September 2021).

Koolmatrie, J. and R. Williams (2000), 'Unresolved Grief and the Removal of Indigenous Australian Children', *Australian Psychologist*, 35 (2): 158–66.

Laub, D. (1992), 'An Event Without a Witness: Truth, Testimony and Survival', in Felman, S. and D. Laub (eds), *Testimony: Crises of Witnessing in Literature, Psychoanalysis and History*, 75–92, New York: Routledge.

LeBaron, M. and J. Sarra (2018), *Changing our Worlds: Art as Transformative Practice*, Stellenbosch: SUN Press.

Machel, G. (2012), '2nd Annual Desmond Tutu International Peace Lecture', Cape Town: University of the Western Cape, 02 October 2012. Available online: https://www.tutu.org.za/peace-lectures/annual-lecture-2012/ (accessed 16 September 2021).

Martin-Beristain, C., D. Páez, B. Rimé, and P. Kanyangara (2010), 'Psychosocial Effects of Participation in Rituals of Transitional Justice: A Collective-level Analysis and Review of the Literature of the Effects of TRCs and Trials on Human Rights Violations in Latin America', *International Journal of Social Psychology*, 25 (1): 47–60.

McNamee, E. (2013), 'Fields of Opportunity: Cultural Invention and "The New Northern Ireland"', in P.D. Rush and O. Simić (eds), *The Arts of Transitional Justice: Culture, Activism, and Memory After Atrocity*, 1–24, Berlin: Springer.

Mendeloff, D. (2009). 'Trauma and Vengeance: Assessing the Psychological and Emotional Effects of Post-conflict Justice', *Human Rights Quarterly*, 31 (3): 592–623.

Moon, C. (2009), 'Healing Past Violence: Traumatic Assumptions and Therapeutic Interventions in War and Reconciliation', *Journal of Human Rights*, 8 (1): 71–91.

Moffett, L. (2019). 'International Reparation Initiative for Conflict-Related Sexual Violence: Four Challenges', *OpinioJuris*. Available online: http://opiniojuris .org/2019/03/28/international-reparation-initiative-for-conflict-related-sexual -violence-four-challenges/

Muid, O. (2006), *Then I Lost my Spirit: An Analytical Essay on Transgenerational Theory and its Application to Oppressed People of Color Nations*, M.A. Diss., School of Social Welfare. State University of New York.

Niezen, R, (2020), 'Human Rights as Therapy: The Healing Paradigms of Transitional Justice', in D. Celemajer and A. Lefebvre (eds), *The Subject of Human Rights*, 153–71, Bloomington: Stanford University Press.

Reis, B.E. (2020), *Creative Repetition and Intersubjectivity: Contemporary Freudian Explorations of Trauma, Memory, and Clinical Process*, New York: Routledge.

Ross, F.C. (2003), 'On Having a Voice and Being Heard: Some After-effects of Testifying Before the South African Truth and Reconciliation Commission', *Anthropological Theory*, 3: 325–41.

Rush, P.D. and O. Simić, (eds) (2013), *The Arts of Transitional Justice: Culture, Activism, and Memory After Atrocity*, Berlin: Springer.

Seidman, J. and N. Bonase (2015), 'Khulumani Support Group: Using Art-Making and Oral Narrative to Address Land Dispossession, Popular Resistance and Restitution', *Oral History Journal of South Africa*, 3 (1): 25–31.

Seidman, J. and N. Bonasae (2016), 'Tsogang Basadi: Finding Women's Voice From South Africa's Political Conflict', Available online: http://www.judyseidman.com /tsogang%20basadi%20paper.html (accessed 10 September 2021).

Shefik, S. (2018), 'Reimagining Transitional Justice Through Participatory Art', *International Journal of Transitional Justice*, 12 (2): 314–33.

Simić, O. (2014), 'But I Want to Speak Out: Making Art From Women's Testimonies', *Australian Feminist Law Journal*, 40 (1): 51–67.

Solms, M. and P. Gobodo-Madikizela (2016), 'Has South Africa Healed From the Agony of Apartheid?', *The Friday Stand-In: Radio 702*, 22 July 2016. Available online at http://www.702.co.za/articles/15231/mental-state-of-the-nation-has -south-africa-healed-from-the-agony-of-apartheid (accessed 10 September 2021).

Sonyka, V. (2017), '"Phka Sla" Dance to Help KR's Forced Marriage Victims Heal', *Khmer Times*, 17 January 2017. Available online: https://www.khmertimeskh .com/60315/phka-sla-dance-to-help-krs-forced-marriage-victims-heal/ (accessed 10 September 2021).

South Africa (1999), *Truth and Reconciliation Commission of South Africa Report: Vol. 4*, Ch. 10, Cape Town: The Commission.

Young, S. (2004), 'Narrative and Healing in the Hearings of the South African Truth and Reconciliation Commission', *Biography*, 27 (1): 145–62.

Zlotowski, L.J. (2014), *Justice Taken Personally: A Conversation About Truth, Reconciliation and Forgiveness Following Mass Atrocity*, Irvine: University of California.

CHAPTER 13

EmbodiMap I

Trauma survival and refugee experience

Lydia Gitau

In 2011, I was part of a team of Kenyan volunteers conducting 'trauma awareness' workshops at Dadaab Refugee Camp in Northeastern Kenya. Dadaab is now the third-largest 'Refugee Complex' in the world, established in 1991 to host refugees fleeing civil war in Somalia. A second influx of 130,000 refugees arrived in 2011, fleeing drought and famine in Southern Somalia (UNHCR 2020). The workshops we ran focused on helping the refugees to acknowledge and name their feelings and emotions. Using a 'manual' prepared by an absent expert from the United States, we invited them into large groups to discuss and give words to 'their trauma'. Not wanting to disappoint, they endeavoured to find words that fitted our descriptions of trauma, though I myself could not find a word to translate 'trauma' in my mother tongue.

One of the 130,000 arrivals was Halima (name changed). She had walked more than 500 kilometres over many days, crossing the semi-arid plains between Somalia and Dadaab to escape the drought. She had set off with her six children, but arrived at the camp with only two. Halima's other children had either died on the way due to starvation and exhaustion or she had to leave them behind when they were too weak to continue, since she could not carry them all. How could we ask Halima to access and name the feelings and emotions that arise from this experience?

In 2013 I carried out research among South Sudanese Refugees in Kakuma Refugee Camp in Northwest Kenya, established in 1992 following the arrival of the 'Lost Boys of Sudan', a group of about 20,000 boys who fled their villages in Southern Sudan in the late 1980s. The camp hosts 184,550 refugees, mostly those fleeing war in South Sudan, and also from Somalia, Ethiopia, Eritrea, Burundi and the Democratic Republic of the Congo (DRC). For most of the refugees, the camp is practically the only home they have known. The South Sudanese refugees – survivors of ongoing conflict and mass violence lasting over five decades – have constantly suffered direct attack, insecurity, death of or separation from loved ones, destruction of homes, scarcity of basic necessities and experienced loss of identity and a pervasive sense of hopelessness. These observations left me with an overwhelming sense of the need for trauma-sensitivity in the interventions and support structures for refugees. But how could this be achieved practically?

In 2016, I began working with the Service for the Treatment and Rehabilitation of Torture and Trauma Survivors (STARTTS) in New South Wales, Australia: a non-profit organization that provides psychological treatment and support to help individuals and communities heal the scars of torture and refugee trauma and rebuild their lives. My work involved running training programmes on trauma-informed ways of working with people from refugee backgrounds and asylum seekers, and in 2019 I went to work as a trauma counsellor with the Yezidi refugees in Armidale, a regional city in New South Wales. The Yezidi are an ethno-religious minority group mainly coming from Northern Iraq and Syria, forced to flee their homes as a result of persecution by Islamic State (IS) militants. Most Yezidi refugees are survivors of the August 2014 genocide (Sinjar Massacre) by IS in which thousands of men were captured, killed or held in captivity, while women and children were abducted and forced into sexual slavery. No words or pictures capture the depth of horror experienced internally by the Yezidi, which always seemed to me to be indelibly imprinted, as if painted in eternal colours (Gitau 2020: 1).

The search for a means to work directly with such an imprint led me to join a creative research team at fEEL (felt Experience and Empathy Lab) at the University of New South Wales, where I work with artists and psychologists developing arts-based 'tools' or creative projects for application in trauma and mental health support. For me the overriding questions are: How can we design interventions that are sensitive to the complex and culturally varied ways refugees experience trauma (Bracken 2002)? How can we support refugee survivors of trauma to access and identify their feelings and emotions in ways that help them move forward in the direction they would like to go? How can we create spaces to capture and hold their experiences with respect – while also cultivating capacities for what is often called 'resilience'.

The construct of resilience is double-edged – equated with the ability to withstand the negative consequences of trauma, to recover quickly from any symptoms of pathology, remain enthusiastic, committed and engaged in life tasks and produce positive outcomes (Hobfoll & de Jong 2014: 70–1). Confining resilience to a particular set of characteristics and outcomes risks oversimplifying the complex realities of people's experiences of survival, producing a dichotomy that implicitly casts 'traumatization' as a failure of 'resilience' (Lenette, Brough & Cox 2012; Liebenberg & Ungar 2009; Ungar 2011). This has the pervasive effect of eroding the identity of the survivors, casting them as helpless victims of adversity (Bottrell 2009; Harrison 2012) much like Frantz Fanon's (1963) *damné* – 'the wretched of the earth', implicitly left to internalize a dehumanizing and negatively defined identity. In prioritizing the goal of resilience, we may therefore fail to address power imbalances while simultaneously curtailing the freedom to explore varied possibilities for survival or mental and emotional well-being. How, then, can we begin to address not only trauma and survival within a framework that enables 'trauma-informed' psychosocial support but also the self-defining, creative work that enables people to escape harmful designations?

In what follows I discuss working with a media arts tool in virtual reality (VR). This is not to propose that a singular 'tool' is adequate to the immense challenges that Halima's story (among many others) presents. Rather, I want to propose the necessity of exploring a creative approach that not only provides a practical support tool but, more importantly, an imaginative exploratory framework grounded in experience.

Using EmbodiMap

EmbodiMap is a VR experience, designed as a 'tool' for engaging with the embodied aspects of trauma and anxiety and developed through an iterative participatory design process with people with lived experience of trauma. It supports a phenomenological exploration of what is directly felt in the body (Bennett, Froggett & Muller 2019: 185–201; Kuchelmeister 2020: 134–53). The tool allows participants to generate a tangible 3D visualization of the effects of trauma, anxiety or nervous system activation in the body – and then to engage directly with this imagery, ideally developing a creative agency that enables changes to be effected. EmbodiMap is accessed by wearing a head-mounted display, which allows the participant to enter a virtual space with a backdrop of their choice, and to virtually interact with a life-sized avatar body. Through a guided process, users map feelings, emotions and sensations onto the avatar figure, using hand-tracking technology to draw using their hands with a variety of colours. Participants can walk around or step inside the avatars and the drawings they have created, also interacting with avatars by changing their posture and position (Figure 13.1).

Such functionality, designed to enhance the feeling of agency and control, is informed by somatic approaches to trauma therapy, for example the work of Ogden and Fisher (2015), which explores 'movement vocabulary' to understand how the body is experienced and how posture facilitates shifts

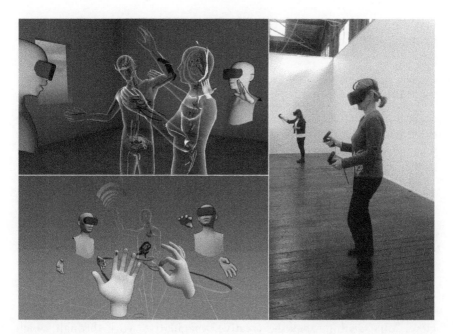

FIGURE 13.1 *EmbodiMap, felt Experience and Empathy Lab (fEEL), 2020. Courtesy fEEL, UNSW.*

in psychosomatic awareness. EmbodiMap may be experienced as a self-directed exercise or as a guided meditation with a voiceover directing the participant to slow down, pay attention and become aware of sensations in their body and draw them onto the avatars.

I invited Anjie – a therapeutic practitioner specializing in bodywork – and Sol (name changed) – a community engagement officer working with refugee communities– to EmbodiMap sessions to explore the possibilities of working with this tool in their areas of work. Anjie is originally from Bosnia–Herzegovina. She had previously worked as a volunteer at The Big Anxiety festival, and says that through this exposure she came to understand the value of art in terms of trauma recovery. Moreover, working at the festival provided Anjie's first experience of finding 'help' with processing trauma. She had found the arts uniquely accessible as a first line of support. Sol is originally from South Sudan, and formerly one of the 'Lost Boys of Sudan'. In his work helping build capacity in refugee communities, Sol engages with creative arts such as dance and music. He described the potential he has witnessed in such creative projects to help people from refugee backgrounds cope with the effects of war and the stressors of resettlement.

EmbodiMap may be used to directly advance the kind of work that may be undertaken in somatic trauma therapy. However, it is designed not as a clinical tool per se but as a creative media experience available to individuals outside clinical settings. My conversations with Anjie and Sol were focused on their perceptions of how this tool might be used.

Creating space

If art in general offers a means to explore and express internal, subjective experience, EmbodiMap directly transports participants into spaces where what is experienced internally can be represented externally, as Sol remarked of the experience:

> Art is one of the best tools you can use because what it does, it externalizes, you know. So you can engage with it in your own way.

As Anjie noted, the EmbodiMap experience:

> helps create a space where imagination is used more to create a *possibility* of wellbeing rather than causing the wellbeing.

Here, Anjie distinguishes the creative, imaginative work through which possibilities for new experience are self-generated, from simply engaging in a passive 'feel good' activity. This intuitive 'play' or imaginative work highlights the agency of the participant using the creative tool. The term 'tool' is used advisedly in this context to convey the 'use value' of EmbodiMap. However, as Anjie points out, such a creative engagement differs from the use of a more mechanical tool, directed towards a single purpose.

Art is grounded in embodied, sensory experience but arguably derives power from its ability to reconfigure experience, while speaking to it at the same time (Lederach 2005). This involves accessing feelings with an increasing sense of perspective, often speaking from the 'edge'. As Fadiman (1997: viii) says, 'the action most worth watching is not at the centre of things but where edges meet . . . and often, if you stand at the point of tangency, you can see both sides better than if you were in the middle of either one.'

The EmbodiMap experience facilitates such vantage points, whereby the extent of what can be seen is greater than 'in real life' scenarios, and the possibilities for action more varied and immediately accessible. Engaging interactively with an avatar as a transparent container for one's felt experience is a distinctively proximate experience, enabling one to travel inside the body and shift perspective with ease and rapidity so that the gap between feeling or action and observing one's body is easily negotiated. Further, as Anjie remarked, the experience helps:

> to create a larger capacity for the body to have an experience, because that's what you want. To expand the body's capacity to feel . . . a variety of

feelings. . . . Expanding our . . . place [so] that we can hold the unpleasant and pleasant.

The expansion of the capacity to hold a variety of feelings resonates with what psychotherapists might term a container or holding space (see Chapter 4). Inhabiting such space and spending time within an internal landscape suggests a further dimension to the process of repair – somewhat at odds with the functional notion of resilience. The expansion of capacity afforded by the EmbodiMap experience allows for freedom to explore, contain, envision and represent a range of fluctuating feelings and emotions.

Language and experience

By creating spaces for holding and representing emotions, feelings and sensations, EmbodiMap also allows for an expression and articulation of experience that may be felt and known at some level, even as it is not put into words. As such, it is a bridge between the inchoate language of trauma and its verbal expression, as Anjie points out in relation to people in the 'freeze' state of the 'fight, flight, freeze' nervous system response:

especially [for] people who can't move – to expand their vocabulary of . . . emotions to physical sensation. People who probably have real difficulty in connecting language, sensation, body . . . I think it's quite curious, it can allow stuff, curiosity to come up.

In other words, by means of an immersive visualization experience, this tool supports a process of attunement to internal cues and sensations, which in turn enables the recognition of emotion and feeling and an investigation of the ways in which trauma may manifest in somatic symptoms (Ogden & Minton 2000; Ogden & Fisher 2015).

Trauma is classically defined as an unassimilable experience, beyond language. As Pierre Janet observed over a century ago, it sits outside normal memory, unable to be formulated within conventional narrative (van der Kolk, Brown & van der Hart 1989). As such, the shift from repetition or 'acting out' of trauma to 'working through' or processing, generally implies assimilating traumatic experience into the framework of narrative language. But as I learned in Dadaab, the gap between shared language and embodied trauma is vast and challenging to navigate.

From Anjie and Sol's explorations with EmbodiMap and with art more broadly, it appears that the experiential visualization tool not only helps to identify experience but holds that experience (sensation, feeling, remembered phenomenon) in place so that it can ultimately be spoken. This in turn promotes wider communication.

Sol spoke of the way in which art encapsulates and communicates a depth beneath what is seen and known on the surface:

> I'm telling you what works . . . the point is nothing beats art. When you are looking at that [artwork], it is art, yes, but inside, it is more than art. Those are the things that actually help the community.

This idea that something is seen and subsequently carried forward in a way that helps the community is envisaged by Anjie in a different way:

> Could you make yourself feel specific things that are not there? You know, could this then allow you to explore how to feel something without you causing [it] yourself . . . and then you can cause it . . . you've got an option.

In the phrasing, 'make yourself feel specific things that are not there' and 'explore how to feel something', Anjie infers growth through creative imagination; in other words, using this tool to imagine a feeling into being. She further described how EmbodiMap could be used to help give language to emotions that one would otherwise not be able to trace, giving the example of anger. She speculated on the question of how a person might know, within their body, that they are angry or not angry. Could they identify where the anger is located? Anjie pointed out the need for this exploration because 'usually people are cut off from it', and EmbodiMap can help us to track these feelings:

> I think this is a really good tool to go track it. If it's not in you, if you were to know that that person is angry, just like you, where would you know, to show? So the body becomes a landscape of emotions.

Reclaiming connections

Anjie explained that

> the body work that I do is about reclaiming connection. So I think that's what art does. And that's why [EmbodiMap] is such an interesting tool. It is constantly trying to create synapses as it's constantly trying to create bridges to something that is removed from us.

The question of connection is of particular importance in the refugee context since the very fact of displacement has disconnected refugees from all that previously gave them a sense of belonging. The essence of trauma is precisely this total overwhelm and disconnect. Judith Herman underlines the sense of disconnection that survivors of traumatic events feel, once all that gave meaning to their lives seems to have been shattered:

> Traumatic events have primary effects not only on the psychological structures of the self but also on the systems of attachment and meaning

that link individual and community. . . . Traumatized people feel utterly abandoned, utterly alone, cast out of the human and divine systems of care and protection that sustain life. Thereafter, a sense of alienation, of disconnection, pervades every relationship, from the most intimate familial bonds to the most abstract affiliations of community and religion. (Herman 1997: 51–2)

Anjie stresses the importance of connection, saying:

It should be almost mandatory. You have to make a connection. You are making your connection with me. It can be quite a solitary experience. And that's the problem with mental health care. It becomes such a solitary experience. . . . That's part of life to make a connection with another human being . . . what makes us really resilient, even though it's such a politicized word, is our connection. Our ability to ask for help, like you've asked me, our ability to reward, to gift, to exchange stories.

EmbodiMap for Anjie enacts connection in the sense that there is another figure, ready to receive one's feelings, emotions and sensations, which is perceived as comforting. Anjie excitedly expressed, while in the virtual space:

It looks like me. It looks like a human, but it isn't human . . . which I actually like . . . a lot of people have this fear of machinery, but when you know what the difference is, you are constantly in control, you feel you are there, there are people there, there's a support, that it's not too busy. You feel open, but then I push myself as well. It's quite an emotional moment when you have the second figure, the first figure when it disappears, you have this moment of like, aah! Like 'is that me?' I've just shaped myself. There is a moment of, so that's really nice. Marks are left. And it's really nice when you come in. I love the idea of walking to the figure, walking out of the figure, so that you have that ability to be in the figure . . . you have this idea of stepping in and stepping out.

'Pulling' time

EmbodiMap allows the user to engage in a slow, unhurried, calm setting (with or without a guided mediation), paying attention to thoughts, emotions and sensations. As Sol remarked about his experience in the virtual space:

You wonder and think a lot of things . . . it makes you really transported there, you know. And then as you do that, you feel you are grounded, you know, especially when you do the breathing, you are now there.

At first Sol experienced a kind of resistance to this slowing down, being a rather unfamiliar practice for him. But as he allowed himself to calm down, guided by the voiceover in the app, he found the benefit:

> Sometimes . . . it's really hard to calm yourself down and be grounded. . . . This is the problem I always have, you know, it's too slow for me, for my pace. But that's what it is for . . . it's like, there is a resistance. I don't have time to calm down like that. It's too slow. But then once you allow yourself for that and you calm yourself down, you actually feel the benefit. But that resistance in the beginning is there.

How art allows for the slowing down of time, and in this case how EmbodiMap 'pulls' time – giving opportunity for a range of emotions and sensations to be felt, was poignantly captured by Anjie:

> art has always been a space where time slows down. So for us to process trauma, we need, in my opinion, to slow down. It's easy to say, and it's easy to write about, but art has the ability to somehow expand that time. A little bit like . . . the timeline can be pulled so that an hour is not an hour as we know it, but an hour can be expanded in our body and experienced fully. You know, it's not like from one to two or from two to three o'clock, it's actually between one breath to another to another.

Control

Support that helps restore a sense of safety and control is clearly significant for refugees who have left their homes and sought refuge in a different country as a result of a threat to safety.

Anjie identified several salient features in this regard. First, there is the opportunity for playfulness, as one is introduced to the virtual space and invited to make marks in an exploratory way, devoid of judgement or the expectation of a specific outcome. As Anjie points out, this free play allows one to feel safe in the space:

> The point is to relax and be in a safe place. So that's what it is . . . the body needs to feel safe, to be able to express that. If the body is not safe, you can't express your truth because it's vulnerable.

The second part of establishing safety is the ability to mark one's territory, a place where one feels in control:

> like mark the outside of the body, legs and then people would feel like, okay, I'm giving it the shape. Now I'm marking the territory, you know . . . go around it, mark the back, the head.

The next step is when one begins to feel in control. A sense of dejection, vulnerability and powerlessness is replaced by a feeling that one can make things happen. Anjie expressed this while in the virtual space:

> This is so pretty. You can make them close their mouth and not speak. Isn't it, you can just say, I don't want you to speak.

Importantly, this progression engenders a sense of being in a place where options emerge and are felt as possibilities for action. Thus Anjie suggests that EmbodiMap helps

> get to the place that I'm comfortable with another human being, who I cannot control how they will react to me, but to go: Now I can look somebody in the eyes. I can feel the anxiety I want to please them. I don't have to . . . it's okay. I have got an option to leave and I still have options to be with them . . . now I know how to behave in that this is a safe distance for me. Thank you.

Building resilience

The ability to know one's limits and take control is central to what might be termed 'resilience', as this is key to re-establishing the life goals and autonomy that are often destroyed by experiences of mass violence. As Anjie pointed out, this differs from certain 'Western' conceptualizations of resilience:

> You only build resilience when [your] capacity . . . to feel and ask for help is better. . . . Resilience in Western terms, from what I've understood . . . you just get up and brush yourself off and off you go again. Well, you know what? Sometimes there is no off again. What I want to achieve might not be similar to you. What you want to achieve. Maybe I don't want to have all of this. Maybe all I want to do is have a little garden and paint every Sunday. And that's me. I don't want to own a flat. I don't want to have a degree. I don't want to, you know, I just want a really simple life. So, resilience in a way, sometimes it's a bit pushed, harassed to achieve, but it's actually the skill of being able to understand when it's too much. I have now got resilience to say, this is too much for me. I can back off. I can take time out.

This expression serves to underline that what constitutes a 'good outcome' may not be standardized but is rather determined by the participants themselves – what is most important to them, and how they define their own outcomes (van Breda 2018). Resilience is less a list of qualities than a lived world of possibilities.

In summary

Indications are that the use of arts-based engagement for psychosocial support for refugee survivors of trauma may allow for interventions that are sensitive to the complex and culturally varied ways refugees experience trauma. These interventions need to create spaces to capture and hold the survivors' experiences with respect and to help promote capacities for resilience that are unique and meaningful to the survivors.

As a creative media tool, EmbodiMap allows participants to have an 'experience near' encounter with an avatar body that not only is figured as one's own, embodying one's feelings, emotions, pain and trauma but also yields remarkably easily when the participant effects subtle changes. This proximate experience is important as it allows both for a 'holding place' of one's trauma and a vantage point for any action and change one may want to make. The micro-interventions and small actions that the participant effects on this body figure can translate into micro-acts of regulation and agency in their own bodies, thus promoting a sense of control and self-determination. This is all the more important when we consider the internalized sense of wretchedness and dehumanized identity at the centre of the experience of trauma.

It is indeed hard to imagine what kind of intervention would be of help to Halima in the face of such devastating loss. I do not suggest that a VR tool like EmbodiMap would be sufficient for dealing with the immense challenges that Halima's experiences present, but in such desperate situations, we need to offer something imaginative and radical. Nothing conventional will do. We need to come up with something that allows for a 'bottom-up' engagement with a self/body over which one has agency. A continued exploration of interventions that are creative, generative and grounded in self-determination is called for to support the psychosocial well-being of survivors of refugee trauma.

Acknowledgements

Ethics Approval reference for this study is HC200508.

References

Bennett, J., L. Froggett, and L. Muller (2019), 'Psycho-social Aesthetics and the art of Lived Experience', *The Journal of Psychosocial Studies*, 12: 185–201.
Bottrell, D. (2009), 'Understanding Marginal Perspectives: Towards a Social Theory of Resilience', *Qualitative Social Work* 8, (3): 321–39.

Bracken, P. (2002). *Trauma: Culture, Meaning and Philosophy*, London: Whurr Publishers.

Fadiman, A. (1997), *The Spirit Catches you and you Fall Down: A Hmong Child, her American Doctors, and the Collision of two Cultures*, New York: Farrar, Straus and Giroux.

Fanon, F. (1963), *The Wretched of the Earth*, New York: Grove Press.

Gitau, L. (2020), 'The Plight of Yezidi Refugees and why my Heart Bleeds', *Pearls and Irritations*. Available online: https://johnmenadue.com/the-plight-of-yezidi-refugees-by-lydia-gitau/ (accessed 17 June 2021).

Harrison, E. (2012), 'Bouncing Back? Recession, Resilience and Everyday Lives', *Critical Social Policy*, 33 (1): 97–113.

Herman, J. (1997), *Trauma and Recovery*, New York: Basic Books.

Hobfoll, S. E. and J. T. V. M. De Jong (2014), 'Sociocultural and Ecological Views of Trauma', in L. A. Zoellner and N. C. Feeny (eds), *Facilitating Resilience and Recovery Following Trauma*, 69–90, New York: The Guilford Press.

Kuchelmeister, V. (2020), 'Experience Design for Virtual Reality. From Illusion to Agency', *International Journal on Stereo & Immersive Media*, 4 (1): 134–53.

Lederach, J. P. (2005), *The Moral Imagination: The Art and Soul of Building Peace*, New York: Oxford University Press.

Lenette, C., M. Brough, and L. Cox (2012), 'Everyday Resilience: Narratives of Single Refugee Women With Children', *Qualitative Social Work*, 12 (5): 637–53.

Liebenberg, L. and M. Ungar (2009), 'Introduction: The Challenges in Researching Resilience', in L. Liebenberg and M. Ungar (eds), *Researching Resilience*, 3–25, Toronto: University of Toronto Press.

Ogden, P. and J. Fisher (2015), *Sensorimotor Psychotherapy: Interventions for Trauma and Attachment*, New York: W.W. Norton & Co.

Ogden P. and K. Minton (2000), 'Sensorimotor Psychotherapy: One Method for Processing Traumatic Memory', *Traumatology*, 6 (3): 149–73.

Ungar, M. (2011), 'The Social Ecology of Resilience: Addressing Contextual and Cultural Ambiguity of a Nascent Construct', *American Journal of Orthopsychiatry*, 1: 1–17.

UNHCR (2020), 'Dadaab Refugee Complex', *United Nations High Commissioner for Refugees (UNHCR) Global Website*. Available online: https://www.unhcr.org/ke/dadaab-refugee-complex (accessed 17 June 2021).

van Breda, A. D. (2018), 'A Critical Review of Resilience Theory and its Relevance for Social Work', *Social Work*, 54 (1): 1–19.

van der Kolk, B. A., P. Brown, and O. van der Hart (1989), 'Pierre Janet on Post-traumatic Stress', *Journal of Traumatic Stress*, 2: 365–78.

Part VII

Thinking in action with creative resources after trauma

CHAPTER 14

Unnerved

Anita Glesta

I'm not wrong am I? To seek the pumping heart in the head, little rose on fire . . . excerpt from the poem, 'Tongue on Fire', developed by Abigail Wender in response to Anita Glesta's animation, Tongue on Fire (2019)

My father died suddenly four years ago. The loss was shocking in ways I had not anticipated. Though he had heart problems and was not in great health, his passing felt abrupt. The only way I could connect with how I felt from my loss was through the act of painting. Though I had been a multimedia artist for decades, I never stopped painting. Mostly, I work with ink on paper. However, for some reason, I turned to my very early training in oil painting.

Through a process of layering the canvas with thick impasto, I began to paint an oversized heart (Figure 14.1). I squirted the paints out of their tubes and onto the palette. Lining up the blobs of colour, I arranged them like the colour wheel – secondary, primary and complementary colours in hefty blobs on an oversized disposable paper palette. Blue, red and yellow daubs formed the primary trio, and between each of these, the secondaries: orange, purple and green.

The smell of the oils and turpentine offered familiar comfort. I surrendered myself to the over-loaded brush, laden with a generous amount of paint. Though it felt a little like rolling around in the mud, I knew how to handle the paint – physically, working it onto the canvas. I had stopped painting with oils many years before, but with decades of experience I had the confidence that it would lead me into a process of discovery. I allowed

FIGURE 14.1 Untitled, *oil on canvas, 48 inches × 72 inches. Anita Glesta, 2017.*

sections of colour to bleed into one another, juxtaposing muddy areas with bright, clear colour. From these messy applications of paint the image of a heart emerged – a volumetric, almost three-dimensional form.

It was as if – in this state of uncertainty, unmoored by grief – painting offered a means to navigate the unknown, to find my way back to something known, something that, in this creative process, could be rendered in concrete and visible terms. Donald Schon, the theorist of 'intuitive practice', refers to this use of skilful practice as 'knowing in action' (Schon 1983). He points out that we do not always think before acting: 'in much of the spontaneous behavior of skilful practice we reveal a kind of knowing which does not stem from a prior intellectual operation' (Schon 1983: 50). It was in this intuitive manner that I was able to capture an embodied experience of grief as it unfolded in advance of any conscious processing. Our knowing, says Schon, is 'ordinarily tacit, implicit in our patterns' (Schon 1983: 49). What I consciously 'knew' was that I was attracted by the sensual and oleaginous texture of oil paint because it seemed like a very direct way to connect with my grief. In my struggle to understand what happened to my father, painting was the only possible means to navigate unfathomable loss. And, not only the wrench of loss itself but my anger at the abruptness of my father's passing. The distressed heart, as it emerged in my painting, was indeed an 'angry heart'. I tentatively gave this name to the painting-in-progress (Figure 14.1). Perhaps I understood that something of our relationship might be kept alive for me in the action of painting an internal organ.

I cannot give a precise account of how, when and why I chose to depict the heart, beyond its literal association with my father's death. That is to say, I am not aware of having made a conscious choice of subject matter.

The heart in painting has a history – most obviously through Catholic iconography. But my process-driven inquiry has little to do with this, or with the ironic commentaries on sentimentality that characterize the iconic heart images of Andy Warhol and Jim Dine. I experienced a driving force to simply do it.

Schon (1983: 49–50) suggests that a practitioner in the act of doing might ask these questions of themselves: 'What features do I notice when I recognize this thing? What procedures am I enacting when I perform this skill? How am I framing the problem that I am trying to solve?' Through this self-questioning we may not only make sense of the thing in question but uncover an implicit 'understanding', which can surface in action. For me, the unconscious or intuitive process was also a profoundly embodied one.

It was around five months after my father's death when I found myself engaged in this act of painting the heart. The process began sometime in November. About three weeks into working on the painting, I began to feel little skips in my chest – as though a small pony were galloping across it. Such episodes lasted for just a few seconds. I ignored them. I registered a feeling, a sensation, but made no cognitive association, aware only of my need to connect with the physical act of painting. Grief, I suppose, is characterized by the desire to hold on to an object rather than 'find out' or 'know' categorically that it is gone. By 'ignoring' the skips in my chest, I wilfully (if unconsciously) reverted to a connection through the painting process that was intensively felt rather than thought.

My need to paint was less a method of illustrating something known or even something that happened – an event in episodic memory – than of capturing an unconscious process that was still overwhelming. It was in essence the feeling of grief and of the anger and distress accompanying loss. In *The Feeling of What Happens*, Antonio Damasio describes this experience as a biological process:

> We often realize quite suddenly in a given situation that we feel anxious or uncomfortable, pleased or relaxed and it is apparent that the particular state of feeling we know then has not begun on the moment of knowing but rather sometime before. Neither the feeling state nor the emotion that led to it has been 'unconsciousness' and yet they have been unfolding as biological processes. (Damasio 1999: 11)

The complex psychological and neuropsychological process that was 'known to me' experientially was an unconscious, unthought known (Bollas 2017). But it was also a somatic experience, linked, it seems now, to a biological process, itself analogous to my painting of the distressed heart. In *Being a character,* Bollas (1993: 12) writes that we 'constantly endow objects with psychic meaning . . . we walk amidst our own significance, and sometimes long after we have invested in a thing, we encounter it again, releasing its meaning'. Though I did not know this at the time, through the experience of painting the heart, I was engaged in an emotional relationship with an object whose 'meaning' was later 'released' to me as a physiological response.

Persuaded by a friend that my chest pain should be investigated, I finally saw a cardiologist around a month after the skips in my heart began. 'Just to be safe', he equipped me with a heart monitor halter to wear for a weekend, along with a cell phone to tap whenever I felt the heart skips. The cell phone would relay the real time data back to the hospital.

Wearing the monitor but otherwise feeling fine, I went to a cocktail party on the Saturday before Christmas. At the event, I found myself standing talking with two amiable art dealers, when a blackness surged through my head. It felt as if my brain was whipping itself into a swirling vortex. My phone was on the table about two feet from me, but I was frozen in place, unable to reach for it. I hoped that I wouldn't fall. I experienced an acute awareness of my surroundings, which prompted anxiety and a desire to fight against the feeling that at any moment I might be entirely enveloped by darkness. The feeling wore off after about three seconds. I politely excused myself and left the party.

The day after the party I went back to the studio to continue to work on my painting. I sat in front of the huge, brightly coloured, drooping heart that seemed to glare at me. After a few hours in quiet dialogue with the image, I received a call from the cardiologist instructing me to 'go to the hospital immediately'. Apparently the last night's black vortex experience registered 200 beats a minute, and the data indicated crisis.

Beth Israel Hospital in downtown Manhattan was already emblematic of my relationship to my father, who had been an attending physician there for over fifty years. I was met in the emergency room by a medical team with a gurney. Defibrillation paddles were slapped onto my chest, and an intravenous needle stuck in my arm. My immediate assumption was that I was the object of attention as the daughter of Dr Curtis – as I had been as a child, visiting him at work. But they had no idea who he was, or who I was.

I had experienced a ventricular tachycardia and was sent on to the Cardiac Care Unit (CCU) for a battery of tests: angiogram, electrocardiogram, stress tests, radiology, cardiac sonogram, x-rays and nephrology studies. None of the findings indicated any severe abnormalities or need for a stent. I prepared to leave after three days in the CCU with no conclusive evidence of serious heart issues besides early signs of hardening of the arteries. Before I left, the cardiac electrophysiologist arrived to explain that, though they had not found anything significant in all the tests, sometimes a rogue electric current from the heart fires up and causes a ventricular tachycardia. He added that he felt it was unlikely that this was the cause of my ventricular tachycardia. 'The circuits went a little haywire' was all he could tell me. He then remarked, 'And sometimes this can be triggered by shock, grief and/or anger.'

In reflecting on how and what I knew of this feeling in my chest, I wonder if there was a direct connection between what was happening in my body and my intense involvement in painting, and more specifically, my focus on working with an image of a heart in some distress. This emerging formulation of experience evokes both the 'distressed heart' and the process of working in a state of distress.

A cardiac event triggered by grief

After my three-day hospital stay in the CCU, I researched the various causes of ventricular tachycardia. Via the Harvard Medical School (2020), I learned that there is something called Takotsubo Syndrome, or 'Broken Heart Syndrome', first described in 1990 in Japan. In Takotsubo cardiomyopathy – so named because the heart takes the shape of a ceramic octopus-catching vessel known as the Takotsubo – the heart muscle becomes suddenly stunned or weakened. This is a temporary condition that mostly occurs following severe emotional or physical stress. Apparently more than 90 per cent of the recorded cases are women between the ages of fifty-eight and seventy-five (Harvard Medical School 2020). Little has been written of the psychological experience of this 'heartbreak' and its nexus with biology.

The subjective dimension of experience does not yield to objective scientific analysis in any obvious way. There is, however, growing interest in the emerging field of neurophenomenology – a field that systematically explores the interface between the data of neuroscience and internal or experiential knowledge of brain processes, highlighting an 'explanatory gap' (Thompson, Lutz & Cosmelli 2005). My inquiry may be understood in this light. However, the language of *my* experience is, in the first instance, painting. The painting process was not simply a means to understanding a prior medical event. Painting served as the means of surfacing embodied knowledge in real time, as the cardiac event unfolded, and *before the fact* of the medical occurrence.

While a neurophenomenologist might investigate a biological process in an experiential register, I wanted to look closer at the entanglement between the biological event of ventricular tachycardia that I experienced, and the 'shock, grief and/or anger' from which it may have stemmed. Initially, my inquiry through paint was surfacing *the feeling of what happened* – loss, the loss of my father. Then, as I began to experience tachycardia, my painting surfaced the feeling of what *is happening* – those skips in my heart. My practice has since broadened to explore dynamic relationships between events past and present, and their somatic effects.

On the one hand, my grief seemed to have precipitated a cardiac event. But I was also predisposed to stress and anxiety. I experienced a range of childhood traumas that included what might be classified as text-book neglect. I did not receive the consistent care deemed necessary for 'secure attachment' or emotion regulation. According to John Bowlby (1969), the originator of attachment theory, neglect (that is, the absence of a functional caring relationship in childhood) essentially compromises self-regulation, which must be learned through a process of co-regulation; the feeling of being soothed and nourished by a carer.

I sought and enjoyed the company of adults from an early age, and often understood the nuances of their conversation in a precocious way. However, the denial of the protection a child needs to navigate their world left me without the resources to assuage anxiety, no doubt contributing to my often-worried state. Perhaps this predisposed me to the cardiac condition of ventricular tachycardia?

It is well established in trauma theory that trauma manifests in the body (Van der Kolk 2015) and plays a cumulative role in how our internal systems develop and function. The implication of this is that the way the body responds to stress in adulthood may also be conditioned by early development. Everything, it seems, is connected. My broken heart, the way it skipped – all part of the continuity of my life, which extends, too, into paint.

What's more, I got to thinking: it's not just me, it's me in relation with others, all of us with our shared mammalian evolutionary history. I found the ideas of Stephen Porges (2001, 2003, 2009) helpful. He writes about the vagus nerve, which is the longest and most complex of the cranial nerves and has a key role in the parasympathetic control of the heart, lungs and digestive tract. The vagus nerve begins at the base of the skull, the brain stem, and from there its sensory and motor fibres transit between many areas of the body. It is just one part of the autonomic nervous system, which controls the visceral functions of the body and its fight-or-flight response. Porges writes about the multi-directional communication between the viscera, the brain and the environment. He writes, too, about how social engagement provides another source of input into this system. In other words, he argues that we co-regulate ourselves in relation to others. The functions of our bodies – our guts, our lungs, our hearts – are linked in complex ways to the sensory and social inputs we receive from the world around us and are linked, too, to our deep evolutionary drive towards safety and social connectedness.

In how many ways, I began to wonder, is the beating of my heart connected to everything else? Stress, feeling unsafe, loss, feeling grief. Paint, the feeling of it on my brush, letting it move itself across the canvas. Heartbroken.

Seeking relief

I left oil painting behind after my Takotsubo experience. Its visceral qualities had been necessary to capture my grief. Oil painting is a slow medium and requires time and patience. It helped me express the feeling of being in that state of grief – the difficulty of letting go of the lost object that I sought to animate, to keep alive.

I began to think more about the anxiety and tension that I was feeling at the time of my ventricular tachycardia. In thinking about this, I began to visualize a rock moving along the pathway of the vagus nerve. Its trajectory began at the brain stem, moving down a constricted throat corridor and into the heart and the intestines. I found this visualization helped me process my feelings. I decided to turn this visualization of a rock moving through my body into an animation – a return to my multimedia practice. Movement and dynamism took on both psychosomatic and formal registers. I was interested in exploring all that moves under the surface of our skin, of which we are largely not conscious. I was interested in exploring the way stress lodges within and moves around the body. To do this in my video, I returned to ink (Figure 14.2). I like this medium because of its fluidity. I employ it, I make it move, using old-fashioned stop motion animation. In the doing, my relationship with my own practice shifted from simply expressing to processing my feelings associated with trauma and loss.

In relational psychotherapy, the therapist does not simply help regulate a patient's emotions but is also engaged in a two-way relationship: a series of shared moments that aim to engender self-awareness (Wachtel 2010). The ultimate outcome should foster a sense of relief. Allan Schore (2012), noted for his work in neuropsychology and trauma theory, speaks of the therapeutic encounter as 'emotional co-regulation that occurs moment to moment'. Since we experience vicissitudes of emotions from moment to moment and we are impacted constantly by one another's emotions, my interest is in the potential for something akin to co-regulation to occur in an encounter with my video animation.

In my own personal experience, making art is a kind of co-regulation. Returning to oil painting was a retreat – a place to go, to make an object as

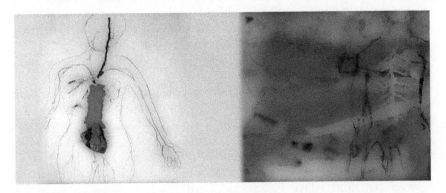

FIGURE 14.2 *Still from the animation,* UNNERVED. *Anita Glesta, 2021.*

the recipient of my emotions. Noreen Giffney (2021) suggests that cultural objects can perform a function akin to self-regulation. Like the nurturing relationship between a mother and her nursing baby, a painting or a moving image might just enable a kind of secure attachment that is forged through the processing of emotion – albeit without the support that may occur in partnership with a therapist.

While painting allowed me to arrive at a place of awareness of feeling that is inherently embodied, the method of animation helped me to visualize the weight of my broken heart – stress and anxiety, trauma, like a rock, travelling along my vagal nerve. Pat Ogden, the founder of sensorimotor psychotherapy, asks her patients to lean into the pain by asking them to find the place where it is felt and to stay with it. For Ogden, 'tuning into these cues can help regulate arousal, enhance self-understanding, alter negative internal states, and establish new meanings' (Ogden & Fisher 2015: 2). In my practice, I draw on my intuitive knowledge and a capacity for visualization that stems from my arts training. I give form to feeling – and to a process of seeking relief.

Through my animations I want to offer my audience the kind of relief that I have found in the process of making them. When we talk of viewers and audiences in an arts context we tend to homogenize, even though it is widely understood that such notional viewers may resonate with content in different ways. But what if the viewer can use my work in a way that might be analogous to my own process? Can the viewer experience the work in a way in which they are attuned to it as a process that affords relief; that engages with and acts upon a state of anxiety or distress? Perhaps it is more accurate to ask whether the work can act *with* rather than upon – co-regulate rather than regulate? In other words, can we imagine a form of interaction in an emotional and even neurobiological register?

Teresa Brennan's theory of entrainment suggests that we have a propensity to be affected in this way by images. In Brennan's (2004) book, *Transmission of Affect*, she proposes that the physiologic underpinnings of our emotional states are derived from multiple sources, including our environment. Referring to the multiplicity of ways in which we experience 'being', she states: 'sights and sounds are physical matters in themselves, carriers of social matters, social in origin but physical in their effects. Every word, every sound, has its valence; so, at a more subtle level, may every image' (2004: 71).

Entrainment and co-regulation require a reciprocal relationship with another person. But, not exclusively. My animations offer an expression of my own process of co-regulation. Through moving ink, I create the impression of a journey from a state of anxiety, and of heartbreak, to one of relief. I wonder if this imagery could be of 'use' to others. In other words, is my process one of subjective description, or can the dynamic interaction between self and image be enacted third hand, between an image or animation and a viewer? I also wonder, can I support not only a momentary relief, stabilization or calming, but a longer-term reflective process? This raises the question of how far such 'use' can go.

Certainly, animation can offer a graphic and dynamic visualization of an embodied process. It is thus a stimulus to imagination; a vehicle to 'hold' an image of felt experience. Perhaps when the rock exits the body, a viewer feels a relief that is akin to a catharsis. Allowing themselves to surrender to the audio/visual imagery in the animation they might experience a transferal – recognizing the trauma in their own bodies and learning how to shift it.

As survivors of trauma, we must live with states of grief. How wonderful if we might be able to actively 'use' visual art, not just to identify a feeling, but to engage in a process with it. Since my cardiac event, I have a heightened awareness of my process when I create audio-visual works. Not unlike a meditation, I experience a surrender. The rock in my brain, in my body, shifts. I am grateful to lose myself in a process which encourages this transition into a 'parasympathetic' state, a more peaceful state.

While painting enabled deeply embedded feelings to surface, literally in my heart, the moving image animation gives form to dynamic sensations and feelings of anxiety and relief that form a constant conversation within the network of the nervous system for all of us.

References

Bollas, C. (1993), *Cracking up, Psychoanalysis and Self-experience*, New York and London: Routledge Press.

Bollas, C. (2017), *In the Shadow of the Object, Psychoanalysis of the Unthought Known*, Oxon: Taylor & Francis.

Bowlby, J. (1969), *Attachment and Loss: Volume I*, New York: Basic Books.

Brennan, T. (2004), *The Transmission of Affect*, Ithaca: Cornell University Press.

Damasio, A. (1999), *The Feeling of What Happens: Body and Emotion in the Making of Consciousness*, New York: Harcourt: Harvest Books.

Giffney, N. (2021), *The Culture-Breast in Psychoanalysis*, London: Routledge.

Harvard Medical School (2020), 'Takosuobo Cardiomyopathy or Broken Heart Syndrome', *Harvard Health Publishing*, 29 January 2020. Available online: https://www.health.harvard.edu/heart-health/takotsubo-cardiomyopathy-broken -heart-syndrome (accessed 06 September 2021).

Ogden, P. & Fisher, J. (2015), 'Exploring Body Sensation', in *Sensorimotor Psychotherapy: Interventions for Trauma and Attachment*, 197–217, New York and London: Norton.

Porges, S. (2001), 'The Polyvagal Theory: Phylogenetic Substrates of a Psychosocial System', *International Journal of Psychophysiology*, 42: 123–46.

Porges, S. (2003), 'The Polyvagal Theory: Phylogenetic Contributions to Social Behavior', *Physiology and Behaviour*, 79: 503–13.

Porges, S. (2009), 'The Polyvagal Theory: New Insights Into Adaptive Reactions of the Autonomic Nervous System', *Cleveland Clinical Journal of Medicine*, 76 (Supplement 2): S86–90.

Schon, D. (1983), *The Reflective Practitioner: How Professionals Think in Action*, New York: Perseus Books.

Schore, A. (2012), *The Science of the Art of Psychotherapy*, New York: Norton Professional Books.

Thompson, E., A. Lutz, and D. Cosmelli (2005), 'Neurophenomenology: An Introduction for Neurophilosophers', in A. Brook and K. Akins (eds), *Cognition and the Brain: The Philosophy and Neuroscience Movement*, 40–97, Cambridge: Cambridge University Press.

Van der Kolk, B. (2015), *The Body Keeps the Score: Brain, Mind, and Body in the Healing of Trauma*, New York: Viking Press.

Wachtel, P. (2010), *Relational Therapy and the Practice of Psychotherapy*, New York: Guilford Press.

CHAPTER 15

Wau-mananyi

The song on the wind

Pantjiti Imitjala Lewis, Rene Wanun Kulitja, Angela Lynch (Uti Kulintjaku), translated by Beth Sometimes

For a long time our spirits have been crying for our children, across our communities. Many are stuck, confused, they cannot recognise their position in their families. They are isolated and in personal difficulties. We are deeply miserable inside our spirits about what to do about this.

(ILAWANTI KEN)

This is also a story of how strong women are, how they help the men who are falling down, some of them all their lives. They crack, they get sick, they have trauma. In our families it's always the woman, helping.

(MARGARET SMITH)

Uti Kulintjaku – which means to think and understand clearly – is a collective of senior *Anangu* (the Pitjantjatjara word for 'people') women from remote Aboriginal communities of Central Australia, who work in collaboration with Western trained mental health practitioners to develop a shared, cross-cultural understanding of mental health and well-being. *Uti Kulintjaku* have produced a range of award-winning resources to share this understanding with their families and communities.

In the mid-winter of 2019, the group gathered at Kulpitjata, a homeland south of Uluru, not far from where the borders of the Northern Territory, South Australia and Western Australia meet. Over a week, they enacted and recorded the traditional story of *Tupul-Tupul*, a man who becomes trapped in a hollow log. In collaboration with the University of New South Wales' felt Experience and Empathy Lab (fEEL), this ancient story became a virtual reality (VR) experience, where the viewer takes the perspective of the trapped man, looking out through the cracks in the log at the women trying to set him free. These women are his wives, played in the VR production by Pantjiti Imitjala Lewis and Rene Wanun Kulitja. The piece is titled *Wau-mananyi*, which comes from the song within it. *Wau-Mananyi* is not a word; it's a sound, the sound of the wind, when sung (Figure 15.1).

Rene Wanun Kulitja: Yes, so in the past, our grandmothers and grandfathers lived in the bush. They lived really good lives, collaboratively in their family groups; together. One group would be in one place, with extended family living in other neighbouring areas. Other people would be living in their extended family groups and they would all travel extensively. And when people would arrive in places where other family members were camping, there would be great celebration to be together. This is the good and proper way it was back then. People were happy.

In the evenings and early mornings some would give speeches to the group, and people would listen attentively. '*Alpiri*' is our term for the type of speech where senior people impart significant information, ideas and reiterate laws and ways to live in order to plan and care for the group – so

FIGURE 15.1 *Uti Kulintjaku, 2019. Photo Volker Kuchelmeister; courtesy fEEL Lab.*

that they would travel cohesively. That is an important part of how it was in the old days. And this law is not extinguished – we continue to reflect on these practices, and that which has been foretold for us.

Pantjiti Imitjala Lewis: For many years we *minyma* (senior women) have gathered to talk about the mental health and well-being of our children. In our *Uti Kulintjaku* group, we began to develop and practice ways of using story and our law to aid people we're concerned about – those with mental health struggles, confusion, people in crisis. People who are wondering what they should be doing, people who are paralysed by addiction, whose worlds are closed to them, people who are living in a half-life. We thought to retrieve an old story about a man who became trapped in a hollow log, and we set about making something that might be of assistance to people who are unwell and struggling with mental health issues.

We hoped that seeing a production of this story could be an opportunity for healing and a way of regenerating healthy thought patterns. We learned this story ourselves from three senior women. As they shared this ancient story with us, we also began to understand new things, seeing the connections. It was a learning experience for us too, creating something similar to a film, and having the opportunity to act in it also. We saw that – like the man in the story – there are many people in our communities who are suffering: people who are isolated, people who are in such altered mental states that they talk to themselves as they walk down the road or to the shop, even though there might be nobody else around.

Yes, so in the story we produced, the man who enters the hollow log speaks in the traditional way of our people in the past. The two women who were his wives throw themselves on the ground crying, devastated that their husband has become trapped while hunting for meat. The hollow tree he entered had grabbed onto him, and he fell down into a trap. The tree closed in around him and he became totally ensnared. Then, he had to try and travel while remaining fully enclosed in this log, the poor thing! He said, 'My dear women, hunt meat for yourselves! I've gotten into serious trouble here and I cannot escape! I can't get out and so you two will have to seek out your own meat to eat!'

The poor thing! So it is told that in the afternoon the two women hunted and ate their own meat. They travelled along with their husband towards a place where there are powerful *ngangkari* (healers). Their hope was that the *ngangkari* could break the tree open, but they had to make camp along the way, the wives crying and the man unable to sleep, standing up vertically inside the tree. Poor thing! But those two women were caring for him along the way, it is told. Dear things!

Well us two, Wanun (Kulitja) and I played the two women as they travelled along, escorting the poor man to help. And those two women hunted along the way, worrying dreadfully for their trapped husband. As we played the parts of these women, it was as if the picture became clearer to us too, like we were experiencing it ourselves: the two women and the man who had become trapped in the tree and couldn't escape. Playing these parts made available the idea that our minds can similarly become trapped, and it can become incredibly difficult to escape certain ways of thinking, and to heal.

We, the women of *Uti Kulintjaku*, often reflect on practices and ideas from the past. We create things via a deep consideration of knowledge that has its roots in our history, and record this knowledge, law and story. For this re-enactment, we did our hair in an old style called *muli-muli* – how they used to bind long hair in the old days. It's similar to how these days we might tie our hair up towards the back of our heads, but in those days people tied their hair to the front.

Mr Miller came along to help us, and he played the part of the man. He recorded the man's voice, and sang the song of the one who became trapped inside the hollow log. And he was speaking from the position of travelling along inside the log, and we were camping along the way.

To make this film, we all travelled to a place called Kulpitjata – not far from Uluru, in between two of our communities. Wanun chose her homeland. She wanted us all to get together in her homeland and make the movie there, and so that is where the story was filmed. A bushfire had burned through there and it was really lovely, the ground was clean. So, after the bushfire we made camp there, in a little creek bed. All our tents were set up there, wonderful little shelters. It was a good site, and we saw lots of stars, and heard foxes calling out at night.

And we heard some really wonderful stories and law. Another person who has the same name as me was telling stories – Pantjiti McKenzie. She was talking in our style of *alpiri* – the early morning address to the camp, sharing a lot of important ideas and we were listening. She told the story of the man in the log, singing the associated song as she spoke the story. We listened and learned, and I was thinking, 'Hey! When we were little children, we would hear stories lying in bed, told by our grandfathers, or grandmothers. We would listen and fall asleep.' So, we remember the knowledge that was shared with young children, the old stories. Sometimes I tell stories to my granddaughter. She really loves stories, but the ones that are in books; you know, there's one about three goats, and one about the three pigs. What are some other ones? She always asks for those ones. 'Granny! Tell me a story! The three pigs! Tell the story with the fox in it.' So, I tell the story with the fox. And she listens until she falls asleep.

The part of the *ngangkari*, the healer, was played by Roy Yaltjanki, the other Pantjiti's husband. He acted as the *ngangkari*, and retrieved his internal life force from his stomach; you know, the special power he has as a healer, similar to *mapanpa*, his healing force. *Kuuti* is a Pitjantjatjara concept for this. He used his *mapanpa* – his power – to strike the hollow tree and break it open. And as it is told, the trapped man then fell to the ground, emaciated. So, then the healer retrieved the man's *kurunpa*, his spirit, as perhaps it had become lost. The healer sent out his *mapanpa* to search for the man's spirit, and the *mapanpa* found it, brought it back and dropped it on the ground beside the man. Then the *ngangkari* picked the *kurunpa* up and returned it to the man's body, and he was healed. He started to feel better. He healed when his spirit was back in his body.

The film we made at Kulpitjata was taken to Sydney and turned into a VR experience, to be watched through VR goggles. We took this back home and showed it to lots of young people. They were laughing and finding it really clever. And we explained, my older sister and I,

> We are using this story to explain something that is real for us today, you know, for young men and women, people who live here in this community. About things which also constrain people's minds, like ganja [marijuana]. People get confused and hazy, they become stubborn and resistant and they get addicted. They lose interest in listening to their families, their mothers and fathers. And so maybe this story will open your minds and help you to understand how things are. Perhaps it will lift your motivation and be a healing force. Maybe it will inspire you to also get involved with positive activities, maybe it could help.

We did it for them. And they said, 'Hey, this is really great!' They were really impressed, listening to these positive ideas (Figure 15.2).

FIGURE 15.2 Wau-mananyi: The song on the wind, *Stills from VR and installation, 2019. Photo Volker Kuchelmeister; courtesy fEEL Lab.*

Rene Wanun Kulitja: Do you want to know why we made it as a VR? So someone could sit down in a chair and put on the VR goggles and experience what it might be like to be locked inside a tree. From in there someone could see and experience that sensation. It is like you are really inside that tree and you can really get inside the feeling of that. Does it feel alright? Say, I might come along, sit here and put the goggles on, and experience something really incredible. The VR is accessing the spirit to teach me something. And then I might think, 'True!' And by being really touched by it, I can start to understand and believe what it is showing me. And, I will understand that this is a significant concept to consider.

It's an experiential learning process, that someone might see with their own eyes and be deeply touched by. And then this will give rise to someone's capacity to comprehend, and contribute to solutions to the issues it describes. It's a very comprehensive experience. When I look at that VR picture, the scene is really entering my whole body. It's inside my head. As I am looking at this picture, it's lodging in my mind and my spirit; in my body. It's a full-body experience.

CHAPTER 16

EmbodiMap II

An auto-ethnography

Sophie Burgess

We become good at abandoning our bodies. This idea crystallizes as I'm reading the work of poet and writer Molly McCully Brown (2020), who lives with cerebral palsy and writes of the experience of living with chronic pain. I write this line, paraphrasing McCully Brown, as I begin what is to be an experimental auto-ethnography focusing on the use of EmbodiMap, an arts-based virtual reality (VR) experience. EmbodiMap immerses a patient in the manifestations of trauma and anxiety in their body through interactions with a virtual avatar. This chapter reports my experience with EmbodiMap in two registers – my experience as a patient, a survivor of traumas with chronic pain (who has been in therapy long term), and my interpretations as a clinical psychologist who works psychodynamically.

In 2021 I found myself, like many of us, confined to an apartment for many months – a space in which I work and live alone. The injunctions of Covid lockdown ('stay at home', 'keep distant', 'mask up') felt like the constraints and punishments associated with earlier traumas, echoing the commandments embedded within those past experiences – 'don't move', 'you can't leave', 'stay small', 'shut up'.

Lockdown was a painful – at times dread-inducing – space to inhabit, triggering memories of trauma, while limiting access to the external resources that may have helped. Getting through isolation called for a radical acceptance of passive rather than active responses to these challenges. This seemed the only way to both contain a struggling 'self'; conserving my internal reservoir of psychological structures at a time when the world's external structures had largely dissolved, shut down until further notice.

I turned to EmbodiMap to help process the psychological difficulties, activations and annihilations of 'living' in lockdown. I hoped this virtual immersive experience might yield some imaginal opening-up, building agency through creative engagement. With EmbodiMap, users can generate an avatar that assumes their own posture, pose and form – like an instant 3D snapshot of their body. Within the virtual environment, users may then 'play' with their translucent avatar bodies, their fingers becoming instruments that can draw and paint into the spaces inside and around the avatar body. A guided introductory session encourages use of the drawing function to represent feelings and emotions at the places these are experienced – and thus to visualize and record the ways in which trauma is carried in the body. Users can effectively reach through the 'fourth wall' into the virtual space, hold, touch and carry their avatar. They can step into their avatar body, examine what is drawn or represented there and then step out of it again, contemplating actions and posture both from within and outside.

Over the course of four months, I underwent a number of EmbodiMap sessions, recording what happened and the feelings that arose in the process. The following reflections are drawn from diary records from five of these sessions, edited for clarity. The conceit of separating the voice of patient and therapist – two facets of myself – I deploy as a means to capture unfolding experience, and thereby to empirically test the VR tool rather than simply to theorize about it. Readers interested in the nature of the experience may also access it online via video.[1]

Session one

The patient

By accident, I select a dark room from the menu of available environments (which apparently includes a sunlit studio with ocean views). I find myself in total blackness, untethered, weightless. I am at first aware of the weight of the headset (this strikes me as symbolic – I carry so much in my head).

My hands emerge into the virtual space. I imagine I'm meant to do something with these hands, but they remain limp. I wiggle them. That is the extent of movement I can muster. Looking out into the darkness of the virtual space, I see three coloured blocks. I'll have to adapt, I think: make do, as always. Following some prompts, I create an avatar: a translucent, life-sized, mannequin-like figure that I recognize as myself. Discovering colours on my fingertips, I find that I can create lines in the air.

My immediate instinct is to draw a thick, red, curved outline around the avatar.

I move my hands around the body of this avatar and suddenly feel a surge of compassion towards it. Beyond that red line, I don't have the capacity for moving or drawing.

In response to the dark abyss, I've drawn a boundary around myself. And then I remain still.

The therapist

Reviewing this session, I am struck by the vulnerability of the patient (this aspect of myself). She is lost and immobile in a dark and unfathomable space. She finds her hands but not her feet. With no mobility she cannot navigate the darkness. She remains without footing, adrift. Harlem (2010) describes exile as a dissociative state when a self is 'lost in transit'. A person in exile isn't simply one who can't (physically) return; she is someone who cannot 're/member' other versions of herself, or is unable to make connections to versions of the self, forged in more secure relationships in different times and spaces. In this sense, the patient enters the virtual environment with no 'remembered' capacity for movement. She finds herself in an abyss, small and overwhelmed and unable to 'do'. Fairbairn (1944) speaks of this as an experience of 'not-ness'.

Drawing a line is *something*, though: an instinct to protect oneself, enacting some kind of 'holding' within the experience of 'not-ness'. Patients with histories of deprivation can display, in different ways, a need for their external environment to compensate for the nihilism of their internal world. This can happen in concrete terms through lots of material things, or in non-concrete terms through lots of validation and reassurance – a counterpoint to the patient's feeling of living in nothingness and powerlessness. I wonder if the thick red line might be an attempt to 'secure' something – what Balint ([1968] 1993) called ocnophilia, where we cling to external objects/people with great intensity in order to fashion a sense of security and/or avoid danger. Beyond this holding on – the patient has not been able to 'potentiate'. She has, in a way, 'failed to launch'.

Session two

The patient

This time I'm able to select a brighter room. This environment (that is, the virtual representation of natural light flowing into the space) opens up in me a feeling of welcome and safety. I click to generate an avatar that mirrors my own posture, and I notice that she stoops. The avatar's head is lowered in what looks like subjugation. I am moved to intervene. It seems I have the

FIGURE 16.1 *EmbodiMap, fEEL Lab (screenshot from VR session). Photo: Sophie Burgess/Volker Kuchelmeister; courtesy fEEL Lab, 2021.*

ability to move and carry this weightless avatar. My instinct is to hold her hands, to gently move her upright.

I try to adjust her head, but I can't. I know, technically, that I should be able to shift the avatar body, but she remains downcast. I try to stand her up, so that her head might look straight ahead, but instead I turn her entire body on its side. The avatar has fallen. I try again; I'm able to stand her up, but her head still looks down (Figure 16.1, left). I feel sorrow at the sight of my own postural form reflected back at me, but also a visceral acceptance of the avatar's plight. By accident, I draw a yellow line near the avatar's throat, and feel a release. I exhale. Yellow feels like light or hope.

Having tried to tilt the head of the avatar, I want to be with her in this posture. I accept her as she is. I push my hands through into the virtual space. I wriggle my fingers. I reach forward and hold her hands.

The therapist

'Before the advent of language', wrote Dosomantes-Beaudry (1997: 521), 'the body becomes the theatre in which distress is played out'. I think of these words as I observe myself as patient in this second session. I'm aware of my own somatic response to the experience of the patient – a warmth in my stomach. I notice (and share) the compassion and acceptance the patient feels towards the avatar's 'downcast' posture. It's as if the patient's history of hurts is projected onto the avatar in this stooped position of helplessness. The avatar seems to manifest the heaviness of trauma in the body.

Yet I also see the love of a parent towards a child communicated through touch and connection in the holding of the avatar's hands. In this, the patient is manifesting the analyst's ability to offer a 'container' or space for the patient's affect and experiences to be metabolized (Bion [1963] 1977, 1967), doing so with an appropriate restraint or minimalism (Balint [1968] 1993). Trauma can leave survivors ill-equipped to tend to their own inner (vulnerable or 'downcast') child, let alone work towards reparation. This second session reveals the ability of the patient to act as a care-taker and care-giver (an ability that has been developed and internalized through ongoing therapy). Reaching with her hands and making this connection, she is no longer in exile.

Session three

The patient

Today, I'm on the cusp of a migraine. EmbodiMap provides direct and in-the-moment feedback about my constricting posture. The avatar I generate (a 3D snapshot of me) has bent legs, although I wasn't aware going in that my knees were buckling. Such feedback also corresponds to the extreme lower back pain I have today; without my knowing, my body has reflexively adjusted to squat, a way to manage that pain in my back, my shoulders and neck. I feel heavy and squashed.

I draw huge areas of blackness inside and outside my avatar's head, and a long strip of blackness across her back. Taking several steps, I pick up and shift the avatar across the space. She is drifting and floating. I pull her back towards my own body and draw orange arrows from her feet to signify how they have moved. I'd like to do more, but the pain I'm feeling is blinding. The orange arrows I draw articulate how my avatar was able to do what today I cannot.

The therapist

The patient wants to take steps to overcome her pain but knows simultaneously that she is unable to achieve this. I see both acceptance and purpose – an awareness that recent triggers must have been suppressed or repressed to manifest as various pains, but there is no compulsion to un-assimilate the pain. We cannot live without hope, but we cannot adapt if our hope is unrealistic. There is a life-affirming tension between two the moves enacted by the patient in this session – the black markings attest to pain and futility of effort; the orange arrows point outward to something else, a way of visualizing or imagining the action that the patient yearned to take.

Session four

The patient

I am back in the EmbodiMap virtual space and my first instinct is to move around. The technology asks me to 'define the boundary' of the play space, which I determine. I then use my hands to move the avatar around this defined play space, infused with a sense of discovery. A red line appears, as if to stay, 'Stop!' when I reach the end of the play area. I feel an urge to push the boundary away, to expand the territory. But I have to tolerate this bounded 'space'; these are the 'real limits'.

I draw purple lines to mark the boundary in the air, so that I can gauge when I'm approaching an edge as I move around, rather than hit red lights or meet a wall. Purple came to me in the moment for its association with power. I swing my arms from side to side, air drawing – and paint blue lines across the arms of my avatar. I also draw in blue on the inside of my avatar's head. I want to express a feeling of being present. I extend the blue drawing into her chest and stomach, filling her with a calm presence. I keep up this exploratory activity, walking around, adding some red squiggles inside my avatar, each representing sensation – because it feels like, in this moment, anything is possible. It's wondrous.

The therapist

What strikes me the most about this session – and the feeling state of the patient – is her playfulness, her exploration of security and bounds and an increasing potentiation and agency (by which I mean capacity to enact intentions effectively). She is open to possibilities. No longer frozen as she was in session one, or subdued as a result of pain as in session three, the patient 'thaws', coming into a new aliveness. The feeling of freedom within bounds is 'wondrous'; the patient has found her legs.

Now she makes choices and sets bounds (soft and hard), going where she will within them. She has resolved a tension between the potential of the self and the limits imposed by the ego/drive (Freud 1905, 1923). For instance, she feels the urge to push the boundary away, but recognizes that such boundaries are real and thus tolerable.

From the perspective of the patient, the avatar is like Winnicott's (2005) 'container' for the developing self. EmbodiMap provides a form of visual encouragement in the absence of a sense of entitlement or deservingness: a permission to go further.

Drawing purple lines, she navigates the potentially triggering boundary, avoiding the system's instruction to stop. The purple line is ecotone; a safe space, signposted by a careful 'note to self'. By means of this line, the patient exercises some soft power over her own destiny; she acts wisely to protect her own well-being, resulting in a new sense of freedom, which she experiences as wondrous. She sets up a sort of amber light in the way a parent might switch on a bedside lamp or hold a torch for a child at night, allowing her to avoid the trauma she anticipates she'll feel.

In this fourth session, the patient negotiates the implicit dialogue between the personal shadow (the part that instinctively wants more freedom from boundaries) and the internalized therapist – both of which are present in the new forms of play – to discover a new freedom, and to pave a realistic way forward. In this session, there is integration (Freud 1905) and, arising out of that, what Jung (1964) called 'individuation'.

Session five

The patient

This time I generate two avatars: it's as if one bears witness to the other, who is able to move, generate and 'be alive'. I identify the first avatar as 'me' and have her draw purple lines with an upward movement, as if in a dance. I draw symbols around her. Then I outline the second avatar in blue for safety (Figure 16.1, right). I pause the first avatar's movements and walk inside her. I'm smiling; I'm seeing from within!

I continue to play with the first avatar, lifting up her arms, tilting her hands in an elegant dance. She is pretty graceful. I am moved at the sight of the avatar's arms, reaching upward, towards something she hasn't known before. She is no longer limp, no longer 'folding' with nothing to reach out for. Standing within her, I feel I could leap! Inside the avatar, I feel a kind of happy anticipation or waiting.

I paint purple across her chest – in the past, a site for the short breaths of anticipatory terror. Now, purple marks my chest as a resource, a reservoir of breath. Inside the second avatar, I draw three round, red-filled circles (Figure 16.1, right). Looking at these, they might be haemoglobin. I seem to have infused the avatar with life blood – in her head/brain, her heart space and gut. I connect both avatars by a red line, since they are both alive to me.

I move away to get some perspective on the dancing figure of the first avatar with her arms reaching up, and the second avatar bearing witness. Each to me represents exactly how I am at present: one absorbed in the dance, the other bearing intense and tender witness, immersed in the environment. I feel proud of this. I feel alive, I feel whole. It all feels magnificent!

The therapist

There is joy here. In this session, I see the patient integrating creative instinct and intuition – she is 'alive' in the libidinal sense (indicating a life drive and vitality), compared with the earlier sessions where there was apparent ego death (no drive to act). She is anchored by intuition; whereas before she was uncertain, now she trusts – both herself and the virtual environment.

I've watched the experiential understanding of the patient build from the inside over these sessions – she has effectively internalized the therapist and stands ready to hold, guide and potentiate feelings. The two avatars articulate two aspects of self: one who dances – with whom the patient identifies, and the figure who bears witness – connected via a red line to the vitality of the dancing self, looking on in delight.

The body, I would note, is an agent of change. The patient's avatar has progressed from immobility and subjugation ('downcast') to one who dances and delights in witnessing the dance. The self is now present within the body. The avatar body functions as a container or vessel, which, in giving form to the patient's abilities, prompts new ways of seeing, free-associating and linking increasing interpretations. Moreover, the patient feels alive and whole. She holds steady on the ego-self-axis (Edinger 1960) ('I feel proud', 'happy waiting'). She has moved from illusion to spontaneity and realization (Turner 2002). Whereas at the beginning, anguish dis-abled her and pain weighed her down, she has arrived at a place of freedom, choice and aliveness. You could read the dancing avatar in this session as Winnicott's (1953, 2005) 'true' (spontaneous, creative) self, the witness (mirroring the dancer) as the 'good-enough mother' looking out for her and delighting in the vitality of her child (omnipotence comes to the 'child' self in the safety of the caring gaze: 'I could leap! It feels magnificent!').

There is rich expression in the fifth session, dense with action, symbol, texture and figures relative to earlier sessions. Although old psychic material may still be present, the virtual experience has effectively transported the patient into a potential space where this expression can manifest. It is important to note the shift here, and the degree to which this freedom was not possible in session one.

The patient has survived (perhaps triumphed over) a series of castrations through this process, yielding pride (rather than shame) and 'bigness' (all that the patient feels capable of feeling and doing). Through the process of interacting with the avatar over these five sessions, the patient has become able to potentiate, overcoming her 'failure to launch' at the outset. The patient also seems to have equipped herself through the sequence of sessions with mental–emotional skills she did not earlier possess (Klauber 1987), which feel 'magnificent'. We see her follow these feelings to embark on healthy risk-taking and exploring, to carve a path to authentic being (Freud 1923; Bateson 1972). The patient has begun to safely surrender to the process (that is, to let go of anxieties) and at the same time has been able to take her life actions into her own hands.

In this EmbodiMap session, I also see how the witness avatar might function as a surrogate therapist: this second, 'other' avatar is not a passive viewer – her empathic participation as a mirror/mentor facilitates the choreography of movement. Both avatar figures are mobile and can be adjusted, which enables a micro exchange of holding and containment, moment to moment (Bach-y-Rita 2009). From this final session, I understand how EmbodiMap might allow patients to experience exchange, communication, co-construction and rhythmic synchronicity, all of which play a vital role in trauma therapy (Herman 1992; van der Kolk 2014).

Freud (1905) asked whether there is such a thing as a natural end, to which object relations theorists, speaking of the revival of instincts, say, 'Yes': if the patient has worked through transferences, frustrations and conflicts to arrive at the experience of parting (Grotstein & Rinsley 1994). At this closing juncture, there is an implication of possibilities being born or re-born, emerging as an inhabited self in the open (Klauber 1987). When the dancing avatar holds her dance pose, the witnessing avatar holds this figure in her delighted gaze, and the patient contemplates this, feeling alive and proud, articulating this natural end.

Conclusion

Meissner says, 'all psychological stories . . . narratives, fantasies, defences, symptoms . . . no matter how we conceptualise them, bear the primeval trace of the body's signature' (Meissner 1997: 435). My experience as a patient, reported and analysed in this chapter, shows how the EmbodiMap VR tool allows a unique experience of relating to one's embodied 'self'. Through this relation, patients can represent the debilitating experience of pain, the safety of attachment, the joy of exploration and of building agency, facilitating a profound shift in their relationship to their trauma. Object relations theory (Grotsein & Rinsley 1994) would see the VR avatar as an object in relationship with a patient. In this case study, we've seen how the avatar is a container for projection – or perhaps a vessel for engendering a deeper understanding of the many dimensions of self. We've also seen how the avatar – as a witness, mirroring and watching over the dancing 'self' – also functions as a surrogate therapist. But the avatar does something a therapist cannot – entering 'into' the body of the patient, as it were, or becoming the body of the patient's 'self'. The avatar allows a patient to engage with their 'self' in an embodied (rather than purely verbal) way. As with Freud's (1923) body ego – the avatar's body (with which the patient both identifies and engages) becomes an object and an agent, without ever being separate from the patient.

EmbodiMap allows a self-directed or self-choreographed venture by the patient into experience that may be unexplored, hard to verbalize, envisage, grasp or relate to. It can therefore radically enhance the therapeutic process, allowing patients to experience aspects of self and enact change by means of their own creativity and physical movement. With this tool, a patient's 'self' or history (in this case, of childhood trauma) takes on a virtual shape in the world, and the patient gets to inhabit that shape (or at least observe and interact with its form). A user of the EmbodiMap tool comes to articulate in various embodied ways (via drawing, colouring, holding and/or entering into the form of the avatar) her own feeling states in response to the avatar's embodied enactment of her own experiences of self, in pain and in freedom from pain.

EmbodiMap thus goes to a place where traditional analysis cannot. The body (not just verbalization about the body) becomes the language through which the reparation of trauma is essayed. This tool cannot replace a therapist but can complement traditional 'talking therapies', and may be of particular value in the trauma field. Many patients arrive to therapy without a language for their experience, and trauma patients are likely to be confronted by a degree of alexithymia – a problem with identifying, feeling and expressing emotions (the term meaning 'no words for emotion'). Under these circumstances, a non-verbal language for articulating experience is of tremendous value – it may, in fact, make a critical difference.

The EmbodiMap tool may help locate various somatic markers of trauma in the assessment phase of treatment. In this process, language is bypassed and instead somatic markers find a new way of 'speaking'. EmbodiMap may also simply help users identify sensing and feeling states via mark-making and 3D exploration of their avatar body, which in turn may help develop emotion identification, expression and regulation.

The patient's identification with the avatar is of course idiosyncratic and unpredictable. From my own experience, however, I can imagine that EmbodiMap may indeed perform a profound reparative function by enabling patients to move from states of dissociation to states of sensing, spontaneity, connection and play – with both self and others.

Though further study is needed within the VR domain, play with other bodies is well established within the trauma literature as central to recovery, especially in relational/attachment-trauma (e.g. Grotstein & Rinsley 1994; Herman 1992; van der Kolk 2014). EmbodiMap's avatar can serve as a proxy human, an 'object' with which a relationship may be formed, tested and refined with increasing degrees of relational freedom.

The more we know of trauma and other attachment or relational difficulties, the clearer it is they are lodged in the body. Healing must therefore engage the body. In this chapter I have (as the therapist/I) observed my own experience (as the patient/I) with EmbodiMap. The process of engagement with an avatar in the virtual play space led me from a state of dissociation to an experience of inhabiting and being myself – what Winnicott (1953, 2005) would call my 'true' (spontaneous, creative) self. It also facilitated an experience of what it feels like to witness one's vulnerability through the hold of a 'good-enough mother' – and what it feels like to be so witnessed. As a therapeutic experience, the five sessions I undertook were profound. My own experience suggests the possibility that VR tools – particularly those, like EmbodiMap, that use avatar bodies – offer great hope to trauma survivors.

Note

1 Available online: https://vimeo.com/465643239 (accessed 28 September 2021).

References

Bach-y-Rita, P. (2009), 'Sensory Plasticity', *Acta Neurologica Scandinavica*, 43 (4): 417–426.

Balint, E. ([1968] 1993), *Before I was I: Psychoanalysis and the Imagination*, London: Free Association Books.

Bateson, G. (1972), 'A Theory of Play and Fantasy', in K. Salen and E. Zimmerman (eds), *A Rules of Play Anthology*, 314–328, London: Routledge.

Bion, W.R. ([1963] 1977), *Elements of Psycho-analysis*, London: Heinemann. Reprinted in W.R. Bion (1977), *Seven Servants: Four Works*, New York: Aronson.

Bion, W.R. (1967), *Second Thoughts*, London: Heinemann.

Dosamantes–Beaudry, I. (1997), 'Somatic Experience in Psychoanalysis', *Psychoanalytic Psychology*, 14 (4): 517–530.

Edinger, E. (1960), 'The ego-self Paradox', *Journal of Analytic Psychology* (5): 3–18.

Fairbairn, W.R.D. (1944), 'Endopsychic Structure Considered in Terms of Object Relationships', The International Journal of Psychoanalysis, 25: 70–93.

Freud, S. (1905), 'On Psychotherapy', *The Standard Edition of the Complete Psychological Works of Sigmund Freud*, 7: 257–268.

Freud, S. (1923), 'The ego and the id', *The Standard Edition of the Complete Psychological Works of Sigmund Freud*, 19: 12–66.

Grotstein, J.S. and D.B. Rinsley (1994), *Fairbairn and the Origins of Object Relations*, London: Guilford Press.

Harlem, A. (2010), 'Exile as a Dissociative State: When a Self is "lost in transit"', *Psychoanalytic Psychology*, 27 (4): 460–464.

Herman, J. (1992), *Trauma and Recovery*, New York: Basic Books.

Jung, C.G. (1964), *Man and his Symbols*, New York: Bantam Doubleday Dell Publishing.

Klauber, J., ed. (1987), *Illusion and Spontaneity in Psychoanalysis*, London: Free Association Books.

McCully Brown, M. (2020), *Places I've Taken My Body*, New York: Persea Books.

Meissner, W. (1997), 'The Self and the Body: 1. The Body Self and the Body Image', *Psychoanalysis and Contemporary Thought*, 20: 419–448.

Turner, J.F. (2002), 'A Brief History of Illusion: Milner, Winnicott and Rycroft', *International Journal of Psychoanalysis*, 83: 1063–82.

Van der Kolk, B. (2014), *The Body Keeps the Score: Brain, Mind and Body in the Healing of Trauma*, New York: Penguin Books.

Winnicott, D.W. (1953), 'Transitional Objects and Transitional Phenomena: A Study of the First Not-Me Possession', *The International Journal of Psychoanalysis*, 34: 89–97.

Winnicott, D.W. (2005), *Playing and Reality*, London: Routledge.

Part VIII

Soundwork/earwork

CHAPTER 17

Held Down, Expanding

An exchange on trauma through acousmatic sound art practice

Thembi Soddell

Preamble (from me to you to me)

This chapter reflects on my 2018 sound installation, *Held Down, Expanding*, in which I used abstract, acousmatic sound to represent and understand the wordless, non-narratable, felt sense of my lived experience of trauma and so-called mental illness. This work grew from my combined experience of twenty-one years of living with this 'thing' that might be called mental illness and nineteen years of composing with acousmatic sound.

'Acousmatic sound' is a term used to describe sound experienced in separation from its cause – where the sound can be heard, but its source and cause cannot be seen. The term's use in musical and, by extension, sound art contexts (also known as acousmatic music) emerged from the theory and practice of French composer Pierre Schaeffer, the pioneer of *musique concrète* (a genre of music composed through the assemblage and manipulation of recorded and found sounds, played back through loudspeakers, which he developed in 1948). Schaeffer sought to build an objectivity into the language of experiencing acousmatic sound as music, removing personal interpretation or connection to real-world experiences. He saw the role of the composer as 'scientist' who must remove the experience of the self – or anything beyond the 'objectively' intersubjective perception of sound (based on Edmund Husserl's approach to phenomenology) – to experience acousmatic sound as music.

In contrast, *Held Down, Expanding* presents a different approach to understanding intersubjectivity in acousmatic sound, one where the experience of the self listening in isolation becomes central to an empathic exchange between artist and audience members. Through this work, the isolated, then later shared, experiences of acousmatic sound evoke unique memories, senses and imaginings in each individual, while also revealing a shared consciousness of the intersections between individual perceptions. This work was created through an exploration of my own experience of an unknown trauma manifesting as felt senses and somatic 'symptoms' of so-called mental illness, with no clear connection to a cause or story behind them. Creating the work was a process of coming to better understand these felt senses and their relationship to my lived experiences, while also building an experience for audience members akin to being cradled inside one's subconscious, non-verbal mind.

Mind (wordless; projecting outward)

I find it hard to write now because there are no words for what I feel:
'trauma is . . . a wordless story.' (Menakem 2017: 8)
This is why I make art with abstract sound.
Abstract sound is the language I use to describe
   what lives in my body but not as a corporeal form: 'Our bodies have a form of knowledge that is different from our cognitive brains. This knowledge is typically experienced as a felt sense of constriction or expansion, pain or ease, energy or numbness' (Menakem 2017: 5).[1]

In *Held Down, Expanding*, one audience member's body at a time is suspended in a pitch-black box, the energy of acousmatic sound expanding and contracting around them. The sound moves through moments of loud and soft, ease and dis-ease, intensity and silence; the audience member's experience moving through their own memories, affects, perceptions and imaginings. These grow from the abstract sound (and the frameworks around it), which is ambiguous,

   wordless,
         empty – full yet expanding.

         Just like (my) depression

and trauma

(what trauma?)

and this thing we could perhaps call mental illness.

Right now, as I write, I am almost falling asleep again. Often I will be walking and close my eyes for just a fraction too long and feel like my body might collapse, like my mind is collapsing in on itself, like I am half slipping into that other expansive world. I like it there, more than here, even when it is terrifying. At least it is something like sleep, which means not being here. Now. (Where are you?).

Depression means having no words to

tell you what I feel or what my body knows.

But it knows.

I turn to acousmatic sound to reflect on [this 'thing' for which I have no words] because I cannot describe it, but also because my attempts to find words bring a heightened, expanding distress. To find words I must sit in the feeling for a long time, becoming stuck in an endless cycle of trying to figure it out,

understand,

make sense,

find a linear narrative,

find a solution,

know the truth,

know the story,

untangle the confusion,

remove the ambiguity,

find certainty,

tell it 'right',

find an accurate narrative –

One that I can tell and know it *is* the truth.

(what truth?)

In this word (and narrative)-finding process, I no longer know what is real and what is not. Everything becomes a threat. Each narrative is incomplete and my anxiety rises when I say it out loud in its incompleteness. In saying it with words, the multiple ways in which a single experience can be perceived is lost. No justice is given to the depth and complexity of those things I know and feel but cannot say; the 'things' I have experienced but do not know when, how or why. In words, my feelings cease to exist: invalidated.

I feel trapped by words

but not by abstract sound.

I experience abstract sound as a truth within itself. As I listen, all the uncertainty, frantic energy in motion (emotion) and fear become beautiful. It is an easy form of meditation. It is a way for my mind to understand and integrate my felt sense of what I know in my body but cannot see. When composing, I can sit in the sound and feel the complexities,
the confusion,
the ambiguities,
the multiple truths,
and in shaping the sounds a felt sense of understanding begins to take form. My sense memories begin to make more sense. It is a safe space for them to reveal themselves, or hide in comfort if they need – as they wish. There is a narrative without a narrative (a non-narrative); my experiences 'being arranged into a shape that makes more sense, that [can] be understood and integrated'.[2] It is easy. Natural. I have control.

Control (from me to you to me again)

I will take you now (through words) into the experience of *Held Down, Expanding*, where that which has inhabited my body and mind is projected outwards through abstract sound. The process of creating this work involved a contemplation on the impact of insidious abuse, manipulation and control in intimate relationships, and its problematic 'treatment' through (and by) the mental health system. This work is made of a custom-designed, multi-speaker sound system that creates a spatialized sound field, which feels both real and unreal. It uses fourteen speakers and two subwoofers to fill the air with a full frequency spectrum of sound, experienced by one person at a time in isolation. That experience goes something like this:
    You arrive at your appointed time, open the front door of the exhibition space and walk inside. A person – I will call them the operator – wearing all black approaches you and tells you to take a seat. They hand you a small package wrapped in foil. They tell you to unwrap it, read it and to re-wrap it once you are finished. They walk away but watch you from a distance.

You unwrap the package and inside you find a small black book. You open the front page. Black. The next: black. There are many black, blank pages in this book, but also some pages with words in grey. The first one says: 'The dual temporality of trauma as a "double blow" that strikes consciousness in its infancy: while the first blow consists of a cause without affect, the second blow is an affect without cause' (Pedersen 2016).

(The sound to come might be the second blow.)

The words and blank spaces are like a puzzle. There are fragments but no full thoughts – a meaning hidden in the gaps. Themes of trauma, suicide, emotional abuse and fear emerge. On the last page a quote: 'finally, only sounds remained' (Jamison 2011: 79).

You re-wrap the book and the operator approaches you. Holding a black clipboard, they read a script explaining safety precautions, handing you a torch in case you panic and want to leave. They ask you to consent before you continue. If you say 'yes', you follow the operator as they lead you to a large black structure in the middle of a room: 2.2 metres high, 2.4 metres wide and 3.6 metres deep – the structure all black. The operator opens the door. They usher you in, sit you in a reclining chair but tell you not to recline. They lock the door with a latch, both of you inside, the room so dark you can barely see a thing around you – just a faint red glow from a small obscured light. The operator walks behind you. They raise your chair with a foot pedal, recline it by pulling its back down towards them – the chair screeching as it moves. You feel the hand of their control over you; you feel your consenting submission. They then slide you and the chair backwards into place, so your head is aligned between two speakers that are very close to your ears. You can hear the faint breath of the operator behind you. The light goes out and you are suspended in a pitch-black void:

> Void is really a state within. . . . There is nothing so black as the black within. No blackness is as black as that . . . I find myself coming back to the idea of narrative without storytelling, to that which allows one to bring in psychology, fear, death and love in as direct a way as possible. This void is not something which is of no utterance. It is a potential space, not a non-space. (Anish Kapoor quoted in Celant 1998: xxix–xxx)

After not too long a soft faint sound begins right next to your ears. It feels like it is almost inside your head. Here is where my words will fail. I cannot describe what you will hear, what you will perceive–feel–remember–reject–narrate–imagine–understand, nor the experiences I am attempting to convey. Words fail because 'trauma is . . . a wordless story' (Menakem 2017: 8), as are our emotions and our felt perceptions. This is why I am 'speaking' to you through abstract sound:

In complete darkness, you hear the soft faint sound inside (outside) of your head: a rhythm, a low-frequency beating (machine-like, but somehow also organic) at a slightly different rate in each ear.

Something feels not quite right,

the subconscious beating as a heart does
(but not in a beat that makes organic sense).

The sound begins increasing in volume, width and intensity; it is widening out, shifting above, over and in front of you, then filling everything around you. It expands past the bounds of the physical space, feeling both smaller and larger than it is. It is calming, yet disorienting,

the mind expanding outwards,

the subconscious swelling as a fear does.

Time disorienting;

Space ex p a n d i   n   g   ,

filling,
filling,
filling,
filling,
filling.

(The abstracted sound reflects the place I go when I cannot stay 'here' [then], when I am slipping between two worlds, slipping between two moments in time but placed in neither. It is also the place I am escaping to. It is comforting yet not. It is terrifying yet not. It is beautiful yet not. It is where I am disconnected yet profoundly here.)

The sound layers and rises. The frequencies shift upwards as the sound expands outwards. The sound *also* lowers while *also* getting higher, masking what is behind it. Frequencies shift and then the sounds behind them unmask. Fragments jump around and inside of you. (What is it? A voice? Who is speaking? Who is failing to speak?). After some time, or perhaps what feels like no time at all, the sound begins to shrink downward and inward. It is flattening, constricting, drawing back inside your head from where it came.

Then, silence.

A tension:

'Silence like a cry without words; mute, although crying endlessly'.
(Maurice Blanchot quoted in Kofman 1998: 10–11)

The operator turns on the light. They push the back of your chair upright again, lower you, unlatch the door and let you out. They guide you towards an audience journal where you can write about your experience of listening in whatever way you like, and read what others have written before you, such as (quoted from the audience journal):

> Things I felt:
> Weightless – in the screeching chair.
> Heavy – my body a deadweight like the air around me.
> Objectified – by the clinical feeling of being in a screeching chair (akin to the feeling of waiting for a medical procedure).
> Suffocated – as the noise amplified around me, I gasped for air.
> Silenced – with all space around me consumed by sound, I couldn't have made a peep.
> YET . . .
> Empowered – like I wanted to push through and prove my strength.
> Able – Although I felt 'confined' to the chair, I felt like swimming up from the depths of the darkness to the light at the top, so I could breathe again.

You might then turn to another page and find this quote:

> My body felt heavy, there was fear. The priming with the ideas of trauma had opened something in my thoughts and going into the darkness, somehow trapped, felt like terrifying in some way, in the back of my thoughts somewhere. Then the sound was all around me, gently building. The idea of surfaces disappeared and I existed somewhere in a mist of vibrations. They were comforting, surrounding, my weight existed within it. Something in the back of my thoughts was changing and shifting, healing a little, being arranged into a shape that made more sense, that could be understood and integrated.

You turn to another page, then another and another – then to a blank one. You might then write your own contribution, or you might not. Once done, you leave. Later I read the journal and find the words you have left for me. Inside these words I find our exchange, even though we have never met. In the space of my non-narration of my experience you have begun to narrate your own. I have told you something without words and you have given me your words – many of which could almost be my own. Through this exchange I have come to know myself better and my experiences better. I have come to know you better. I have come to know the sound better. I silently thank you.

Trauma and the acousmatic gap (some(no)where in between)

In his book *Sound Unseen: Acousmatic Sound in Theory and Practice* (2014), Brian Kane highlights the structural gap inherent to acousmatic listening in its spacing between source, cause and effect. In an acousmatic listening situation (and by extension acousmatic sound-based art), he explains, it is impossible to have a direct experience of a sound's source and cause (for instance, by seeing who or what is creating it) while experiencing the sound. He emphasizes that because of this, the very concept of acousmatic sound is ontologically tied to a structural gap. Without it, sound ceases to be acousmatic; or, in other words, 'the *being* of acousmatic sound *is* to be a gap' (Kane 2014: 149). Kane argues that to experience sound as acousmatic, the audience must be experiencing the gap between the sound and its source and cause.

Where an ontological gap between source, cause and effect can be seen as inherent to acousmatic listening, trauma, too, could be understood in this way. The post-traumatic symptom of a flashback reflects 'a history that literally *has no place,* neither in the past, in which it was not fully experienced, nor in the present, in which its precise images and enactments are not fully understood' (Caruth 1995: 153). There is a gap between the traumatic event and when its emotional–affective–physical–psychological–spiritual impact is experienced in the consciousness of the person who lives with trauma (the shock of the event making it impossible to feel in full at the time), where what is defined as trauma lies not in the traumatic event itself, nor in its emotional impact, but in the gap between event and effect. It is in no place in its entirety yet somehow in all places all at once; or some(no)where in between. As with Kane's ontology of acousmatic sound, the *being* of trauma *is* to be a gap.

Inside this gap, the traumatic event/sound's source and cause can only be related to and understood through one's own memories, emotion, perception, frameworks of knowledge, imagination or pure affect. For Kane, this creates a specific kind of unease in the acousmatic situation that accounts for its 'gripping tension and mystery' (2014: 148). For me, in the gap of trauma, there is also a gripping tension, mystery and unease. Though, where in acousmatic sound-based art this is a joyous experience, in trauma it brings an annihilating distress.

The creation of *Held Down, Expanding* grew from this distress – the distress of ambiguity, the distress of not knowing what happened, not knowing what is real or imagined, what is true and what is not. It also grew from the joy of listening to abstracted acousmatic sound – the kind created by enhancing the ambiguity inherent to acousmatic listening, choosing to compose with sounds that embody a wide perceptual gap between effect, source and cause. The opening sound in *Held Down, Expanding*, for example, is a voice – a sample of extended vocals performed by Alice Hui-Sheng Chang. But through sampling and performance techniques, once heard, it no longer sounds like a voice; nobody perceives it as a voice. It sounds machine-like,[3]

maybe
(depending on how you perceive),
both real and unreal;
both existing in the real world and extending beyond it

– a gap.

In this gap, the mind wanders. It searches for a cause (always imagined) or it escapes from a cause (just listening). It is within this gap that my contemplations on trauma can take place. In the safe, joyous space of acousmatic sound contemplating the ongoing imprint of trauma becomes manageable. While composing, I am inhabiting, exploring and navigating the gaps in my memory and their connections to my frameworks of knowledge. In the gap between source, cause and effect, I can use the sounds as metaphor for concepts, thoughts, memories, imaginings or sensations (and so on) evoked by the feelings I find in the sounds. I order the sounds, arrange them, all without the need for words; all without a need for certainty. A single sound can embody many thoughts or ideas, including those that are contradictory. The wordless abstraction of acousmatic sound can embody the many narratives that underpin my experience of trauma, as well as no clear narrative and the gaps between them all.

In doing so, *Held Down, Expanding* holds an essence of my experiences without being explicit as to what they are. This leaves a gap for audience members to also wander through their own mind. I shape where that wandering goes by framing the listening experience with textual and relational elements (the book, the encounter with the operator, the implicit references to clinical settings, the suspension in pitch-black, the journal of multiple perspectives), but there is still space for audience members to perceive their own reflection. This provokes a shared, intersubjective consciousness that, in contradiction, is also a private, unique experience for each person – their experience of the work a self-reflection entangled with, yet separate to, my own.

A story in the gap (an interlude with Vanessa Godden)

Vanessa Godden is an Indo-Trinidadian and Euro-Canadian media and performance artist whose work explores their lived experiences of sexual assault, cultural heritage and the body's relationship to geographic space through material engagements with the body. As a collaborator and peer, they experienced *Held Down, Expanding* during its development. I remember the look on their face after first doing so. I cannot describe it, but it prompted my concern: 'Are you okay?' 'I think I need a cup of tea and to sit in the sun for a while.' That was all they said; or we may have laughed, as we often do to release any unspoken tension. I made the tea and we sat out the back of my house in the sun. They told me about their experience inside the work – inside their mind while listening – how it felt like they were stepping inside my subconscious mind. This took them into their own subconscious, evoking memories of their own trauma, but not in a bad way. We did not talk about what trauma it had led them to – it remained unspoken – but through the sound we felt a shared sense of understanding. This understanding existed in the sound's embodied wordless story, in our shared knowledge of the 'felt sense of constriction or expansion, pain or ease, energy or numbness' inherent to the body's storage of traumatic knowledge (Menakem 2017: 5), in this case projected outwards through the expansion and contraction of abstract sound. Later, Vanessa emailed me about the memories and sensations that filled the acousmatic gap while they listened. In part, they describe not the sounds in the work, but their sound-based memories that surfaced as they listened: 'All I can hear is the buzzing of fluorescent lights and the clicking of the gurney wheels. All I can see is black.'

Black

After creating *Held Down, Expanding*, my nights became haunted. Darkness had always been a safe space of comfort for me: I need pitch-black to sleep; I love sensory deprivation. But I began to notice that at night my fear, for an unknown reason, would begin to rise. At home, when walking into different rooms I would feel a slippage into another time. My dreams became something I had not experienced before. I would move through strange, complex, hyperreal situations with figures-objects-places from the past. I would be lucid dreaming, then at some point start to feel frightening physical sensations without a clear cause. Everything would turn to pitch-black and I would say to myself, 'I don't want to remember'. Then I would wake up –

everything stopping but the fear

At the time, my depression was a thick, heavy sludge. It would not budge, no matter how hard I tried. I was also in therapy (I always am, have been for years) and began sharing memories I had not shared before; experiences from the past I had not given much heed. I twice undertook an inpatient, trauma-focused therapy programme to help process these memories. In the safety of therapy, I wandered through the unseen but felt horror, looking for the point at which it could end. I could not find it – always stuck in that room in my mind, not quite able to get out.

Although, somehow, I did.

Now the still unseen horror in my dreams has stopped. Blackness feels (mostly) safe again. Creating *Held Down, Expanding* ushered me into this space of collapsing-expanding distant time, then led me to a place I could find present-day presence again.

At the core of this ushering is complete blackness, a blackness where I could hear better; listen better – to not just the ambiguous, acousmatic sound, but my ambiguous thoughts–experiences–sensations and those 'things' hidden in my mind I could feel but not see. The audience journal – the shared stories of my peers and unknown audience members – helped to transform my understanding of my experiences to a new, more organized form – although one which I still cannot explain to you in words.

Words always fail.

Of course, this is just one way to tell my story. Many others versions exist, all true (in so much as truth exists), even in their contradictions. My creation of *Held Down, Expanding* was premised on this idea, on the question of, 'How might I reflect the multiple ways in which I perceive a single experience of trauma, and the multiple ways in which people each perceive the same experience differently? Can a shared connection between us be found in isolation?' In this process of non-narration through acousmatic sound, knowing what is real and what is not was no longer a threat. The narrative feels complete in its incompleteness, in that it gives space for my emotions. My feelings are validated. There is also space for audience members to be as they are, to feel their own (non)narrative, to wander through their own imaginings–thoughts–sensations–memories, which may or may not be connected to my own. In coming to know myself better I also hope that audience members can come to know themselves better, or each other better or find ways to connect in their disconnection. Remembering,

I am no singular narrative.

And neither are you.

Notes

1 Resmaa Menakem's work (e.g. 2017) uses somatic understandings of trauma in anti-racist activism to assist in healing racialized trauma caused by, and through, white-body supremacy. As *Held Down, Expanding* was not created, on my part, as a specific exploration of racialized trauma, this key aspect of Menakem's work is not discussed in this chapter. For more information on how a body-centred approach to trauma can aid in the abolition of systemic racism, please refer to his work on Somatic Abolitionism. Available online: https://www.resmaa.com/movement (accessed 30 September 2021). It is also important to note that I write this chapter through the lens of my own experiences of trauma in a white-body.

2 This is a quote from an entry in the *Held Down, Expanding* audience experience journal. They are not my own words; rather a quote from someone unknown, yet they articulate my working process as well as I could.

3 This sound is also the opening sound of the track 'Object (im)Permanence' on my album *Love Songs* (Soddell 2018). It can be streamed online through *Room40*, or is available in hardcopy alongside a book of concrete poetry – the same book that is presented at the beginning of *Held Down, Expanding*. The album and installation are companion pieces.

References

Caruth, C., (ed.) (1995), *Trauma: Explorations in Memory*, Baltimore: The Johns Hopkins University Press.

Celant, G. (1998), *Anish Kapoor*, Milan: Charta Books.

Jamison, K.R. (2011), *An Unquiet Mind: A Memoir of Moods and Madness*, Oxford: Picador.

Kane, B. (2014), *Sound Unseen: Acousmatic Sound in Theory and Practice*, Oxford: Oxford University Press.

Kofman, S. (1998), *Smothered Words*, Illinois: Northwestern University Press.

Menakem, R. (2017), *My Grandmother's Hands: Racialized Trauma and the Pathway to Mending Our Hearts and Bodies*, Las Vegas: Central Recovery Press.

Pedersen, C. (2016), 'Encountering Trauma "One Moment Too Late": Caruth, Lyotard, and the Freudian *Nachträglichkeit*', paper presented at the 6th Global Conference *on* Trauma, Budapest, Hungary, March 11–13.

Soddell, T. (2018), *Love Songs*, Brisbane: Room40, compact disc. Available online: https://room40.bandcamp.com/album/love-songs (accessed 07 July 2021).

CHAPTER 18

Hold me in a circle of tender listening

Entangled encounters with women survivors from the Mental Health Testimony Project archive

Amanda McDowell

I was conscious of listening from an early age – standing behind my bedroom door, holding my breath. I listened for signs – a slight change in tone of her voice and I knew that everything was going again . . . that my mother was going . . . again. Perhaps this listening is what has led me, years later, to a place where all I can do is listen. Play and re-play women's voices, over and over, listening for something – a breath, a tone, a quality that I can't quite put my finger on, that I don't fully understand but that speaks to me – forces me to listen – to hold my breath and hear.

Twelve years ago, I made a short film with my mum – a performative document of our encounters and conversations over several months while she was living in an acute psychiatric ward (one of countless admissions that had begun years before, since I was five). I wanted to create a film in which we both held the camera and made editing decisions together, an attempt to address the power dynamics inherent in the filmmaker/subject relationship. However, in the end, it felt like a representational encounter in which my mother's confessional speaking presented her as 'Other', someone who could be viewed at a distance. In the aftermath of making that film I experienced feelings of intense sadness, anger, shame and guilt that reappeared periodically for many months.

In 2016 I began working with the Mental Health Testimony Project (MHTP) archive – a British Library oral history collection of fifty whole-life video testimonies recorded in 1999/2000 to document the lives of women and men across the UK who experienced the psychiatric institution in the late twentieth century. My ambition was to create a work that explored women's experiences of psychiatry, that could open a space for long-silenced women to speak, and that could operate beyond the level of representation, engaging with what voices do. From this archive, I selected the testimonies of five women – Kathleen, Carole, Anne, Pauline and Anne Marie – whose voices would become the basis of a multichannel sound piece titled hold me in a circle of tender listening. I had hoped that making this work would resolve the difficult feelings that persisted after the film project with my mother. Working with these voices, however, left me feeling blocked; weeks and months during which I felt inescapably stuck. In the writing that follows, I acknowledge these feelings as part of the necessary conditions for making a work that stages ghosts – my process being 'a form of embodied hauntology' that works with the affective traces of 'submerged narratives' (Blackman 2015: 26), opening up different modes of perception and implicating the researcher intimately within the process.

The embodied methodology that emerged through this process was a practice of listening-*with* (rather than listening to) the voices from the MHTP archive. Listening-with became a way for me to explore haunting and the affective transmission of trauma through the archive – a transmission that became apparent through my embodied responses to the testimonies of women who, like my mum, experienced some of the worst abuses of the twentieth-century psychiatric institution. In listening-*with* I foreground my approach as porous, emergent and relational – where listening does not proceed as a series of static encounters with pre-existing bodies and voices from the archive, but as dynamic and affective 'intra-actions' (Barad 2007) that inform and co-shape one another.

I was working with an 'assemblaged archive of trauma' (Trivelli 2013) that included oral history recordings, *her*stories of madness and psychiatric treatment, my memories of childhood and both my own and my mother's experiences of psychiatry. These archive materials were not simply 'things' captured on tapes and in transcripts held in the British Library but active elements of my research process, and demanded a methodological approach that could take into account my own entanglement, 'investments and emotions' (Trivelli 2015). Listening-with women's voices, words, breaths, stories and the spaces and sounds of the oral history interview, my embodied responses and feelings became a performative part of the process, animating the archive. In an uncertain space of liminality, I was somewhere in-between remembering and forgetting, past and future – listening-with voices that were very present but not actually 'there', women whose lives I had come to know intimately, without ever *knowing* them. Temporal and spatial shifts occurred as voices entered me, articulating 'present' moments of crisis, telling me things that I didn't always want to hear. Listening always 'invokes corporeality . . . envelops listeners, and . . . resounds within the body' (Drobnick 2004: 10). The longer I listened-with these women the more I felt their many voices working on me, producing new understandings, feelings, thoughts and actions; transforming me in the process in ways I had not anticipated.

Locating me in hold me in a circle of tender listening

I didn't set out to make a piece that was personal, or to express my*self*. The 'me' in the work's title refers to my attempt to engage the social in a staging of traumas 'too deeply embodied for an *I* to speak them' (Clough 2000: 20). It speaks to my desire to be held within a shared listening space, away from my self-enforced isolation of listening-with voices through headphones over so many months. In early summer 2019 I shared the almost-finished sound piece with people working in 'mental health', many of whom had their own experience of psychiatric treatment. Sitting with these audiences, I felt their listening as a form of tenderness for my own experience. Although my own voice is not present in the piece, simply being in a collective space – listening together – was a form of sharing that felt intimate. I became part of a body of listening, held and heard.

I made this work with the hope of creating a collective, 'tender' listening space[1] for those women, one generation removed, that I had come to know solely through their testimonies. It was an attempt to address the isolation of these women in particular, and others like them (including my own mother) who had been held at a distance from their communities and families within psychiatric institutions for weeks, months and years at a time. I hoped the work would bring these women into dialogue with each other and away from their secondary isolation within the British Library archives. My intervention within the archive was an attempt to create opportunities for these long-silenced women to finally be heard. In its final iteration, the listening circle of the multi-speaker sound piece[2] became a place of tenderness, a space to sit and recognize the catastrophic loneliness of trauma and the terrible failure of psychiatry to listen (Harpin 2018). As Carole (MHTP 2000) says of her experience of being in hospital, 'there [was] very much a feeling of being lost from the world, of being stranded'.

Voice

Is not voice always already intervening, as a sounded body that searches for its place. (LaBelle 2014: 1)

Rather than seeing voice as sound projected from the vocal cords of a vocalizing body towards the ears of a passive hearing body, I follow Brandon LaBelle in recognizing the voice as 'always already intervening' (2014: 1), or perhaps *intra*-vening, to follow Barad's new materialist logic (2007). This vocal intra-vention is 'lodged within the power dynamics of particular structures – linguistic, familial, pedagogic, governmental etc. A voice that is often underrepresented, overheard and interrupted' (LaBelle 2014: 1). Voice can articulate resonating structures of power and the lived experiences of those who might otherwise remain unheard. Human voice is created through a performance of the mouth that involves the depths of the body, including respiration and breath. Voice brings us into a confrontation with the mouth as a cavity that includes 'the tongue, teeth, lips, and the throat' (LaBelle 2014: 1). The mouth is wrapped up in the voice and vice versa, such that to theorize the performativity of the voice is to 'feel the mouth as a fleshy, wet lining around each syllable' (LaBelle 2014: 1).

This assemblage of mouth, mucus membrane, vocal sounds and respiration comes into sharp focus when listening-with psychiatrized women's voices, where medications might dry the oral cavity, swell the tongue and create involuntary movements and tics, with effects on the sounding voice. If, as LaBelle (2014: 2) argues, 'the mouth functions to figure and sustain the body as a subject . . . within a network of relations', then listening to the operations of voices/mouths from the MHTP archive might reveal relations at play within psychiatry, as medications and other physical treatments affect the way voices/mouths sound and behave. An example can be heard in the testimonial recording of Kathleen (MHTP 1999b), who speaks in slow, considered sentences with long pauses in-between. Listening-with these pauses, I notice the constant clicks, clucking, licking and sucking noises that fill the spaces between her words. These sounds are the result of facial spasms and tics, involuntary movements of her mouth and tongue resulting from Tardive Dyskinesia, a condition brought on by years of psychiatric treatment with drugs like Chlorpromazine (Largactil) or 'liquid cosh' as my mother calls it. Listening-with the fleshy sounds of Kathleen's constantly moving tongue, the power of the psychiatric institution and the disfiguring impact of its over-zealous drug regime become apparent as all the parts of her moving mouth vocalize, transmitting bodily affects.

Through listening-with and reassembling the MHTP archive, the horizons of voice begin to reach beyond the fleshy interiors of throats and mouths to include non-human voices; for example, the beeping of a fax machine. This inclusive framing moves me towards new materialist and posthuman conceptions of voice that extend beyond 'humancentric vistas' (Tiainen 2013: 394) and beyond an idea of voice as something that interacts between bodies (self/other, human/media technology) that exist separately from their relating. Rather, voice is better conceived as always, already relating and co-constituting, a Voice without Organs (VwO) (Mazzei 2013: 733) that never arises from a singular subject, but is always produced in 'enactment[s] of entanglement'. Voice as produced in the staging of oral history recordings, listening bodies, memories, silences, transcripts, objects, spaces and sounds; voice, like the archive itself, as 'an assemblage, a complex network of human and nonhuman agents' (Mazzei 2013: 733).

Earwork

> If . . . studying ghosts allows us to rethink a society's relationship to its dead, particularly to those who are subject to some kind of injustice, the ghost and its haunting effects act as a mode of memory and avenue for ethical engagement in the present. (Cho 2008: 29)

Listening-with or 'earwork' engages my ears as sensory instruments to practice 'listening, hearing [and] attuning' within the contexts of memory and forgetting in the testimonial archive (Mody 2005: 176). The idea of earwork as a mode of research comes from studies that argue for 'multi-modal' sensory approaches to lived experience of organizational space (Brown et al. 2020). As the following examples explore, my earwork becomes a form of 'critical listening' through which I develop a 'different sensibility' to the 'acoustic environment' of the oral history interview (Brown et al. 2020: 1543).

The earwork of listening-with a testimonial archive can be understood as a form of 'diasporic' listening that apprehends the transgenerational transmission of trauma through 'scattered [sounds], affects and voices' (Cho 2008: 24). Listening-with testimonies of trauma – out of sync with the earwork of other archive listeners, past present and future – is a form of distributed, 'machinic' perception across space and time; a perceptual, technological and social assemblage that Cho (2008: 174) after Johnston (1999: 46) calls a 'collective psychic apparatus'. Attending to the distribution and reassembly of memories, silences, unheard, lost and forgotten voices across a multiplicity of listening bodies allows for a polyphonic exploration of the affective potential of haunting. This affective earwork also involves listening *beyond* the whole-life testimonies of individual speaking subjects in order to attend to that which is 'nonnarrativizable' (Cho 2008: 24).

My diasporic earwork is also memory-work. As Jill Bennett (2005: 42) argues, the memory-work of trauma and violence draws on somatic memory stored in the body at a cellular level. This memory is 'felt as a wound', triggered by the senses and lends itself to performance in which 'the past seeps back into the present, as sensation rather than representation' (Bennett 2005: 42). As a form of memory-work, my praxis of listening-with the transmission of trauma across time and space attempts to understand the MHTP testimonial archive via an 'acoustic epistemology' of 'knowing-with and knowing-through the audible' (Rice & Feld 2021: 1). What complicates this process is my attention to the archive's 'nonnarrativizable' acoustic phenomena – the sound of a page being turned, a fax machine bleeping, my own panicked breathing. These sounds direct my listening away from a story about loss, and towards an affective encounter with sound that registers the 'loss of loss' (Butler 2003: 467).

The fax machine as bona-fide agent

One sound that opened my ears to the possibility of 'things that have voices' (Ihde 2007) was the vocalization of a fax machine that sounds eighteen minutes into Kathleen's testimony, piercing the moment of her speaking and recalling a memory. Kathleen is being interviewed in an office in The Haven – a care home built to house elderly, long-term residents of the psychiatric institution (Horton Mental Hospital) that had formerly existed on the same site, demolished in 1997. Puncturing the membrane of temporality, the fax machine is never named or acknowledged in the interview, and is represented in the transcript simply as a 'loud beeping noise in the background'.

> Interviewer: How old were you when you were evacuated?
> Kathleen: Eleven.
> Interviewer: And how old were you when you returned back to your family?
> Kathleen: Well, we came back when the Bath bombs were dropping . . . the headmistress was very unhappy and she . . . got the government to allow us to [noise in the background] . . .
> Interviewer: Just carry on . . . just carry on . . .
> Kathleen: What's happening?
> Interviewer: Just carry on . . .
> Kathleen: . . . she got the government [loud beeping noise in background] . . . to allow us to return, so we didn't wait 'till after the war, which was the original idea, you know . . .
> Interviewer: Do you want to cut; you want to stop? [loud beeping noise persists]. (MHTP Archive 1999b)

The fax machine intrudes like an emergency warning, insistent and disorientating. 'What's happening?', Kathleen asks in a childlike voice.

Through this interruption, the present moment collapses and the past returns. It is uncanny that the sound of the fax disrupts the interview at the very moment Kathleen recalls returning to London during the 1942 Bath Blitz. The fax breaks through in a moment of emergency, interrupting the oral history interview neither as object or subject, but as 'intervener' (Latour 2004: 75).

The fax appears as a ghost: a 'psychic apparatus' with agency, an 'unconscious mechanism' that cannot be contained (Trivelli 2013: 59), circulating as an ephemeral voice. Playing with this sound in the Pro Tools editing suite timeline, the fax becomes a structuring device around which I assemble different voices and narratives that allude to being in a state of emergency. I isolate and repeat the fax's familiar, nostalgic tones, bringing it into play with other voices, narratives, feelings and memories. It becomes a psychic catalyst evoking a fire alarm, air raid siren and multiple moments of crisis. Removing it from Kathleen's vocal track, I give the fax its own track and space to sound; playing with its insistent call, separating one shrill pulsating moment, repeating it several times. Underneath the pulsating *'dadadadadada'* of the fax's high notes is a lower humming sound which, brought together with the displaced voices of the interview, creates a sense of urgency that propels the listener towards panic.

The fax resonates in multiple ways with descriptions of memories from the other oral history interviews in the MHTP archive, intra-acting with other moments in which an alarm is remembered. In Anne's testimony, for example, she speaks at length about the experience of being sectioned after going into hospital voluntarily:

> I went in voluntarily and they put me on a seventy-two-hour section . . . and they said that I had been actively aggressive . . . I was shouting and bawling and it was worse in a way . . . it was the time out room again and I hated it, but I thought I can't, they took everything away from me, my handbag and everything. . . . I was being disruptive and they, put me in the time out room again and as I went down, as they took me down to the time out room I smashed a fire alarm, cos I thought 'I'm letting people know what's going on in this place' you know, you don't need this when you're ill, and the fire alarm went off and I was in the time out room [laughs]. (MHTP 1999a)

In Carole's testimony, the fax is brought into play with her description of setting fire to a waste-paper bin in her office, and listening for the fire alarm that would allow her to leave the building, 'My overwhelming need was to get out of the building ' (MHTP 2000).

At some point, I realized that I had selected three testimonial recordings from twenty-three potential narratives that featured an 'alarm' sounding in some form – either within the form of narrative retelling or, as in Kathleen's testimony, the fax machine interrupting the interview. The voices were already intra-acting through my listening. However, in the *Pro Tools* timeline, which separates individual voice tracks (one for Kathleen, one for Anne and another for Carole), the testimonies had to be troubled for this intra-action to become apparent. To unsettle the chronology and linearity of individual narratives, I experimented with forms of layering, foraging and disfiguring that involved 'raiding for fragments upon which other narratives can be spun and misshaping the testimony through selective quotation and . . . amplification' (Hartman 1997: 12).

Listening-with the turning of pages

About three hours into the interview with Anne – and in her lengthy response to the question, 'and when they gave you all these different drugs, what did they explain about why you were being given them?' – I hear paper rustling. I'm not sure whose paper it is, but as Anne speaks, it becomes apparent that she has prepared for this part of the interview by writing down the names of all the drugs she has been prescribed. As Anne responds, the pages are turned over, one by one.

> Stelazine: I had mania with it.
>   I've had Chlorpromazine/Largactyl, high doses in the early days.
> Haloperidol: paralysed my legs, unable to walk.
> Sodium Amytal: could not get out of bed the next day.
> Amitriptyline: that's what I'm on at present, sleeping all around the clock.
> Long-term Lithium: good, but got too high and had to be sectioned. Also kidney trouble and chronic psoriasis and weight gain. Sectioned three times for up to ten weeks.
> Prozac: can't remember.
> Carbamazepine: I came up in a rash all over and that had to be stopped.
> Lustral, Procyclidine, Largactil, Sodium Valproate and Zopiclone: my eyes really hurt, I've had heart palpitations and breathlessness, panic attacks and feelings of fear and terror that I've never had before, they said it was the illness, not the drugs. Acute exhaustion, depression, mood swings, sometimes physically, but mood always down and that was in the last . . . fear, fear and agitation. (MHTP 1999a)

In the simple action of turning the page many things become apparent: the pressure applied on Anne as 'patient', the insistence on and of the drugs, the impossibility of the side effects and the inseparability of all these forces. The noise of the page being turned becomes a reminder of memory loss and the difficulty of keeping track of everything that has happened when your brain has been electrocuted by Electroconvulsive therapy (ECT) and tampered with by toxic medications. The urgency of writing it all down, the importance of getting the order right, of telling a story that *makes sense,* answering questions no one outside of those with a prescribing/psychiatric agenda has ever asked before.

Responding to a question like, 'Were you given any medication?', in the context of the oral history interview, Anne's reply becomes a challenge to recover her experience, to remember with accuracy what has happened and to be heard as a reliable witness. Listening to the turning of pages is a reminder of the institutional context of the oral history interview as a research process that seeks to recover 'truths' about the experiences of psychiatric patients in a particular moment of time. It highlights the epistemological context of a research project concerned with hearing the voiceless. In listening-with these interviews, it becomes apparent that the women speaking are far from voiceless, and that the spaces and contexts of the interview have voice too. The sound of the page turn itself becomes a vocalization, an autobiographical utterance that is social in the Bakhtian sense, 'engag[ing] the embodied knowledge, memory, history and identity of much larger entities than the self' (Lebow 2008: xv). The page turn becomes part of an assemblaged archive that brings to bear my own memories of being in front of professionals who only ever heard my words as further proof of their own diagnosis and symptomatology.

Breath tracks

Nothing more than the act of breathing is able to testify to the proximity of human beings to one another. (Cavarero 2005: 31)

November 2015: I can't think for all of the speaking. I can't listen anymore – these voices are too real and the stories they tell, too difficult. These questions seem only to reveal history recounted in chronological order. I know you are not all that is told in these words.

At home with only the audio to hand, the task of listening-with these dense spoken narratives for clues about what I might do with them feels impossible. I begin taking words out. I find myself longing to hear less; longing for silence, or at least for voices that seem to convey more than they say. Without a clear sense of what I'm doing, I decide to strip back the spoken words, to give back to these voices the breath or 'vital energy' (Järvïö 2015: 28) which somehow got lost in all this listening. Perhaps it is me that needs reviving; sitting and listening have made me listless and despondent, and a dull ache has developed in my left side. I have to remove the headphones and walk away from the computer to find my breath. Perhaps this is just a 'momentarily immobilizing encounter' of the sort Jane Bennett (2010: 5) describes in her work on enchantment, a moment of 'feeling . . . disrupted or torn out of one's default sensory-psychic-intellectual disposition' (Bennett 2010: 42) and which Elena Trivelli (2015: 129) describes feeling 'every morning' as she 'descended into the basement' of the asylum at Gorizia to rifle through piles of yellowing patient's files, untouched for decades. But, I am not in a haunted place surrounded by old clinical files, not researching the physical remains of a 'buried' archive in the damp basement of a crumbling asylum. I am at home, wearing headphones and listening-with women's voices. Repeated listening is having unsettling effects on me. The ache in my side worsens and my nightmares return, after years of absence. I wake in terror as women's voices call out to me – returning me to my childhood, searching long hospital corridors for my mother as women cry out from behind closed doors.

January 2016: Listening to Carole for several hours today, extracting pieces of her testimony and editing out her words, I am struck by the enormity of this task. What does it mean to use this testimony? Am I distorting personal stories? Are these performances I can even use?

Doubts paralyse me. Now I am not only trying to edit Carole's words; I am removing speech altogether. As I sit for long hours extracting words and sentences, the feeling of guilt attached to deliberately stripping these testimonies of their apparent meaning is making itself felt as a bodily tension. Is this some sort of transference? The somatic effects of too much listening? I feel 'my whole body . . . responding to these voices' imparting 'a discomforting feeling of powerlessness' (Trivelli 2015: 127). I create a 'breath track' for Carole, and the results on listening back are surprising. Underneath the calm, controlled delivery of apparently well-rehearsed speech is the breathing of a person who sounds panicked. As I listen to her sharp intakes and quick out-breaths, I find my own breath responding. I am *breathing-with*, my body tuning into Carole's breath, our 'breathing co-ordinat[ing] bodies-in-time' (Lande 2007: 100).

My bodily listening – tuning in to the breathing of Carole – is one way of attending to the terrible loneliness of the traumatized person whose experience of solitude is otherwise inaccessible. Perhaps my breathing-with could be considered a form of 'enactive witnessing' – a form of analytic practice that allows for memory in all its forms, without an attempt to recreate or make individually comprehensible experiences of trauma (Clough 2009). Enactive witnessing becomes a way to engage acts which are outside self-consciousness – experiences which are 'sensory, prelinguistic and devoid of agency' and 'exist only in the ephemeral somatic present' (Grand 2000: 4). Being-with, breathing-with, enables the circulation and transmission of both individual and 'deindividualized' traumatic diasporic memories (Cho 2008: 25), allowing my body to become part of an assemblage of voices, breaths, narratives, symptoms and practices. Like Trivelli (2015: 128), recognizing my own responses 'as entangled *with*, rather than by products of', listening-with enables me to find 'excesses' where others might perceive nothing – an 'entanglement beyond all possibility of disengagement' (Ramadanovic 1998: 62).

Summary

Working with women's voices from the MHTP archive encompassed much time feeling blocked. The labour of listening-with oral history recordings – replete with meaning, stories and so much speech – demanded I find new ways of attending to the trauma that haunted this archive. If haunting occurs as a result of 'endings that are not over' (Gordon 2008: 139), experiences that have for decades been silenced or erased from public record can continue to create psychic and material affects into the future. Working with recordings of women from which I am one generation removed, I have become increasingly alert to the feeling of being haunted. The somatic effects (sensations and feelings) of listening-with reveal 'psyche-body-world entanglements' (Blackman 2012: 24) as I become caught in strange relational dynamics with the women of the MHTP archives. Such dynamics are apparent in my 'breathing-with' Carole whose calm, measured sentences mask the panic belied by her breath, only revealed as I strip words from her voice. They appear in my listening-with the long pauses in Kathleen's speech, and her ever-present tongue-clicking and lip-smacking from years of over-medication with Largactyl. They emerge through listening-with the sound of Anne turning the pages of her hand-written notes as she reads a long list of drugs she has been prescribed, and their terrible side effects. My own memories mingle with these moments of intense listening to create bodily effects: aches, nightmares, a feeling of being trapped. I become part of an assemblaged listening body, entangled with archival voices, narratives, objects and spaces that reorient my perception towards new ways of feeling- and listening-with.

Notes

1   Like Anna Harpin (2018: 10) I use the word 'tender' for its multiplicity of meanings: the early verb 'to tend' meaning 'to turn one's ear, hearken'; the French and Latin uses of the word '*tendre*', 'to hold out, offer' and *tendere*, 'to stretch, hold forth'; as an adjective, 'tender' – 'to become soft or be moved'; as a noun, 'a tender' – 'one who tends, or waits on another'. As Harpin explains, 'to be tender or to tender is to make an offer without assurance of its reception' (ibid.).

2   The sound piece was set up using eight speakers arranged in an outer circle, each speaker amplifying different voices, words, narratives and sounds. The audience sits in a circle within the ring of speakers, creating a collective listening experience.

References

Barad, K. (2007), *Meeting the Universe Halfway: Quantum Physics and the Entanglement of Matter and Meaning*, Durham: Duke University Press.

Bennett, J. (2005), *Empathic Vision: Affect, Trauma and Contemporary Art*, California: Stanford University Press.

Bennett, J. (2010), *Vibrant Matter: A Political Ecology of Things*, Durham: Duke University Press.

Blackman, L. (2012), *Immaterial Bodies: Affect, Embodiment, Mediation*, London: Sage.

Blackman, L. (2015), 'Researching Affect and Embodied Hauntologies: Exploring an Analytics of Experimentation', in B. T. Knudsen and C. Stage (eds), *Affective Methodologies: Developing Cultural Research Strategies for the Study of Affect*, 25–44, Basingstoke: Palgrave Macmillan.

Brown, S., A. Kanyeredzi, L. McGrath, P. Reavey, and I. Tucker (2020), 'Organizing the Sensory: Ear-work, Panauralism and Sonic Agency on a Forensic Psychiatric Unit', *Human Relations*, 73 (11): 1537–62.

Butler, J. (2003), 'Afterword', in D. Eng and D. Kazanjian (eds), *Loss: The Politics of Mourning*, 467–74, Berkley: University of California Press.

Cavarero, A. (2005), *For More Than One Voice: Towards a Philosophy of Vocal Expression*, California: Stanford University Press.

Cho, G. (2008), *Haunting and the Korean Diaspora: Shame, Secrecy and the Korean war*, Durham: Duke University Press.

Clough, P.T. (2000), *Autoaffection: Unconscious Thought in the age of Teletechnology*, Minneapolis: University of Minnesota Press.

Clough, P.T. (2009), 'Reflections on Sessions Early in an Analysis: Trauma, Affect and "enactive witnessing"', *Women and Performance: A Journal of Feminist Theory*, 19 (2): 149–59.

Drobnick, J. (2004), 'Listening Awry', in J. Drobnick (ed.), *Aural Cultures*, 9–18, Toronto: YYZ Books.

Gordon, A. (2008), *Ghostly Matters: Haunting & the Sociological Imagination*, Minneapolis: University of Minnesota Press.

Grand, S. (2000), *The Reproduction of Evil*, Hillsdale, New Jersey: Analytic Press.

Harpin, A. (2018), *Madness, Art and Society: Beyond Illness*, London: Routledge.

Hartman, S. (1997), *Scenes of Subjection: Terror, Slavery and Self-Making in Nineteenth-Century America*, New York: Oxford University Press.

Ihde, D. (2007), *Listening and Voice: Phenomenologies of Sound* (2nd edn), New York: SUNY Press.

Järviö, P. (2015), 'The Singularity of Experience in the Voice Studio: A Dialogue With Michel Henry', in T. Konstantinos and B. Macpherson (eds), *Voice Studies: Critical Approaches to Process, Performance and Experience*, 25–37, London: Routledge.

Johnston, J. (1999), 'Machinic Vision', *Critical Inquiry*, 26 (1): 27–48.

LaBelle, B. (2014), *Lexicon of the Mouth: Poetics and Politics of Voice and the Oral Imaginary*, New York: Bloomsbury.

Lande, B. (2007), 'Breathing Like a Soldier: Culture Incarnate', in C. Schilling (ed.), *Embodying Sociology: Retrospect, Progress and Prospects*, 95–108, Oxford: Blackwell Publishing.

Latour, B. (2004), *The Politics of Nature*, Cambridge: Harvard University Press.

Lebow, A. (2008), *First Person Jewish*, Minneapolis: University of Minnesota Press.

Mazzei, L. (2013), 'A Voice Without Organs: Interviewing in Posthumanist Research', *International Journal of Qualitative Studies in Education*, 26 (6): 732–40.

Mental Health Testimony Project Archives (1999a), [video Recording] 'Ann D'Arcy Interviewed by Judy Mead: C905/41', London: British Library.

Mental Health Testimony Project Archives (1999b) [video Recording] 'Kathleen Haddrell Interviewed by Pauline Abbott-Butler: C905/05', London: British Library.

Mental Health Testimony Project Archives (2000) [video Recording] 'Carole Bressington Interviewed by Judy Mead: C905/25', London: British Library.

Mody, C.M. (2005), 'The Sounds of Silence: Listening to Laboratory Practice', *Science, Technology & Human Values*, 30 (2): 175–98.

Ramadanovic, P. (1998), 'When "To Die in Freedom" is Written in English', *Diacritics*, 28 (4): 54–67.

Rice, T. and S. Feld (2021), 'Questioning Acoustemology: An Interview With Steven Feld', *Sound Studies*, 7 (1): 119–32.

Schilling, C. (2007), *Embodying Sociology: Retrospect, Progress and Prospects*, Oxford: Blackwell Publishing.

Tiainen, M. (2013), 'Revisiting the Voice in Media and as Medium: New Materialist Propositions', *European Journal of Media Studies NECSUS*, 2 (2): 383–406.

Trivelli, E. (2013), *Assembling Memories and Affective Practices Around the Psychiatric History of Gorizia: A Study of a Remembering Crisis*, PhD Dissertation, Goldsmiths, University of London.

Trivelli, E. (2015), 'Exploring a Remembering Crisis: Affective Attuning and Assemblaged Archive as Theoretical Frameworks and Research Methodologies', in B.T. Knudsen and C. Stage (eds), *Affective Methodologies: Developing Cultural Research Strategies for the Study of Affect*, 119–39, Basingstoke: Palgrave Macmillan.

Part IX

Lived experience, activism and survival

CHAPTER 19

Being together in a neurodiverse world

Exploring with Project Art Works

Kate Adams, Sonia Boué
and Chloe Watfern

Project Art Works is a collective of neurodiverse artists and activists, based in the UK, whose work evolves through creative practice and radiates out to awareness-raising in the cultural and care sectors. They were joint winners of the Jarman Award 2020, have been shortlisted for the Turner Prize 2021 and are one of fifteen global artist collectives chosen to lead *documenta fifteen* in 2022. In this chapter we explore how Project Art Works centres neurodivergent experience in their work, and why that is important. The text has unfolded, like a conversation, through a back and forth of written segments between three women, each with a different relationship to the organization. Our writing aims to evoke both the complexity and the potential of the practice of the Project Art Works collective. Its lyric and intuitive approach helps give space to things that are hard to articulate – what it means to care and be cared for, what it means to make and to view an art that values neurodivergent ways of being in the world.

Chloe: My first encounter with Project Art Works was via film. It was a three-channel video installation called *The Not Knowing of Another* (Adams 2008). The film took me on a walk from a semi-decrepit railway bunker, over a bridge, down some steps and out to the seashore. In it, I saw

Kate Adams for the first time – the maker of the work and the co-founder and artistic director of Project Art Works, based in the small seaside town of Hastings. I also saw Kate's son Paul Colley – a maker too, and a man who mostly communicates without words. I saw them touch briefly, more than once. I saw him clap and rock and heard him make some sounds and noises. I saw Kate help Paul down the stairs.

I saw them from all kinds of perspectives: a GoPro strapped to Paul's chest, a camera tethered to a weather balloon from up high, a close-up of Paul's face, longshots of figures in the distance and at the end a beach at sunset with all its glitter and glimmer and the bobbing up and down of the sea and of the camera attached to a body. In those moving images in that darkened room, I didn't know who they were or what it all meant. They were just humans, walking together, in the world: the vastness of it, the beauty of it (Figure 19.1).

But I have thought a lot, since I first saw that film, about what it means. *The Not Knowing of Another*. I've turned those words, its title, around and around in my head and over my tongue. The not knowing of another. I think those words, that work, get at something central to the grander mission of Project Art Works, where art and film are used, quite explicitly, as a means of connection across neuro-types.

At Project Art Work's studio base in Hastings, nestled under the three arches of a road bridge next to a railway track, neurodiverse artists and makers work together, sometimes over the course of many, many years. Artworks and moving images act as a record of interactions – the frame of a canvas, or a camera, are spaces within which things unfold – a dance with paint and paintbrushes, perhaps, or a walk through a favourite place.

I've learnt that at Project Art Works, art and film are often intertwined with advocacy – raising awareness about unique lived experiences of

FIGURE 19.1 The Not Knowing of Another *(Adams 2008), still and installation view at MK Gallery, 2011, Courtesy Project Art Works.*

neurodivergence, and modelling modes of engagement that allow for alternative forms of communication and connection. This involves sharing what they do, and how they do it, with different audiences – from social care organizations to cultural institutions.

Kate, I wonder if you could step in here to tell us more about what drives you to do the work that you do?

Kate: What I know is that if I take care to actively listen and see, make eye contact when talking in a calm and clear way, am observant and responsive to the inconspicuous signifiers in Paul's presence, then we have the possibility of connection. I know not to sit down too close or abruptly or to make assumptions or try and interpret but to be calm and baffled and open.

These are lessons on being and Paul is a patient and stoic teacher. He is enigmatic and uncompromisingly truthful. Without guile or malice. Just very purely himself. This is disarming and challenging because it holds trust and innocence – perhaps more of the latter than the former. He reveals these qualities in every particle of his being.

It took me a while after our clear-eyed, angelic child had been replaced by a devastating litany of clinical labels and inabilities to find my way back to him. To do this I had to be quiet and develop an approach to finding out about him through a form of open and loving research. Like an artist's practice; if I do this what happens? Not too much! Perhaps by approaching it another way – connection. Input and output. By incremental degrees non-verbal communication became so much more expansive than reductive, training the senses and opening out an extraordinary world.

Without the assimilation of neurotypical concepts of what things are and how they work – 'rules' – the world is confusing and wondrous every moment of every day. A shadow on the pavement is not to be trusted. Is it a hole or a shady fissure? Whatever. It needs to be manoeuvred around. Spatial transitions. Very tricky. Doorways, portals and thresholds between one world and another; without knowing what a room is for or what it holds; imagine. Just giving yourself up to this. Trusting. Neurotypical minds tend towards focus blindness and filter out stimulus and minute observations when absorbed by intention.

To share these wonders and to retrieve the identity of Paul and others is a motivating factor in the films and creative activism of Project Art Works. To retrieve the essence of people who have these different ways of being in and seeing the world from labels and crudely applied assessments of needs and capabilities.

In the studios, sensory materials and processes that are direct and unequivocal allow for a primal form of engagement with the viscosity, physicality, hues and tones of the material world. When fully immersed in exploring materials, we make ourselves visible through spontaneous and intuitive decisions. It is these moments that we try to capture and then show alongside the objects and artworks that emerge from these interactions.

Very often, however, the art is in the focus, the action and the process rather than the product.

Project Art Works uses film as reflective practice and reveals different ways of being that avoid categorization or traditional narratives. We employ a process of monitoring assent and dissent to arrive at consent, balancing on an ethical tightrope of sometimes not knowing.

Sonia: Kate sends a link and I enter the wilderness through my desktop (Project Art Works 2019; see Figure 19.2).[1] 'Lockdown' and 'agoraphobia' are big words. My eyes are thirstier for rain than I know. Outdoors is a privilege, the wilderness more dreamlike still, connecting me to the child who had such freedoms through the back gate of a suburban family garden. My screen and my old friend (the gate) are portals to other worlds momentarily fused, as they propel me towards a universe of sensory delight. I am connected in ways I can't easily describe.

What if my eyes are suddenly like a child's hands stroking the curly fronds of ancient ferns, or whose nose has been pricked by pungent fungi? Can I say that my eyes seem to brush like a shin past a clump of dock leaves, grateful it's not stinging nettles? Am I allowed to speak such gibberish? Poets can, and it's called poetry. Poetry is the privilege of those who can use language.

Years clocked scrambling up the banks of the drained reservoir my family home nestled in, seep in with the rainfall in the opening scenes of this film. I am back, I am back, and this is all part of the great unlearning of my neuronormative conditioning. That girl knew plants and soil are essential. This woman's forgotten, though she can still recall the earthy potatoes of

FIGURE 19.2 Illuminating the Wilderness *film still (Project Art Works 2019). Courtesy Project Art Works.*

that first kitchen, the one before the kitchen with a window that looked out onto the gate. In *that* kitchen potatoes were brushed and washed before peeling, and her friend soil came inside to be rubbed between fingers and thumbs, an early 'stim' perhaps?

I've unlearned all my 'stims', but the body is wise and art is a medium for truths if you pay attention. I now realize that through my art I have been slowly reconnecting, including rubbing sand between fingers and thumbs, which incidentally taught me to speak complete sentences in public. Yes. I closed my eyes and manipulated ('stimmed' with) the sand and suddenly, with the flow of the grains through my fingers, words came tumbling forth. From unknown and unknowing I became known and came to know myself.

I observe others knowing themselves in the wilderness too. Often the sure-footed are the neurodivergent adults with complex needs. I see how the wilderness confers space around them and opens up curiosity. I'm aware of the scaffolding this requires, although it's off-camera it is evident in the tentative approach of Project Art Works staff. If there are awkward moments (spoiler, there are) it is staff who are adrift, and bravely so. Neuronormative culture seems petrified of social blunders; the mistimed interaction, the joke which falls flat. Small talk can feel irrelevant when there's so much else to notice and drink in, though. I like that the neuronormative people are trying so hard, but that the gaps are real too. The mask slips. Yes, it does for me too. I've lived a very long time as a bilingual autistic but fluency is never a given. We need scaffolding and bridges.

I ask myself how often I have failed to locate myself in a cultural product. I can't count this number, but what I feel inside this filmic universe is very different. It unleashes a hunger for 'stims' past. How were they unlearned, I wonder suddenly? What delights me especially is the language of the camera and I'm inspired with reference to my own filmmaking. *Illuminating the Wilderness* was with me recently, while I was shooting footage of a short sensory walk for a film by Dorothy Allen-Pickard (2021) called *Three Bodies*. For me the need to translate a particular lived experience through my work has become a primary concern; any discomfort in the viewer echoes my own discomfort in neuronormative spaces. I agree with Kate, not knowing sometimes feels brave, fertile and important.

Chloe: We are dancing around these words – knowing, not knowing. The academic in me wants to go deep into questions of epistemology or hermeneutics. Bigger words, ones I can barely get my head around. I'll try sticking with the subject by taking it sideways a little bit.

I imagine Eva Kittay sitting in a room full of philosophers. The rustle of papers. There are stony stares, and the walls are probably sandstone. Coffee in paper cups. They are focused on defining the parameters of morality: Who do we enclose within the circle of personhood? They list cognitive capacities.

They consider the capacities of non-human animals like chimpanzees and dogs and magpies. All of a sudden, Kittay must defend her daughter Sesha from comparison with, 'What did you say – a pig?' (Kittay 2009: 621). Elsewhere, the bioethicist Jeff McMahan had written that people like Sesha – people with, as these philosophers put it, 'profound cognitive disability' – are 'almost entirely unresponsive to their environment and to other people . . . [and] incapable of deep personal and social relations, creativity and achievement' (McMahan 1996: 5).

Why am I repeating this to you here, now? Well, first, it shows how deep-seated prejudices and discrimination go into the heart of our ivory towers. They extend across all kinds of other spaces too. Stigma surrounding cognitive difference pervades all aspects of our social worlds (Scior and Werner 2016, Scior, Hamid et al. 2020). But I have also turned to Kittay here because her response helps illuminate the ethics of care that she has done so much to develop, while coming back to these words – knowing, and not knowing.

Kittay uses the concepts of epistemic responsibility and epistemic modesty to challenge McMahan. In other words: 'know the subject that you are using to make a philosophical point' and 'know what you don't know'. She shows how he has failed on both those fronts. She shows what she does and does not know, as a mother and carer, about the inner life of her daughter. She tells of a deep and loving relationship that is constantly surprising. In the telling, she reframes the question of moral status to rest not on the 'cognitive capacities' of an individual but on complex webs of interdependence. 'Because what it is to be human', Kittay tells the philosophers, 'is not a bundle of capacities. It's a way that you are, a way you are in the world, a way you are with another' (2009: 621).

From her battlefield in moral philosophy, Kittay is enacting what she calls an invisible labour of care. This labour, in part, requires us to challenge those who presume to 'know' another. This unknowing is, in part, a response to fixed narratives – whether of tragedy or inspiration (Grue 2016).

This unknowing is, in part, what watching a film like *Illuminating the Wilderness* does for a neurotypical viewer like me. I let myself drift and meander with the flow of people and places, the small intimacies. But if I'm really paying attention, I begin to find things out. I look with Gabby beneath the rock and notice the intricate threads woven by a spider. I listen to Sharif ask Dan, 'Has your cat had any dreams before though Dan?' And I hear him respond, 'I tried to ask it, but it wouldn't tell me. It went "meow".' I listen to the rain and wonder at it, wonder at what it might sound like to someone else.

'I love the clattering sounds, the staccato, the ripples, the appoggiatura and trills, the sudden drop in levels, the pitter patter of rain like crisps dancing inside a foil coated box', writes autistic artist-researcher Dawn Joy Leong. 'It unpacks our meanings, our world, on our terms' (Leong 2020).

Kate: I very much like Eva Kittay's (2013) words: 'the struggles of marginalized, subordinated and endangered others.' These words seem profoundly and additionally resonant in 2021, as we tentatively emerge from these many months of contagion in the UK and around the world. So many people in places of care have died. How can this be? Why have those who may rely on the support of others been so imperilled? I shudder when I read the news:

> COVID-19 has had an unequal impact on disabled people who have been among the hardest hit in terms of deaths from the virus . . . 6 out of 10 people who have died with COVID-19 are disabled. Today's figures clearly show that current measures to protect disabled people are not enough and that there is an urgent need for more and better support. (Suleman 2021)

Our right to care and support from others has been wholly compromised by categorizations, labels and attempts to provide ethical frameworks for clinical decisions.[2] This has exposed a value system that exists and provides the absolute conditions for 'endangering others'. The pathologization of otherness has been disastrous for so many people. Overall, it has been far safer to be out of care establishments than resident in them. The group ethos of care presupposes a standard can be applied to groups of people who all have such distinct specificities of spirit, ways of living and needs. There is so far to go.

> Each of us has been shaped by the care of others. From the first touch of the midwife's worn hands as she pulled you into the world, your life has been sustained by a long catalogue of people who have nurtured and supported your development and wellbeing up to this point. Ahead lie more experiences of being cared for, possibly from those you love and certainly from many strangers, whom you may completely depend on for your most basic needs for comfort, food and cleanliness. No one can afford not to be interested in care. (Bunting 2020)

Yet, despite immeasurable goodness in many who devote their lives to this fundamental aspect of life everywhere, we still fail to deliver systemic care for each other that measures up. There are, of course, pockets of brilliance and in some countries the possibility of empowering ourselves and others to take better care through much more personalized and individual routes.

Not knowing should enable us to take more care. Michael Sandel suggests that 'from the fact that people are very different it follows that, if we treat them equally, the result must be inequality in their actual position, and that the only way to place them in an equal position would be to treat them differently' (Sandel 2007). So we return to observation, active listening and open-heartedness that allows the 'other' to be more visible and present in determining how we live and survive in such mixed societies. I use Sandel's insight as a framework for creative self-determination and agency. This alongside Joseph Beuys' exhortation in 1973 that

> Only on condition of a radical widening of definition will it be possible for art and activities related to art to provide evidence that art is now the only evolutionary–revolutionary power. Only art is capable of dismantling the repressive effects of a senile social system that continues to totter along the deathline: to dismantle in order to build A SOCIAL ORGANISM AS A WORK OF ART. (Beuys 1973)

Many artists and collectives are engaged in this endeavour, exploring how creativity and care can so closely align with fundamental ethics and equity in the recognition of others.

Sonia: My working memory is very compromised, but being in the moment and an innate ability to improvise are great advantages which compensate. It's hard to follow a sequence, *ergo* it's hard to learn sequentially or embed sequences in my long-term memory. It can be very trying and disabling, of course. I start each day anew. Certain avenues are closed to me but many vistas open up to a brain like mine, which others may not be able to perceive. I completely relate to Kate's observations of Paul's perceptual experience in this piece and also as demonstrated in the film *The Not Knowing of Another*, which uses a GoPro camera. Reflective filmmaking makes perfect sense as a means to enter into another's perceptual realm. The act of filmmaking with Paul, at times only intuiting consent, feels like a vital act of love which, although vulnerable to criticism, is nonetheless important and brave. The potential of filmmaking to connect us across neurologies feels immense due to the camera providing an eye. We witness, and in *The Not Knowing of Another* we experience, as directly as possible, another's sensory world.

My thoughts fly to filmmaking itself as an act of care (curation) which is very different from viewing and I'm interested in these two experiences as being quite distinct, one active and the other passive. *Illuminating the Wilderness* also features GoPro footage (I believe) but involves multiple perspectives and also employs wider views than *Not Knowing of Another*. *Illuminating the Wilderness* is more cinematic in this sense. I want to explore the two films further but first I'll revisit motherhood, which feels like a powerful undertow.

I'm humbled by Kate's artistic practice and her vision for Project Art Works. It comes from such a truthful place. It's enriching to read this account of her approach to unknowing in the most intimate of relationships, that of parenthood. I share aspects of Kate's lived experience of prolonged maternal care, while observing that good practice in parenting a newborn is to be calm, open and attentive to the minutiae of 'non-verbal' communication, precisely as she describes her approach to her adult son, Paul. Sleepless and often baffling nights are expended, trying one way and another to calm and soothe a newborn's distress. Intense and extreme at times, such practice can be instinctual and straightforward, or experienced as a burden leading to complex feelings. It's from this observation that I begin to make sense of Kate's suggestion that 'not knowing should enable us to take more care' when so often the opposite seems to be the case at both individual and societal levels.

This period of most intense parenting is generally fleeting as the infant becomes known and attention to the minutiae of non-verbal communication is lost. There's no schema for when intense parenting extends beyond infancy into adulthood. Space for gentle and attentive unknowing seems to close down. Stigma is so readily applied in its place.

Kate's model of calm bafflement is close to mindfulness perhaps? A much overused term but also a concept audiences might recognize and buy into, but this is a stray tangential thought. My feeling here is that Kate's creative journey holds a narrative of its own.

Back to filmmaking itself as an act of care, which in *Illuminating the Wilderness* and *The Not Knowing of Another* also provide witness to and model care. Viewing is thus thrice removed in a way, and the films can also be consumed in multiple contexts as an online experience which may create further distance. Viewing may or may not elicit caring responses. Viewing may equally elicit discomfort and unease.

I don't have any answers but I'm curious about the impact of the camera as eye in both films, and how *Illuminating the Wilderness,* though a Jarman Award 2020 winner, received an off-piste critical reception from an established mainstream critic like Adrian Searle (2020).[3] I'm also fascinated by the fact that Project Art Works' films have multiple diverse audiences as Chloe notes – from social care organizations to cultural institutions – and that in many ways I feel *The Not Knowing of Another* is more recognizably an art piece than *Illuminating the Wilderness*. By which I mean it has more obvious equivalencies in style and content with a particular species of art film.

This last observation is because *The Not Knowing of Another*, while containing a narrative arc of sorts (a journey with a resolution), is literally narrower in focus, and an even more direct and sustained centring of the neurodivergent sensory experience as fragmentary (abstract) and here largely non-verbal. The subject is less observed and more inhabited by the viewer. This directness seems to lend power and provide the opportunity for more active viewing. More is demanded of the viewer, I feel.

I'm reminded of how much I've had to learn about supporting audiences in creating and presenting cultural products. As a neurodivergent creative this is unintuitive and often painful labour. I now also wonder if it sometimes gets in the way in the mission of cultural translation of the lived experience of neurodivergence.

A final note to readers

Our intention has been to work accessibly across continents and neurologies and to enable this conversation to flow freely and unfettered by convention. In listening to one another we have been open, generous and undemanding, a style in keeping with the subject at hand. We have chosen to adapt the surrealist game of exquisite corpses, where each player takes a turn to draw part of a body, then folding the paper to obscure it from the next player. Here, we have taken turns to write with the paper unfolded (as it were) and *carte blanche* to proceed intuitively, each knowing our thoughts would be held by the others if we went too far astray. Our writing can thus be viewed as a series of calls and responses, enabled by a commonality of purpose and a trust (across diverse perspectives), which feels precious and rare. Our exquisite corpse therefore comprises a free-form conversation, traversing many of the complex relational dynamics involved in working at the intersection of arts practice and social care for those with complex needs. We make no claim to cover all bases, or to provide answers to the many questions raised. This is a hope-filled beginning of a much longer conversation, though we don't yet know what form it might take.

Notes

1   Here, Sonia describes watching *Illuminating the Wilderness* (Project Art Works 2019).

2   For example, the Clinical Frailty Scale in the UK treated people's need to be supported with daily tasks as a reason to de-prioritize critical care treatment. Available online: https://www.disabilityrightsuk.org/news/2020/april/fury-over -do-not-resuscitate-notices, accessed 11 May 2021.

3   In his review of the Jarman Award for *The Guardian*, Searle (2020) dismissively concludes a brief paragraph on *Illuminating the Wilderness*: 'The upbeat voices of carers cut through indecipherable chatter. "It is very boring here," Sharif says in the gloaming, truth speaking to power. I find all this problematic.'

References

Adams, K. (2008), *The Not Knowing of Another*, UK: Project Art Works. Available online: https://vimeo.com/246994674 (accessed 30 July 2021).
Allen-Pickard, D. (2021), *Three Bodies*, UK: Molonglo. Available online: https:// vimeo.com/530154245 (accessed 30 July 2021).
Beuys, J. (1973), 'I am Searching for Field Character', in C. Tisdall (ed.), *Art into Society, Society into Art: Seven German Artists*, 48, London: ICA.

Bunting, M. (2020), *Labours of Love: The Crisis of Care*, London: Granta.

Grue, J. (2016), 'The Problem With Inspiration Porn: A Tentative Definition and a Provisional Critique', *Disability & Society*, 31 (6): 838–849.

Kittay, E.F. (2009), 'The Personal is Philosophical Is Political: A Philosopher and Mother of a Cognitively Disabled Person Sends Notes From the Battlefield', *Metaphilosophy*, 40 (3–4): 606–627.

Kittay, E.F. (2013), 'Eva Fedar Kittay Interview,' *Ethics of Care*, 16 June. Available online: https://ethicsofcare.org/eva-fedar-kittay/ (accessed 11 May 2021).

Leong, D.-J. (2020), 'Illumination,' *Dawn Joy Leong*, 11 December. Available online: https://dawnjoyleong.com/2020/12/11/illumination/ (accessed 11 May 2021).

McMahan, J. (1996), 'Cognitive Disability, Misfortune, and Justice', *Philosophy & Public Affairs*, 25 (1): 3–35.

Project Art Works (2019), *Illuminating the Wilderness*, UK: Project Art Works. Available online: https://vimeo.com/326795036 (accessed 21 September 2021).

Sandel, M., ed. (2007), *Justice: A Reader*, Oxford: Oxford University Press.

Scior, K., A. Hamid, R. Hastings, S. Werner, C. Belton, A. Laniyan, M. Patel, and M. Kett (2020), 'Intellectual Disability Stigma and Initiatives to Challenge it and Promote Inclusion Around the Globe', *Journal of Policy and Practice in Intellectual Disabilities*, 17 (2): 165–175.

Scior, K. and S. Werner, (eds) (2016), *Intellectual Disability and Stigma*, UK: Palgrave Macmillan.

Searle, A. (2020), 'Apocalyptic goo and Detroit in Beats: Jarman Award 2020 is Shared', *The Guardian*, 22 November. Available online: https://www.theguardian.com/artanddesign/2020/nov/24/jarman-award-2020-shared-whitechapel-gallery-london (accessed 30 September 2021).

Suleman, M. (2021), '6 Out of 10 People Who Have Died from COVID-19 Are Disabled', *The Health Foundation*, 11 February. Available online: https://www.health.org.uk/news-and-comment/news/6-out-of-10-people-who-have-died-from-covid-19-are-disabled (accessed 11 May 2021).

CHAPTER 20

Pathologize this

Dolly Sen

Do you want to know what happens to a child that has been abused, neglected and hated for years with nowhere to go and no one to save them? They go mad – either in small ways that can be masked, or in gargantuan ways that cannot be hidden. In my case, the recipe for madness was simple: put a child through rape, violence, neglect, the serious illness of siblings, racism that included being spat on, name-called, physically threatened. Add a sprinkling of poverty, discrimination and then violent and devastating internalized homophobia when puberty kicks in. The question, then, is how does a child *not* go mad when their searing physical and mental pain is hidden behind a silence in which the whole world colludes?

I had my first psychotic episode at age fourteen, not long after my father tried to kill me, twice: once by strangling me, and once by trying to set my bed on fire. My dad was fundamentally a lazy man and couldn't muster enough effort to finish these murderous acts. My heart by then had nothing left to break, so my mind broke instead.

Because of the fear and paranoia of my psychosis – where I thought I was evil and responsible for bringing pain and disasters into the world – I stopped going to school. Social services became involved and threatened to put me in care if I didn't return. They were unable to see the terror in my eyes; they confused terror with laziness. They didn't stop to ask what was happening. Eventually they referred me to a child psychiatrist based at King's College Hospital in London to be assessed.

I hoped this psychiatrist would listen to my pain and save me from terror. I was frantic to speak to someone about what was happening inside and outside my head. I wanted someone to stop me from drowning. What I learned from that first session is that psychiatry does not offer a life ring to keep you afloat. It puts a concrete block around your feet to freeze your life in time, to make every forward step impossible. The first thing the psychiatrist said, without even making eye contact, was: 'So, what's wrong with you?' It was a devastating thing to hear. What was *wrong* with *me*?

The psychiatrist had a checklist of questions, and I felt myself shrink smaller and smaller with each one. I seemed an aggravation to her, like I was wasting her time. She asked highly personal questions – like those about abuse – with such unfeelingness in her voice, I was left wanting to kill myself there and then. She became another person to add to the list of people who did not care, who could not protect me; another reason not to trust. She ended the session by saying I should pull up my socks and stop being *silly*. It was hard to even entertain that notion when I thought that demons were chasing me. My meeting with the psychiatrist couldn't persuade me that hell didn't exist. Funnily enough, I didn't want to engage with her, or the dozens of subsequent psychiatric workers who shamed my mind by calling it disordered, aberrant, abnormal.

Not once through that abnormalizing lens of psychiatric treatment did I feel better, improved, healed. I spent the next two decades in and out of the mental health system, mostly being neglected when I needed help with an abusive father, housing or benefits, or instead being medicated for admitting that I found it emotionally and psychologically hard to cope with these stressors and past trauma. Every time I brought up childhood trauma, they wanted to diagnose me with a personality disorder; an evil and sordid rebuttal to someone's pain. We can't take away the pain, but we can destroy your sense of self, give you more trauma via the system, and give ourselves a 'get-out clause' so that we can be dicks without your being able to do anything about it. If I critiqued their humiliation of me in any way, personality disorder came up again. One time, when I was actively suicidal, I rang the crisis team; I was told to go for a walk or have a bath. I am not the only person who has been given this awful advice when faced with their own self-annihilation. I made a complaint about the person who took my call; my complaint went nowhere. Instead, what hung in the air was the threat of being labelled with a personality disorder for having the audacity to expect to be treated with decency, respect and kindness.

The longer I was in the system, the more the humiliation, abuse, neglect and iatrogenic trauma built up, a mountain of razor blades that I was expected to climb with gratitude and subservience. Psychiatry has extreme self-esteem issues.

As a branch of medicine, psychiatry is looked down upon even by other medics. It is a limping gazelle that can't keep up with its Aesculapian tribe. What's ironic is that psychiatry shot its own self in the leg. It neither follows stringent science by ensuring high levels of reliability and validity, nor can it find biological causes of mental distress, despite decades and trillions of dollars poured into that endeavour. Psychiatry will never be as incredible a health intervention as open-heart surgery or keeping premature babies alive; it knows this. What it could do is say: 'Let's concentrate on kindness and obvious causes of mental distress such as early adverse experiences, trauma and social and political influences that drive people mad. Let's be amazing to people so they heal and gain strength to take on the world.' Instead, psychiatry has done the opposite: it is unkind, dismissing external influences on distress to the point that it pathologizes traumatized people by saying their personalities are disordered, thereby absolving the abusers and the systems that maintain that abuse. Psychiatry is a branch of medicine with the arrogance to insist upon its expertise despite deceptive silence about the bad science and bad humanity practised in its name, low rates of recovery and a horrific history. What is most shocking is that it is granted the power to do this, fuelled by a social control agenda backed by governments or from the pharmaceutical industry's capitalistic clout.

Think about the physics of psychiatry – it's all pointing and plunging downward. The control and restraint techniques; electroconvulsive therapy (ECT); the awful, dragging sedation of psychiatric meds; the pathologizing and labelling. It pushes stuff down; it brings people to their lowest point. Forget about having a personality, dreams, a life of meaning; if you are breathing and not causing trouble, psychiatry regards you as a fine specimen for society.

I won't hold back what I think about psychiatry – a vile monstrosity birthed from a sordid genesis of racism, sexism, homophobia and classism. Psychology is little better. Both disciplines in their early years regarded non-Western/white people as inferior, feeding into and sustaining the eugenics movement that inspired Nazi policy to exterminate 'undesirables'. Most of the early years of both professions were concerned with moral insanity – for example, people behaving in ways that make straight, white, middle-class men uncomfortable, or behaving in ways that they can't control.

In nineteenth-century Europe, women were diagnosed with hysteria if they were seen to have a 'tendency to cause trouble for others' (Maines 1999: 23). Psychiatry saw these women as shamming or attention-seeking, using their ill health as a way to avoid feminine duties and control their families. The psychiatric 'cure' was to punish these women with negative attention – named 'observant neglect' in Victorian times – to show that hysterics didn't deserve sympathy. If things have truly changed from psychiatry's dubious history, this 'attention-seeking' belief about female patients would have died out, too. However, many female psychiatric patients nowadays will tell you this belief is still alive and kicking. Instead of hysteria, the dubious mark furnished by contemporary psychiatry is 'personality disorder'. Look at psychiatry in any given year and you will find the prejudice and power structures in society at that particular time.

What psychiatry has done to me and others is enraging, but anger is seen as part of our madness; complaints will be ignored and invalidated because any criticism on the patient's part is a feature of our delusion. I decided to campaign in other ways. Over the years, I've done the *committee* thing, the *media* thing, the *speaking to politicians* thing, the *anti-stigma campaign* thing, and realized that I was preaching to the converted. I even tried to change things on the inside. I enrolled in a bachelor of science majoring in occupational therapy. The majority of the teaching staff were impeccable, but there were a few who imparted their own ignorance and prejudice as if it were science. There was the usual non-questioning acquiescence to the view that schizophrenia is a brain disease or that the recovery model is a system with which everyone is happy. In the two years I was a student in the course, the only 'teaching' on personality disorder was a lecturer's comment that people with personality disorder were manipulative.

The practice placements were worse and left me completely disillusioned. While there were some mental health hospital settings that treated their patients with dignity and care, the community mental health team I was placed with defied any notion of kindness and decency. During one morning clinical meeting, a social worker recounted how one of the women on her caseload was raped while she was drunk. One of the psychiatrists seated at the table snorted, 'What, again?', to other sniggers in the room. My placement educator – who was supposed to teach me how to be a professional member of the caring profession – was a decent, gentleman who cared about the people on his caseload, but he was impotent both in significant impact on their lives and in standing up to bad practice. When some of the 'professionals' in the room had laughed at the rape of this woman, I had looked desperately to him to say or do something. He was upset by the remark but stayed silent. He had little effect on the lives of his patients because most were struggling with trauma of some kind, or social issues such as unstable housing or poverty. He would refer people to either six sessions of cognitive behavioural therapy (CBT) – knowing that it would hardly touch their pain – or put them on the social housing register, knowing it would take years for them to be housed, if at all. I made a complaint about several instances of bad practice, knowing it would change nothing. I left my occupational therapy degree not long after.

During these times, creativity and humour were my armour and shield to keep fighting. I could see my art and humour connecting with more people, including those who had no association with psychiatry. Art and humour bypass the conditioning on all things about madness and psychiatry. Poking fun at something opens up unique ideas about it for people. You are connecting, human to human. Those who don't know about the mental health system begin to realize there is bullshit obscuring the truth. My work aims to show people who have to go through this humiliation that they are not alone, and that the people who humiliate them will be ridiculed, the power they have exposed. What power does anything have if you laugh at it? What authority do ugly systems have over you if you make your version more beautiful? I do not want indifference, and I do not get indifference to my work. I put normal over my lap and smack its naughty arse. I aim to savage psychiatry's bullshit concepts and sense of its own supremacy.

I have done this in a variety of ways, using artistic licence to do so. Early on I noticed the power of language to demean one group of people and privilege another. Many who work for the mental health system plead innocence or ignorance when it comes to the stranglehold that psychiatric terms like 'disorder', 'abnormal' and 'maladaptive' have on people's sense of being and status in the world. If there is no power in words, I call on every psychiatric institution to purge the word 'normal' and replace it with 'mediocre'. How can anything beautiful come out of a profession that sees your mind as ugly, or your soul as dangerous? Time to return the compliment and give psychiatry its own risk assessment.

By the same token, I despise the term 'service user'; a fundamentally meaningless term. Service is defined by the *Oxford English Dictionary* (OED) as 'the action or fact of helping or benefiting someone or something; action or behaviour that is conducive to the welfare or advantage of another'. Let's define this so-called service. You may be hurting from trauma, social issues or inequalities or other adverse events. Shall we, as a service, advocate on your behalf to tackle inequality, or are we a machine that feeds and maintains the quicksand of the status quo? Are we a service that facilitates a greater sense of control in a devastated person's life, or are we a tool for social control? Psychiatry only appears like a service if you are into sadomasochism – always the submissive, with no right to a safe word when caught in a control and restraint manoeuvre. If I went to Argos for a kettle and somebody pumped me full of drugs I didn't want, pushed me on the floor because I complained my kettle was faulty or electrocuted me by said kettle, I wouldn't want to go back. This 'service' affects more than your statutory rights; there are no refunds or exchanges for a missed life. Just imagine the feedback form after being half-suffocated by a control and restraint hold from a psychiatric service provider: *How would you rate your last restraint? Would you recommend it to others? How likely are you to repeat your business with us? Would you like a loyalty card?*

If you asked a person on the street what causes mental distress or the experience labelled 'mental illness', most would probably say it originates in the brain. Billions have been spent trying to find biological markers for schizophrenia or bipolar, without success. I and many others associated with movements such as *Drop the Disorder* (Watson 2019) would argue most mental health difficulties are not about broken brains but broken hearts. Tablets do not mend a broken heart; neither do attempts to pathologize it. Pathologizing causes devastating and untold damage. It is impossible to be seen as beautiful or even human under such conditions.

The book that vandalizes the soul in this way is the *Diagnostic and Statistical Manual of Mental Disorder* (DSM), which has had several incarnations over the decades. The book's own creators admit there is no science to how they choose which disorders make it into the DSMs, and admit no strong validity or reliability to *any* mental health diagnosis that does not have a known organic cause (Watson 2019). As careful studies have established, the process of creating the DSM boils down to a bunch of people in a room arguing over what should be included (see Paula Caplan in Watson 2019). The DSM is ripe for ridicule and I have ridiculed it in many ways – most notably by creating the book, *DSM 69* (Sen 2017), a subversive look at psychiatry with art, words and mischief. I did miss a trick though – I thought calling it *DSM 69* was funny, but I should have called it *DSM 6*, so the psychiatrist writing the next version would have had to ask my permission to use the title *DSM 6*, or skip to *DSM 7*.

I made *DSM 69* so that people who derived gratification or strength from my work could access it all in one place. I put the idea out into the world on social media, and Eleusinian Press – whose by-line is 'where music, madness and politics meet' – wanted to publish it. I say in my introduction to the book:

> The *Diagnostic and Statistical Manual of Mental Disorders* (DSM), published by the American Psychiatric Association, is . . . a book on the classification of mental disorders, but reads more like an Argos catalogue, where you may or may not get what you ordered, handed to you in boxes by people who don't know you, and are just waiting for the next person in line to be a bastard to. The only difference is there is no warranty when they break your soul. (Sen 2017: 3)

My own experience highlights the common experience that the *DSM* is at best a system of low scientific reliability, and at worst a label-maker that promises an unbearable hell which is both impersonal and deeply personal. The disorder is not within the person; the disorder is psychiatry itself. I have been brutalized by psychiatry, and I am not the only one. Those who have not gone through the mental health system have little idea of its abusive nature. The few decent people who work in the system cannot subtract from the damage done. *Dolly Sen's DSM 69* (Sen 2017: 3) shows how disturbing and fundamentally flawed psychiatric authority can be, and, maybe, that madness can make perfect sense. The book has manifestos, poems, cartoons, art, rants and essays. Because of my love for sheep, I also developed a Diagnostic Sheep Manual (Figure 20.1).

Being labelled with a psychiatric diagnosis does little for your place in the world. You are promised stigma and discrimination in all sorts of places – from work to relationships, to being disbelieved in a court of law, to being a victim of hate crime. In the UK, the anti-stigma campaign *Time to Change*[1] wanted 'normal' people to have a cup of tea with someone experiencing mental distress. Their crusade insisted it was time to sit, have tea and discuss mental health with a workmate or neighbour. This was all very dandy for the 'worried well',[2] but if you talk about being Jesus or seeing demons, or that unstable housing makes you want to kill yourself, people don't tend to want to finish their cup of tea with you!

THE LOST SHEEP
or 'Obsessive Disorientation Disorder'

Symptoms

- Disorganised thought
- Inflexible about orientation
- Pervasive pattern of lostness
- Attention-seeking (wants to be found)

FIGURE 20.1 The Lost Sheep, *2017. Courtesy Dolly Sen.*

Study after study – those not funded by stigma campaigns – show anti-stigma campaigns to have weak or no significant positive influence, and that any effectiveness dissipates over time (e.g. Walsh & Foster 2021). These campaigns also have an unanticipated consequence: promoting the biomedical framework of mental ill health alienates the general public from those people that anti-stigma campaigns are supposed to help, fostering the belief that such people are 'different'. I was part of the *Time to Change* campaign in its first year. In fact, I was part of their first major publicity stunt: turning the inside of a Sheffield commuter train into a padded cell, and planting volunteers with various mental health conditions (me being one of them) to engage bemused commuters in conversations about mental health. It was an interesting experience, as everyone I talked to had their own story to tell about either their own mental health or the mental health of someone they loved. You get such deep, honest responses if you don't bring shame into the equation, something of which psychiatrists should take note.

Most people I spoke with admitted to struggling with their mental health and worrying about loved ones who were going through those kinds of difficulties. Another volunteer spoke with a teenage girl on her way to school who had just lost her mum to suicide. It was heartbreaking, and all the more painful because I knew many people who had taken their own lives. *Time to Change*'s advice – to ask for help from services that will ignore you, dismiss you or tell you to go for a walk in that darkest of times – is breathtakingly cruel. *Time to Change* stopped using me as an ambassador when I questioned why we couldn't challenge discriminatory and stigmatizing attitudes from mental health staff. Everyone who has been a patient of psychiatry knows that the system regularly dispenses demeaning and defaming encounters. I was told the campaign needed the mental health system as a partner and if we were critical, we would alienate them. *What crap!* I have worked in the psychiatric system as both a peer and a clinician; everyone knows there are colleagues who treat patients badly. Wouldn't being part of a service that tackled this bad practice be something to be proud of? There is something desperately toxic about an organization's unwillingness to address behaviour that causes pain in the people for whom they are supposed to care.

The other institution seemingly off-limits for criticism is the government, even when it demonizes disabled people by labelling them scroungers to justify benefit cuts, or makes decisions that keep mad people powerless, poor and pained. Although individual stigma and discrimination is hurtful, discrimination and stigma by systems is the bigger monster. No government is going to champion or fund a campaign which highlights the damage they knowingly inflict upon countless mad people. Instead, they sponsor campaigns fronted by millionaire celebrities to be spokespeople for the lives of the vilified and lonely poor.

I have always wondered what the person on the street truly thinks about mental health and madness. For that reason, I decided to create *Bedlamb*: a bed covered in cuddly sheep, placed in a public place so that I could invite people to sit with me, tell me what they think causes mental distress or madness, and what we can do about it. *Bedlamb* is named in reference to Bedlam, the nickname for the original Bethlem psychiatric hospital in London, and also a word that means 'uproar and confusion'. I included sheep because I've always loved them; it might be their innocence – lambs prancing like fluffy clouds in spring meadows, despite being destined to be killed for our dinner. I thought putting *Bedlamb* at the current Bethlem Hospital was a good place to start, and it just so happened that I was curating a show on art and protest at the Bethlem Gallery on the hospital site. I installed the bed and sheep under the famous raving and melancholy statues, and invited visitors to get into bed with madness and me (Figure 20.2).

I knew I would encounter people who were interested and well-versed in art, mental health and activism at Bethlem Gallery; I also encountered a few dogs who gave me their deep thoughts. Most people who joined me on the *Bedlamb* at Bethlem thought that we needed social and political change for people to have better mental health and autonomy over their own being. For the acutely distressed, things that came up more than once were love, space, time, nature, the right to rage and be listened to. Most thought psychiatry was doing more harm than good.

I then took *Bedlamb* to Great Yarmouth in Norfolk, a deprived seaside town where I lived at the time. I parked the bed on a busy street. Once the first person was brave enough to get into bed with me, others happily followed suit. The responses I got here from the 'ordinary person' on the street were different from those at Bethlem Hospital. While people agreed that things like unemployment and poor or insecure housing harmed people's minds and

FIGURE 20.2 *A young girl telling Dolly that her brother made her mad,* Bedlamb, *Bethlem Hospital, 2019. Courtesy Dolly Sen.*

hearts, most believed the answer was putting more money into mental health services. This is the thing about mental health campaigning – unless you have direct experience of the psychiatric system, who is going to believe a bunch of nutters over doctors and nurses? This is why art is essential to get the message across. Our stories have to be told in ways that are hard to ignore.

The older I get, the less I believe that the mental health system can be fixed in its current form. It is a self-indulgent monster, and making minor changes to it would be like giving etiquette lessons to a savage beast. It needs to be demolished and created again from scratch. The first step: let the lunatics take over the asylum, and let medicine take a backseat.

In the meantime, I fight for my life and a world that doesn't drive people to despair. I am a flame who is not ashamed of the light I shed, even if it is different to that of others. With my fellow survivors, I want us to shine so that we embarrass the moon, the stars, the sun. I want us to shine as hard as we can – not only to cast light on the millions of flames extinguished by psychiatry before us but also to blaze a trail for those ahead of us, so that those in pain find love, rather than more anguish and distress.

Notes

1 *Time to Change* was an anti-stigma campaign launched in the UK in 2007, and which ran until March 2021. Legacy information available online: https://www .time-to-change.org.uk/ (accessed 3 August 2021).

2 According to the *OED*, 'worried well' describes 'people who are excessively and unnecessarily concerned about their physical or mental health'.

References

Maines, R.P. (1999), *The Technology of Orgasm: "Hysteria", the Vibrator, and Women's Sexual Satisfaction*, Baltimore: The Johns Hopkins University Press.

Sen, D. (2017), *DSM 69: Dolly Sen's Manual of Psychiatric Disorder*, London: Eleusinian Press.

Walsh, D.A.B and J.L.H. Foster (2021), 'A Call to Action. A Critical Review of Mental Health Related Anti-Stigma Campaigns', *Frontiers in Public Health*, 8: 569539.

Watson, J., (ed.) (2019), *Drop the Disorder: Challenging the Culture of Psychiatric Diagnosis*, Monmouth: PCCS Books.

CHAPTER 21

Super-fast augmented anxiety

Clive Parkinson

Let us know if you have any feelings of depression or mania, Clive. But what of crystalline clarity – and what of reverie, doctor?

Reverie #1: A field in Boree Creek (the recent past)

Not so long ago, I stood in a parched field in some remote corner of New South Wales with the artist Vic McEwan, having our photograph taken. The sun was setting on us as we stood almost side by side in front of a large Kurrajong tree. We'd been planning a long-term work exploring suicide and grief. Our slow, expansive approach involved gentle conversations with people who had been through the turmoil that surrounds the extremes of mental distress. I am distracted again by my own brother's death a decade ago. Pausing to take a breath, I become aware of a pain in my side, my ribs. Something and nothing. Vic wears a wide-brimmed hat, I do not. The shutter clicks away (Figure 21.1).

That year, I shuddered through the air, buffeted by turbulence on so many occasions without giving a thought to my body or the earth beneath me; prehistoric times when it was easy just to be. The fissures – those we ignored and those that took us off guard – were there, if we'd chosen to see and hear, but now they've spread and run out of control. The twitching anxieties of a world unravelling.

I'll take your drugs if I must, but isn't it true, the medication makes you feel worse than the illness?

FIGURE 21.1 *Vic McEwan and Clive Parkinson, Boree Creek, 2019. Courtesy Vic McEwan.*

Bortezomib
Dexamethasone
Thalidomide

Reverie #2: Before the storm, the Scottish Highlands (the recent past)

I've driven for over ten hours across this failing island in its last days of Europe, to some remote northwestern corner. In part a family holiday, in part an attempt to corral ideas: to cut and paste my thinking into some semblance of order. My much-craved isolation means resources for this work are reduced. I scratch out notes for this chapter with a plastic ballpoint pen. An assemblage – not smooth and linear but disjointed and sometimes uncomfortable, each exploration bleeding into the next. So, I start with what I know to be real and true.

I am in a garden overlooking the Inner Sound between the Isle of Raasay and the isolated mainland hamlet of Camusterrach. I sit by the deepest section of the UK's seas, a little peninsula on the edge of an invisible coastal abyss. The sky is heavy with fast-scudding clouds, but the late summer air is fresh and cool. Grey smears of rain begin to lash the Cuillin Hills on the Isle of Skye. A small fishing boat turns circles in the bay, net cast deep.

I am fifty-six years old and my life is temporary, as is the garden of the old croft in which I sit. Slow-spreading lichen covers the stones of this garden wall that will one day be washed away by the sea; stone, bone and plastic ground into the fundaments of another planetary era.

Against ageing and death

In his only novel, *The Picture of Dorian Gray* (1890), Oscar Wilde presciently explored the lengths to which an individual might go to preserve their youth, beauty and standing in the world. In Wilde's story it is Gray's portrait that ages while the protagonist himself – having sold his soul – lives a wild and dangerous life, never ageing, until of course, one day in a fit of pique he slashes the portrait with a knife. Gray suddenly ages horribly and dies, the portrait miraculously returned to its original eternal youthful beauty. This high Victorian camp translates easily into a twenty-first-century context, where youthfulness, beauty and vigour epitomize health and well-being, and the pursuit of flawless bodies is endlessly marketed.

The rise of cosmetic procedures has normalized the aspiration of eternal beauty and youth. The ageing face, no longer associated with experience and wisdom, is to be avoided at all costs. Botox is the poison of choice for 'preventative ageing' – as younger people request procedures to prevent wrinkle formation rather than to 'correct the ageing process' once wrinkles appear. Beyond the cosmetic, others cling to the fringes of gerontological science and the possibilities of breakthroughs that might extend human life. The Coalition for Radical Life Extension is a US organization whose vision – boldly set out on its home page – reads like Filippo Marinetti's *Manifesto of Futurism*:

> Stand Together
> For an unlimited future
> Against Ageing and Death.[1]

Describing itself as a not-for-profit organization, the Coalition brings like-minded people together 'to stand up for radical life extension and physical immortality'.[2] Led by preternaturally fresh-faced real estate investor James Strole, this group of predominantly white, wealthy, middle-aged men has a board with vested interests, including Liz Parrish, CEO of Bioviva: a company developing and selling advanced gene and cell therapeutics like the Bioviva *Timekeeper™ – Epigenetics Aging Test* retailing at $457.00.[3] Another board member, known only as Bernadeane, is the yin to Strole's yang, having lived an 'ageless lifestyle for over forty years' and hailed as the 'leading advocate for women and immortality'. Death as a personal catastrophe and not the natural end to life, well-marketed incitements to look 'ageless' – these have inevitable impacts on our interior landscape and how we rub alongside each other.

Neal and Chartrand (2011) explored the impact of cosmetic injections on our ability to recognize emotions in others. Their study examined the effect of both Botox and dermal fillers on facial feedback signals, and thus on the capacity to perceive emotion. They found that 'emotion perception was significantly impaired' in those that had received Botox, which reduces muscle feedback. A failure to mirror the facial expressions of people with whom you are engaging compromises the ability to *understand* what they might be feeling.

Epidemics and empathy

The word 'epidemic' is often co-opted by the media to describe an escalating global mental health crisis. From stress and anxiety to depression and psychoses, it feels as if everyone's mental health is fractured and unravelling. Worse still, we are told that Covid-19 has unleashed a fast-approaching 'tsunami' of mental illness (Roxby 2020).

In 2017, the Institute for Health Metrics Evaluation (IHME) Global Burden of Diseases study (GBD) reported some 300 million people suffering from anxiety worldwide, about 160 million with major depressive disorder and another 100 million with milder forms of depression. That means around 13 per cent of the global population – some 971 million people – experienced some kind of mental 'disorder' (Rice-Oxley 2019).

The language of mental illness and difference is used to explain all manner of day-to-day anxieties. Yet, in a series exploring mental health in 2019, *The Guardian* falls back on the default biochemical model, stating in unequivocal terms that mental illness 'is not a disease of western capitalism' (Rice-Oxley 2019). Many would disagree. Psychologist Peter Kinderman (2015) argues that diagnoses are often 'used as pseudo-explanations for troubling behaviours' that frame mental illness as a 'pathology of the body'. As such they risk 'ignoring any psychological meaning in people's "disordered" responses and experiences', and limiting people's ability to 'understand how they might use their own resources to address their difficulties' (Kinderman 2015).

Kinderman and colleagues offer a stark critique of dominant systems of diagnosis and treatment. They reason: '(t)he death of a loved one can lead to a profound and long-lasting grieving process. War is hell. [So] in what sense is it a "disorder" if we remain distressed by bereavement after 3 months or if we are traumatised by the experience of industrialised military conflict?' (Kinderman et al. 2013). They suggest we start by acknowledging that distress is not *ab*normal, but a normal response to difficult circumstances. There is no resistance here to the fact that mental illnesses are centred in the brain, but any attempt to understand behaviour solely through reductive biomedical models obscures the causal role of social and other factors, and risks harm through stigma and social exclusion. Kinderman's argument is persuasive. Our psychosocial contexts and wider environmental and cultural factors demand our attention.

While evidence points to more people experiencing stress, anxiety and trauma during the current pandemic, the approaching 'tsunami' of mental illness seems like a product of lazy journalism. Clinical Psychologist Richard Bentall suggests that, with all its bleak implications, this doom-laden narrative 'carries the risk of becoming a self-fulfilling prophecy':

> we know from previous research that individual, interpersonal traumas (for example, sexual assaults) are far more mentally damaging than collective traumas such as natural disasters. This is at least in part because strong social bonds protect people against stress and, during a crisis, people often come together to help each other, creating a sense of belonging and a shared identity with neighbours. (Bentall 2021)

Seeing mental illness as an individual biochemical problem locates the individual and their faulty chemistry as a mechanism for change, feeding the burgeoning pharmaceutical industry, whose medications serve to create a complaint workforce.

Perhaps the 'epidemic of despair', a term coined by Elizabeth Stein and colleagues (2017), captures what is really at play. Their work revealed that an upward trend in premature deaths among white Americans living in rural areas largely resulted from 'self-destructive health behaviours likely related to underlying social and economic factors in these communities' (2017). Most 'were attributable to suicide, poisoning, and liver disease', the authors noting that while social programmes have generally improved health trends for people from working-class backgrounds in other countries, America lagged behind.

Psychologist Oliver James (2008) suggests that toxic capitalism reinforces the belief that the key to fulfilment is material affluence, seemingly available to anyone willing to work hard enough – if you do not succeed, you yourself are to blame. Bentall (2021) proposes that it is the *economic* threats of the current pandemic that are most closely linked with symptoms of mental ill health.

Rejecting the biomedical approach to understanding mental illness, the cultural critic Mark Fisher argued that our current 'mental health plague' cannot be understood or treated as a matter of individual 'psychological distress' (2009: 19). Fisher affirmed that '(a)ffective disorders are forms of captured discontent; this disaffection can and must be channeled outwards, directed towards its real cause, Capital' (Fisher 2009: 80). Fisher's colleague Alex Niven described how being on temporary contracts made Mark himself 'a kind of precarious labourer on the fringes of academia' (Niven quoted in Cowley 2019), echoing Fisher's own reflections that work culture is impoverished and punitive. It is unsurprising then that the Research Excellence Framework – the mechanism for measuring academic excellence in the UK – assigned a low score to Fisher's 2009 *magnum opus*, *Capitalist Realism*. Fisher experienced bouts of clinical depression through his life, and killed himself in 2017.

Albert Camus' *The Myth of Sisyphus* offers the clearest literary description of the grinding social factors that push people into blank states of day-to-day oppression/depression:

> Rising, streetcar, four hours in the office or the factory, meal, streetcar, four hours of work, meal, sleep, and Monday Tuesday Wednesday Thursday Friday Saturday according to the same rhythm – this path is easily followed most of the time. But one day the 'why' arises, and everything begins in that weariness tinged with amazement. (Camus 1955: 10)

Home has become a 24/7 workplace, and the technology enabling this feeds a culture of constant and compulsive connection – in work and in pleasure. Continuous connectivity confuses the personal and the professional while offering up solutions to life's ills. Rather than making us gregarious and productive, our networked identity is more likely rendering us an 'invisible actor at the centre of the world' (Firth 2007: 109).

In 2010, 21-year-old Swedish student Marcus Jannes began posting on Facebook that he was lonely and, by his own account, vulnerable. He was having suicidal thoughts and altered his status to say that life was too difficult. After a six-month period of mounting distress, Marcus posted a message to the Mental Health Problems forum of Sweden's *Flashback* message boards, stating that he had taken prescription drugs and paracetamol and would be hanging himself, using a webcam to record the event so that others could watch. People began responding, some offering him words of support, some attempting to distract him. Others, however, goaded Marcus, coaxing him to stop talking and get on with it. His final post on *Flashback* was, 'Alright, let's do it', as he is seen securing a computer network cable over a doorway. Marcus' suicide was live-streamed over the next five minutes as people continued to post comments. It was only after another fifteen minutes that an online user asked, 'Did someone call the police?' By the time this thread was locked by a site moderator, it had received a total of 630 posts over 53 pages. In her critique of those who commented, watched, trolled and failed to call emergency services to help Marcus, police spokesperson Lotta Thyni commented that police cannot control how people use online fora, which, she suggests, 'lack empathy'.

Marcus Jannes' troubling suicide is not the only online story of its kind. Since his death, websites dedicated to suicide and self-harm have flourished.

Some are undoubtably well-meaning, but others provide a home for more troubling thinking around the extremes of mental difference and human vulnerability. There was a bitter irony in Jannes' use of computer networking cable as the ligature which would end his life. The very means of modern communication – its hardware – became the material that extinguished life. His death, a literal ghost in the machine; a terrible and seemingly permanent online haunting.

Diet lollipops and candy-coloured vitamins

The pandemic has blurred the edges of our individual and shared realities. Our vulnerabilities – physical and emotional – seep to the surface, and all the while we look for reassurance from our familiars: the phone in our palms, the screens in our homes. Seemingly connected, more often isolated, talking to shadows and reflections of ourselves and our circles of influence.

According to market and consumer data, '(i)n 2021, the number of mobile devices operating worldwide stood at almost 15 million', a number predicted to reach 18.22 billion by 2025.[4] When Harriet Griffey (2018) analysed data gathered from the UK's telecoms regulator *Ofcom*, it suggested that 'people check their smart phones on average every 12 minutes during their waking hours, with 71% . . . never turn(ing) their phone off and 40% . . . check(ing) them within five minutes of waking'. Griffey uses a term coined by former Apple and Microsoft consultant Linda Stone – 'continuous partial attention' or CPA, which already sounds like a habit waiting to be classified in the next *Diagnostic and Statistical Manual of Mental Disorders*. Griffey argues that

> we exist in a constant state of alertness that scans the world but never really gives our full attention to anything. In the short term, we adapt well to these demands, but in the long term the stress hormones adrenaline and cortisol create a physiological hyper-alert state that is always scanning for stimuli, provoking a sense of addiction temporarily assuaged by checking in. (Griffey 2018)

The smartphone industry has swiftly responded by creating a swathe of digital apps to help monitor our online behaviour, restrict our use and advise us of our bedtime. Not only can we account for every waking moment in the cult of the quantified self, but our phones can lull us to sleep with white noise, set our alarms while gently monitoring our circadian rhythms.

According to their own data, 1 billion people use the social media platform Instagram every month, with more than half of those using it every day. In her analysis of the cult of social media celebrity, Irina Dumitrescu (2019) highlights the central place of the Kardashian/Jenner family. As a coercive force for self-promotion, this extended family are currently selling 'laxative teas, diet lollipops and candy-coloured vitamins' (Dumitrescu 2019). Dumitrescu cautions that we 'turn to celebrities to feel emotion, connection and even transcendence' (Dumitrescu 2019) – even as that connection is distorted by the dampened emotional feedback of cosmetically augmented celebrity faces, or by a distributed model of 'friendship' quantified only in 'likes'.

In an interview broadcast by the BBC in 2005, playwright Dennis Potter warned that 'capitalism now is actually about selling all of you to all of you – but they don't know what it is they're selling – the only object is to keep in the game'.

In place of fear: Social prescriptions or social movements?

Within the cult of well-being, does the role of the arts amount to more than a prescription – a formula for 'feeling good'? Like the mindful colouring books that swamped the market a few years ago, the anodyne arts and health agenda is often missing a kick of adrenaline; a hit that might be provided by *people*, in all their diversity. Much well-intentioned work justifies its purpose and impact through biomedical scrutiny, which for all its usefulness is dull, often evangelical and second rate. In the UK, the arts organization Aesop[5] (not to be confused with the soap manufacturer) uses the language of a conjoined free-market-scientism to instrumentalize the arts. Slipping 'enterprise' and 'purpose' into its acronym, Arts Enterprise with a Social Purpose relies on rousing managerial jargon to sell its product: decision makers, measurement, tools, market development. In truth, its ethos and work feel less in harmony with the cultural sector and more arts and health by government decree; a blind-belief in standardized, cost-efficient products. This represents a distinct deficit of vision, a closing down and restraining of the essential experimental nature of the arts, which is in fact the key to how all of the arts – not just those focusing on illness – might be the nuanced, rich determinants of health and well-being in our communities.

In the period immediately after the Second World War, the Arts Council of Great Britain and the National Health Service emerged from a period of terrible austerity, not dissimilar in scale to the cumulative trauma and economic repercussions that the pandemic is seeding. These institutions flourished as part of a grand vision for The Welfare State (Beveridge 1942) through a process eloquently described by NHS architect Nye Bevan in his sweeping overview of the period: *In Place of Fear* (1952). Bevan held a view that artists of all types had a key role in contemporary society and that

> Someday under the impulse of collective action, we shall enfranchise the artists, by giving them our public buildings to work upon . . . it is tiresome

to listen to the diatribes of some modern art critics who bemoan the passing of the rich patron as though this must mean the decline of art whereas it could mean its emancipation, if the artists were restored to their proper relationship with civic life. (Bevan 1952)

In 1934 Bevan married the Scots politician Jennie Lee, who later became Minister for the Arts between 1964 and 1970. Lee was the driving force behind the 1965 white paper, *A Policy for the Arts: The First Steps*; the UK's first national cultural policy. Through their shared vision for health services and culture in everyone's lives, Lee and Bevan arguably sowed the seeds of what would eventually become an arts and health agenda. Increasing government funding to the arts by 30 per cent, Lee wanted the arts, like education, to be available locally, regionally and nationally: to the many, not just the few. In the introduction to her white paper, she stresses the importance of the role of artists and the need for the state to honour the complexity and sometimes provocative nature of the arts:

> The relationship between artists and State in a modern democratic community is not easily defined. No one would wish state patronage to dictate taste or in any way restrict the liberty of even the most unorthodox of experimental artists. (Bevan 1952)

This is a bold statement, especially considering it would be another fifty years before any British government would publish another culture white paper (Department for Digital, Culture, Media & Sport 2016). Drawn up in another era of austerity, the 2016 white paper provides far less passion and vision, other than offering to 'ensure that publicly-funded cultural events and programmes have a cumulative positive effect on health; and to respond to the recommendations of the All-Party Parliamentary Group on Arts, Health and Wellbeing (APPG) when it reports on arts and health policy next year' (Department for Digital, Culture, Media & Sport 2016). In 2017, the APPG produced a report, 'Creative Health: The Arts for Health & Wellbeing', which included a bullet-point list of 'recommendations' to the arts and health community. It made no attempt to wrest money from the government but rather, in the words of then Secretary of State for Health Matt Hancock, presented as 'saving the NHS money because many of these social cures are cheaper or free . . . and it's the role of the state to sponsor the treatments that are often cheaper, better for patients, and better for society' (Hancock 2018).

Cost-efficiencies and undervaluing artists appear central to this new agenda. In the midst of feverish attempts to quantify arts-related health outcomes, a number of researchers with scientific backgrounds have stepped up to the plate. At the head of the pack is psycho-neuro-immunologist Dr Daisy Fancourt, who – through numerous research articles, a synthesis of arts and health research for the World Health Organization and recommendations for the UK government – holds a biomedical lens to the arts and instrumentalizes its impact.

This bland and prescriptive reductionist model fails to take into account how arts and culture resist crude measurements, and how health isn't always best understood by clinical health outcomes, but through factors like social connectedness, lived experience, invisible histories and oppression. Research should nurture diverse opinion – enabling often-silenced voices to be heard and to inform new thinking. It should resist the dominant paradigm and the constraints that medical models arrogantly impose on human creativity. What of contemporary artists pursuing a social agenda in this increasingly narrow field? What of experimentation understood through the language of its own medium? What of reimagining and disrupting ideas about health, our bodies and minds; our histories and futures?

Portraits of Recovery is a visual arts charity and project directed by Mark Prest, which uses photo portraiture to dispel myths and challenge stigmas surrounding recovery from substance use. For this project, Ali Zaidi produced a series of photographic images and short films, including *Per te Mamma* (2014): a film featuring a letter written by Italian participant, Alessandro, to his mother. It's a powerful expression of shame and love; a letter Alessandro wishes he had sent, but never did. Running for less than three minutes, the film focuses on Alessandro's hands as he holds the letter and reads it aloud (in Italian). No translation is provided. Only at the end does the camera reveal his face. A challenge, a confession, direct eye-to-eye contact with the viewer. This film communicates the fragility of human experience, and for Prest, it was the beginning of a long and fruitful artistic exploration of the lived experience of his and others' recovery.

As part of this project, I had the privilege of working with participants across the UK, Italy and Turkey to collectively explore how to give voice to shared experiences and aspirations. Rejecting passivity and resisting the blame and criminality commonly associated with 'addiction', our collective approach gave birth to the term 'recoverism', and a shared *Recoverist Manifesto*. This cut-and-paste international polemic was created in real time – not mediated by screens and phones, but in a relational and embodied process. It calls for those demonized by intolerant attitudes and internalized shame to understand themselves as more than passive recipients of state-sponsored treatment programmes. As with modernist art movements, recoverism argues for social change in which people themselves are central, and where art amplifies the story of social transformation. Recoverism moves away from clichéd representations of addiction, reframing it as a cultural and civil-rights movement.

Reverie #3: Agents of change

In the dead of night and through pitch-black driving rain, I drive my children over one of the highest mountain passes in Scotland – the *Bealach na Bà* – for an early flight from Inverness. The clouds are denser than any fog we've known. It's terrifying, this mountain pass, and exhilarating. Then the children are gone. The rain pours. The sea reaches heights I've not seen before. I sense our very foundations slipping; a different kind of gravity.

Back in the socially distanced thick of things – where the mismanaged pandemic has wreaked its havoc – it's as if I've never been away.

In the United States, another knee to another throat and a life is snuffed out. A family is compensated, a murderer is sent to jail, but it's not enough. One of the founders of Black Lives Matter (BLM), Patrisse Cullors, argues that love and activism are drivers of social change.[6] BLM treads similar ground to the Black Panther Party, blurring the lines between community activism and culture. Building explicitly on the legacy of Dr Martin Luther King, BLM seeks to honour the dignity and humanity of Black lives by centring 'life, love, joy, rest, and pleasure', as systemic inequalities and police brutality underpin a very natural civic unrest.[7] BLM thrives and expands globally, gaining momentum via a social media movement (#BlackLivesMatter) that 'goes beyond symbolic slacktivism' (Williams, Mezey & Singh 2021).

Human rights activist Peter Tatchell – outraged by a dictator whose country criminalizes homosexuality – throws himself in front of the dictator's convoy, his head under the wheel of the president's car. His well-placed anger at systemic homophobia propels him to dangerous and performative activism. Tracey Emin tells the story of her cancer diagnosis in ink, paint and testimony – piss, blood and fear – confronting the extraordinary normality of being alive. Climate change activist Greta Thunberg declares Asperger's her superpower, and galvanizes young people to challenge authority. *Extinction Rebellion* (XR) emerges as a social movement with performance and cultural interventions at its heart, adopting many of the self-organizing principles from community arts interventions in the 1960s and 1970s. Artist Julie Shiels (2019) suggests that XR blurs the boundaries between mass participation and theatrical disruption, where its 'posters, street theatre, music and symbolic actions are part of the vocabulary of calls for social and political change'.

These people, these social movements, draw links between personal, social and planetary health, and see the world beyond selfish individualism. Artists all? Some of them certainly, others perhaps not in the sense we're used to, dictated by systems that neatly compartmentalize us. But these people are all agents of change, speaking truth to power, confronting us with anger and with love, offering performance as activism, urging us to question dominant forces – more often than not, to the detriment of their own physical and mental well-being.

We are faced with a responsibility for action in the here and now. Not unlike Emin, I find myself inhabiting that amplified zone of self-awareness where the present moment has never felt so real and sensate. I am an occupant of the hyperreal present tense, where the fragility of society is illuminated with phosphorescent clarity.

Fucked-up, insecure, neurotic and emotional

As Boree Creek and the Scottish Highlands fade, that persistent pain in my side turns into a diagnosis; diagnosis into a prognosis; prognosis into a new curiosity about the here and now. The pandemic and an invisible change in my body have run seamlessly together. As the pandemic shows no sign of abating – assimilating into new versions of something 'we'll have to live with' – so too the thing that affects my body is something that will never go away.

Laid low in a hospital bed with tubes of plastic worming their way through me as I am infused with toxins to sedate my cancer for a while, stem-cells harvested from my blood are set free again in my roots and bones and imagination. An enforced isolation is imposed. As the world unravels outside my windows, the walls of my room are assertively self-curated, bringing meaning into this clinical space. Places and people I love are like the religious icons of another time. I scratch outlines about this unequal world and my reimagined place in it while another kind of line, pushed into an arm, delivers its knock-out blow.

'Let us know if you feel nauseous', they say, 'we can give you things for that'.
'But what of my imagination, doctor?'

'It will settle – you'll be *fine*.'* The victim of some strange elective mugging sprawled flat on a hospital bed; curiosity runs through my veins. A mix of poisons and possibilities surge. I erase all traces of Litvinenko's fading smile; of the market's co-option of AIDS activist David Kirby's dying moments (Grenova 2016).

This closer relationship to death has disrupted my imagination, made me alive to nowness and more curious than I've ever been. I am rewilded, sustained by the land, trees and skies, by the possibilities of collective kindness, of care and hope.

However uncertain the future, the present drive of social movements will come to be seen as having redefined socially engaged arts practice and direct action. Perhaps too, this could be the moment when the arts and health agenda accepts social change as central to its vision, shifting from narrow individualism towards environmental conceptions of public health. That clarion call from Bevan (1952) and Lee (1965) for the emancipation of artists and the impulse for collective action rings true and clear. But

FIGURE 21.2 *Still from* Still Life, *Sam Taylor-Johnson, 2001. Courtesy Sam Taylor-Johnson.*

artists aren't our saviours. Perhaps they're alchemists, mixing traumas and anxieties, lusts and desires, creating images, movements, thoughts and ideas in which we – in all our complex differences and similarities – might participate, as we are infected with new possibilities for individual and collective change.

I think of a slowly evolving time-lapse film, *Still Life* (2001) by Sam Taylor-Johnson, a three-minute, forty-four-second record of fruit and its super-fast, super-slow decay (Figure 21.2). The work is a meditation on impermanence; a contemporary reimagining of a sixteenth-century *vanitas* and of what traces we might leave behind. It captures something of our stuttering present tense, the grinding of our synthetic lives like tectonic plates, a predictive fossil-record of the future. When all the ripe fruit in *Still Life* has decayed, what remains solid and seemingly permanent? A plastic ballpoint pen.

* Recoverists say people always tell them everything will be *fine*. But they define FINE as: Fucked-Up, Insecure, Neurotic and Emotional.

Notes

1 See the 'Coalition for Radical Life Extension' website: https://www.rlecoalition .com/ (accessed 25 August 2021).

2 Ibid.

3 See the Bioviva website: https://bioviva-science.com/collections/products (accessed 25 August 2021).

4 See the Statista website: https://www.statista.com/statistics/245501/multiple
   -mobile-device-ownership-worldwide/ (accessed 25 August 2021).

5 See the Black Lives Matter website: https://blacklivesmatter.com/black-lives-matter
   -global-network-launches-new-mlk-artist-series/ (accessed 25 August 2021).

6 Ibid.

7 See the Aesop website: https://ae-sop.org/ (accessed 8 September 2021).

References

Bentall, R. (2021), 'Has the Pandemic Really Caused a "tsunami" of Mental Health
   Problems?', *The Guardian*, 09 February 2021. Available online: https://www
   .theguardian.com/commentisfree/2021/feb/09/pandemic-mental-health-problems
   -research-coronavirus (accessed 20 August 2021).
Bevan, A. (1952), *In Place of Fear*, London: Heinemann.
Camus, Albert (1955), *The Myth of Sisyphus and Other Essays*, translated by
   J. O'Brien, New York: Random House.
Cowley, J. (2019), '"Mark Fisher was the Intellectual Leader of a Generation":
   Alex Niven on Lost Futures, Englishness and Corbynism', *The New Statesman*,
   20 November 2019. Available online: https://www.newstatesman.com/politics/
   uk/2019/11/mark-fisher-was-intellectual-leader-generation (accessed 20 August
   2021).
Department for Digital, Culture, Media and Sport (2016), *The Culture White
   Paper* [White Paper], Crown. Available online: https://www.gov.uk/government/
   publications/culture-white-paper (accessed 25 August 2021).
Dumitrescu, I. (2019), 'Heel Turns: The History of Modern Celebrity', *Times
   Literary Supplement*, 20 September 2019. Available online: https://www.the
   -tls.co.uk/articles/modern-celebrity-history-kardashians/ (accessed 25 August
   2021).
Firth, C. (2007), *Making up the Mind: How the Brain Creates our Mental World*,
   London: Blackwell.
Fisher, M. (2009), *Capitalist Realism: Is There no Alternative?* Winchester: Zero
   Books.
Grenova, A. (2016), 'The Story Behind the Colorization of a Controversial
   Benetton AIDS Ad', *TIME*, 14 December 2016. Available online: https://time
   .com/4592061/colorization-benetton-aids-ad/ (accessed 27 September 2021).
Griffey, J. (2018). 'The Lost Art of Concentration: Being Distracted in a Digital
   World', *The Guardian*, 14 October 2018. Available online: https://www
   .theguardian.com/lifeandstyle/2018/oct/14/the-lost-art-of-concentration-being
   -distracted-in-a-digital-world (accessed 25 August 2021).
Hancock, M. (2018), 'The Power of the Arts and Social Activities to Improve the
   Nation's Health', transcript of speech delivered on 6 November 2018. Available
   online: https://www.gov.uk/government/speeches/the-power-of-the-arts-and
   -social-activities-to-improve-the-nations-health (accessed 25 August 2021).
James, O. (2008), *The Selfish Capitalist: Origins of Affluenza*, London: Vermillion.
Kinderman, P. (2015), 'Imagine There's No Diagnosis, it's Easy if You Try',
   Psychopathology Review, 2 (1): 154–61.

Kinderman, P., J. Read, J. Moncrieff, and R.P. Bentall (2013), 'Drop the Language of Disorder', *Evidence-Based Mental Health*, 16: 2–3.

Lee, J. (1965), *A Policy for the Arts: The First Steps* [White paper], London: HMSO.

Neal, D.T. and T.L. Chartrand (2011), 'Embodied Emotion Perception: Amplifying and Dampening Facial Feedback Modulates Emotion Perception Accuracy', *Social Psychological and Personality Science*, 2 (6): 673–8.

Rice-Oxley, M. (2019), 'Mental Illness: Is There Really a Global Epidemic?', *The Guardian*, 03 June 2019. Available online: https://www.theguardian.com/ society/2019/jun/03/mental-illness-is-there-really-a-global-epidemic (accessed 20 August 2021).

Roxby, P. (2020), 'Psychiatrists Fear "tsunami" of Mental Illness After Lockdown', *BBC News*, 16 May 2020. Available online: https://www.bbc.co.uk/news/health -52676981 (accessed 20 August 2021).

Shiels, J. (2019), 'Extinction Rebellion: How to Craft a Protest Brand', *The Conversation*, 06 October 2019. Available online: https://theconversation.com/ extinction-rebellion-how-to-craft-a-protest-brand-123084 (accessed 20 August 2021).

Stein, E.M., K.P. Gennuso, D.C. Ugboaja, and P.L. Remington (2017), 'The Epidemic of Despair Among White Americans: Trends in the Leading Causes of Premature Death, 1999–2015', *American Journal of Public Health*, 107: 1541–7.

Williams, J. B, N. Mezey, and L. Singh (2021), '#BlackLivesMatter—Getting From Contemporary Social Movements to Structural Change', *12 California Law Revue Online*, 1 June 2021. Available online: https://www.californialawreview .org/blacklivesmatter-getting-from-contemporary-social-movements-to -structural-change (accessed 26 August 2021).

INDEX

NOTE: Page references in italics refer to figures.

Aboriginals. *See* First Nations
    Australians
acousmatic sound   11, 211–20
activism   269–72. *See also* resistance
    political   267–8
Adams, Kate
    The Not Knowing of Another
      (video installation)   8, 239–41,
      246, 247
Aesop (Arts Enterprise with a Social
    Purpose)   267
aesthetic   4, 8, 103–4, 108–9
aesthetic intelligence   56, 101, 108
aesthetic third   42, 44
affect. *See* emotion/affect
affective community   156
affordances   9, 10, 11–12, 94–5, 101,
    103, 105, 107–10
afterwardsness   105
ageing   262–3
agency
    assertion of   19, 84
    building/restoration of   11, 96–9,
      144–5, 202–3, 204–5
    civic   141–2
    creative   59–61, 105, 155, 160–1
    embodied   168, 170, 176
    for social change   269–71
    visual embodiment   31–2
AIDS   144–5
alarm sounds   229–30
alexithymia   206
Alford, C. Fred   44, 108
All-Party Parliamentary Group on
    Arts, Health and Wellbeing
    (APPG)   268

American Psychiatric Association
    *Diagnostic and Statistical Manual
      of Mental Disorders*   12 n.2,
      254–5
Anderson, Tom   72
animation
    Unnerved   187–9
anosognosia   20–1
anti-Blackness   139, 149
anti-stigma campaigns   255–7
anxiety   186–7, 263
apartheid   157
architecture
    of healing   135–6
    as torture   134–5, 136–7
artificial memory   22
arts and health   3–10, 46–7
    and social change   267–72
arts/art process
    as generative process   59–60
    as healing in itself   154, 155
    as reparative process   154–5,
      159–62
arts-based psychosocial design   9,
    93–5, 101, 107, 109
    'trauma informed'   11–12, 167–8,
      176
Arts Council of Great Britain   267
art therapy
    detained refugees   137
    effectiveness of   20
    for PTSD   23–4
asylum seekers. *See* detention (indefinite)
Atkinson, Judy   153–4, 155
attachment theory   56–8, 60–1, 63–4,
    186, 188

Australia. *See also* Aboriginals
    assimilationist policy   156–7
    refugee policy   126–7, 134
    reparation measures   158
autobiographical memory
    and suicidality   25, 29–30
auto-ethnography   197–207
Awkward Conversations   93, 95–101,
    119

Bandura, Albert   31
beauty (eternal)   262
Beck, Aaron T.   33
Beck Hopelessness Scale   33
Behrouz, Boochani
    Chauka, Please Tell Us the Time
        (film)   130, *131*
    No Friend but the Mountains   126,
        128–30
Benedetti, Fabrizio   23
Benjamin, Jessica   100
Bennett, Jane   231–2
Bethlem Hospital (London)   257–8
Bevan, Nye   267–8, 271
Bhenji Ra   96
The Big Anxiety Festival   5–6, 9, 113
biological mechanisms   18, 20
Bion, Wilfred   10, 44, 94
    Leaning from Experience   51
Bioviva (firm)   262
birth practices   55–7
birth trauma   57–9, 63
Black Lives Matter (BLM)   270
blackness   221
Black women
    and police violence   143
Bollas, Christopher   3–4, 49, 56, 108
Bonase, Nomarussia   158
border violence   125–6, 131
botox   262, 263
Bouchard, Stéphane   31
Bowlby, John   186
breathing-with   231–3
Brennan, Cecily
    'Melancholia' (video artwork)   47
Brennan, Teresa   188
Bringing Them Home (BTH)
    inquiry   156
Burck, Charlotte   69

Cambodia   159–60
Camus, Albert
    The Myth of Sisyphus   265
capacity   42–3
capitalism   264–5, 266–7
care
    and arts   245–7
    Care Cafés   116–18
causal mechanisms   18–20, 101
children. *See also* Stolen Generations
    detention of Aboriginal
        children   140
    indefinite detention of   136
    institutional abuse of Aboriginal
        children   142
    suicide   24
    teen abuse   21–2
    trauma   250–1
choral singing   20
citations   146–7
Clegg, David   87
The Coalition for Radical Life
    Extension   262
co-design   6, 162
cognitive behavioural therapy (CBT)
    criticism of   22–5, 32
cognitive disability   243–4
colonialism   126–7, 128, 139
colonial violence   11, 24, 55, 57, 140
common third   42
complexity theory   18
confabulation   86–7
connection/connectivity   172–3,
    199–201
    and capitalism   267
    continuous   265–6
consciencism   142, 148
container-contained relationship   44,
    94, 106, 108, 200–1
containment   55–6, 94–5, 107–8,
    109–10
continuous connectivity   265–6
continuous partial attention   266
control
    Held Down, Expanding acousmatic
        sound project   214–17
    over narrative   105, 106–7, 130,
        161
    over self   31, 173, 176

and psychiatry 254
and refugees 174–5
conversations 93
at public venues 95–101 (*see also*
public conversations)
Coogan, Amanda
'Oh Chocolate' (art
performance) 47–8
co-regulation 186, 188–9
cosmetic procedures 262, 263
COVID-19 126, 245, 265–6, 271
economic threats of 264
lockdown 197–8
creativity/creative practice 11, 42,
62–3
agency for 59–61, 105, 155,
160–1
and care 245–7
and intuition 203–4
and partnership 60–1
as reparative practice 154–5,
159–62
as resistance 7, 125–37
Crenshaw, Kimberlé 143
critical psychiatry 7
cultural encounters case study
method 43–4
cultural experience 41–3, 188
Northern Ireland 45–51
curiosity 44, 52

Dadaab Refugee Camp (Kenya) 166
Daniel, Gwyn 69
Davies, Alex 29, 102
death 262–3
and imagination 271
premature 264
decolonization 126–30, 144
deep listening (*Dadirri*) 153–4, 157
deferred obedience 104–5
dementia 80–7
depression
art therapy 23–4
inexplicable 212–14
and overgeneral memory 25
postnatal 19–20
statistics on 263
Designing Reparations project
154–5

detention (indefinite) 7, 127, 131–7.
See also refugees
*Diagnostic and Statistical Manual
of Mental Disorders*
(DSM) 12n.2, 254–5
disabled/disability
achondroplasia dwarfism 99,
100–1
cognitive 243–4
government attitudes and
policy 257
disconnection 10–11, 154
refugee context 172–3
discrimination 255–7
disorders 12 n.2, 22–3, 254
DSM 254–5
indefinite detention refugees 131–2
medical model of 6–7
personality disorder 251–3
statistics 263
distress 19, 181–5
as normal response 263–4
public on causes for 257–8
and trauma transmission 58
Djuric, Bonney 102
Dumitrescu, Irina 266–7

earwork 27–8. *See also* listening-with
Edge of the Present (mixed
reality) 28–9, 30–5
education, denial of 140
ego death 199–201, 204
embodied experience 12
and animation 189
and virtual reality 168–76
embodied self 30, 205–6
EmbodiMap (VR experience) 168–76,
197–207
Emin, Tracey 270
emotions/affect 3–4, 8, 30–1
impact of cosmetic injections
on 263
and language 172
physiologic underpinnings of 188
positive 98–9
and suicide 25
empathy 83, 99–100, 139–40
lack of 265–6
enactive witnessing 232

entrainment 188–9
epidemics 263–6. *See also* COVID-19
epistemic modesty 244
epistemic responsibility 244
epistemophilia 44, 108
The Eradication of Schizophrenia in Western Lapland (theatre) 69, 70–1, 73–7
evidence 4–5, 141–2
exile 199
experience 4, 6
  of art 3–6
  inter-experience 8
  'learning from experience' 51, 101, 107–8
  pattern of 51
  transitions in 52
Extinction Rebellion (XR) (social movement) 270
Extraordinary Chambers in the Courts of Cambodia (ECCC) 159–60

Facebook 265
facilitating environments/spaces 9, 161
  of care 116–18
  and cultural experiences 43–4
  lack of 106
  notion of 94–5
  Parramatta site 103–4, 107
  and psychosocial design 93–4
  public settings as 95–100
Fairbairn, William Ronald Dodds 199
family drama 73–7
Fancourt, Daisy 268
fax machine, vocalization of 228–30
felt Experience and Empathy Lab (fEEL) 167, 192
films
  and advocacy 239–40
  Chauka, Please Tell Us the Time 130, *131*
  Illuminating the Wilderness 242, 243, 244, 246, 247, 248 n.3
  Melancholia 47
  Per te Mamma 269
  as reflective practice 241–2, 246, 247
  Searching for Aramsayesh Gah 126, 134–8

Small Axe 149
  on stigma surrounding recovery from substance use 269
  time-lapse film 272
  and trauma 50–1
First Nations Australians. *See also* Indigenous; Stolen Generations
  Anangu 154, 191–3
  concept of 'Country' 10, 57
  Dadirri 153–4
  institutional abuse 142
  life of 192–3
  mass over-incarceration of 140
  Tupul-Tupul (story) 192
  Uti Kulintjaku 154, 155, 191–2, 193, 194
  Wau-mananyi: The Song on the Wind (artwork) 154, 192–6
Fisher, Janina 168–9
Fisher, Mark 263–4
flashbacks 22, 23–4, 218
flash-forwards 29, 32
forced marriages 159–60
Freud, Sigmund 18
Fuchs, Phillippe 31
future thinking 24, 29, 30–2

gender-based violence 160
gene expression 25
Gerald, Mark 43
Gibson, James J. 101, 109
Giffney, Noreen and Eve Watson
  Clinical Encounters in Sexuality 52
Glesta, Anita
  Unnerved 187–9
  Untitled (painting) 181–3
Gobodo-Madikizela, Pumla 99–100, 154
Godden, Vanessa 219–20
Gould, Stephen Jay 18
grief 181–3
  as trigger for cardiac event 184–6
Griffey, Harriet 266
Groom, Amala 95

hallucinations 71, 83, 85, 86
Hancock, Matt 268
Harlem, Andrew 199

harm 7
    self-harm 103, 131–2 (*see also*
        suicide/suicidality)
    and witnessing 141–2, 149
Harpin, Anna 233 n.1
Hayes, Gypsie 102
heart 181–5
helplessness 200–1
    learned helplessness 31
Herman, Judith 172–3
Hibberd, Lily 102
historical trauma 155, 158
holding environment
    EmbodiMap 204–5
    lack of 106
    notion of 51, 97, 100–1, 203
    of not-ness 199
    of one-to-one conversation 99
    Parramatta site 103–4
    refugees 170–1, 176
Holmes, Emily 29
hopelessness 30
humour 253
Hustvedt, Siri 32
    'Suicide and the Drama of Self
        Consciousness' 30
hysteria 252

iatrogenic trauma 250–5
immersion 30, 86–7
immersive media 12, 22, 102
    The Visit 80–2, 83–5
impermanence 272
Indigenous 60, 64, 130, 145, 146–7,
    157. *See also* First Nations
    Australians
individuation 203
installation art 62–3. *See also*
    sound installations; video
    installations
Institute for Health Metrics Evaluation
    (IHME) Global Burden of
    Diseases (GBD) study 263
institutional abuse 7, 21–2, 93,
    102–9, 141
    psychiatric 224–5
institutional change 144
institutional racism 139–40, 142, 148
    and psychiatry 143–4

inter-experience 8
intergenerational trauma 11, 50
    breaking the cycle of 59–62
    and listening-with 227–8
    transmission of 55–6, 57–8
intersubjectivity 11, 83, 100, 211–12,
    219
isolation 173, 225–6
    listening in 211–12, 214–19
    and pandemic 266

James, Oliver 264
Janet, Pierre 171
Jannes, Marcus 265–6
Joseph, Betty 52
journalism 127–8

Kakuma Refugee Camp
    (Kenya) 166–7
Kane, Brian 218
Kardashian/Jenner family 266–7
Keenahan, Debra 95, 96, 99, 100–1,
    109
Khulumani Support Group 158,
    159
Kinderman, Peter 263–4
Klein, Melanie 108
knowing in action 182–4
knowing/unknowing 241–4, 246–7
knowledge sharing
    Alpiri 192–3, 194
Kuchelmeister, Volker 102
kyriarchal system 7, 129

LaBelle, Brandon 226
Lafargue Mental Hygiene Clinic
    (Harlem, New York) 144
Laing, Ronald David 4, 6, 8, 85
La MaMa Experimental Theatre Club
    (New York) 117
Langer, Susanne 21, 94
language
    of mental illness 263
    and psychiatry 254
    and trauma experience 171–2,
        206
learned helplessness 31
Lee, Jennie 268, 271
Leong, Dawn Joy 95

libraries   117–18
listening
  deep listening (*Dadirri*)   153–4,
    157
  in isolation   211–12, 214–19
listening-with   224–5
  breath tracks   232–3
  earwork   227–8
  somatic effects of   231–2, 233
  turning of pages   230–1
Listen_Up project   153–4
lived experience   3–6, 9, 240–1,
    246–7
  and acousmatic sound   211–12
  Long Table on   114–15
  multi-modal sensory approaches
    to   227
  and scientific objectivity   20–1
loneliness   225, 232, 265
Long Table   113–16, 119
*Long Table on Lived
    Experience*   114–15
*Long Table on The State of the
    World*   115
Long Table on Women in Prison in Rio
    de Janeiro (2005)   114
'The Long-term Impact of Childhood
    Trauma on Adult Mental and
    Physical Health'   50

McEwan, Vic   260, *261*
McKenzie, Pantjiti   194
McMahan, Jeff   244
McNally, Jenny   102, 104–5
McQueen, Steve
  Small Axe (TV series)   149
madness   250
  public opinion on   257–8
Mama, Candice   155
'The Man in the Log' (Aboriginal
    traditional story)   154,
    193–6
Mansoubi, Moones   128
Manus Prison theory   125–6
Maté, Gabor   57
mechanisms   10, 17–19
medication. *See* psychiatric drugs
melancholia   47–8
memory-work   227–8

Menakem, Resmaa   222 n.1
mental health
  alternative definition of   9–10
  psychiatric definition of   9
mental health staff
  discriminatory and stigmatizing
    attitudes of   256–7
Mental Health Testimony Project
    (MHTP) archive   224–33
mental imagery   29
Merleau-Ponty, Maurice   21
Mgoduka, Siyah   155
micro-interactions   101, 102
mindfulness   137, 247
Mira   131–4
mixed reality   28–9, 30–5
movement vocabulary   168–9
Mulqueen, Geralyn   50
mutual recognition   100–1

National Health Service (UK)   267
Nauru Detention Centre   131–7
Nauru Imprisoned Exiles
    Collective   125–6
neglect   186, 250, 251
  'observant neglect'   252
neurodivergence   8, 239–41, 243,
    247
neuroecosocial approach   101
neuronormativity   243
ngangkari (healers)   154, 193, 194–5
Nicholas, Tony (Denise)   102
nightmares   136–7
Niven, Alex   264
Northern Ireland
  cultural experiences in   45–51
not-ness   199

object relations   44–6, 55–6, 62–4
Ogden, Pat   168–9, 187, 188
Open Dialogue   69–70, 71–2, 75,
    77–8
oppression   7, 102
  day-to-day   265
  kyriarchal regime   7, 129
other/otherness
  pathologization of   245–6
overgeneral memory (OGM)   23, 25,
    29–30

pain 201–2
painting
  19th July 137
  Concealed Borders 134
  Nameless 137
  oil painting 186–7
  Untitled 181–3
panel discussion 113–14
parenting/parenthood 20, 246–7. *See
  also* attachment theory
  facilitating environments 61–3,
    108, 204, 207
Parkinson, Clive 260–1
  Recoverist Manifesto 269
Parragirls Past, Present 7, 21–2, 93,
  102–9
Parramatta Girls Home (PGH)
  (Sydney) 102. *See also
  Parragirls Past, Present*
Parrish, Liz 262
partnership 60–1
Paskovski, Lynne 102
performance art 50
Perinatal Dreaming 55, 56, 62–4
personality disorder 251–2
person-centred therapy 82–3
phenomenology
  of acousmatic sound 11, 211–12
Phka Sla Krom Angkar project 159–60
photo portraiture 269
Pine, Emilie
  Notes to Self 46
placebo 23
play therapy 61–2
police violence 141–3
political violence 159
Porch Sitting 118–20
postnatal depression 19–20
post-traumatic growth (PTG) 132–4
presentational symbolization 94
Prest, Mark
  Portraits of Recovery 269
Project Art Works (collective) 8, 239
  Illuminating the Wilderness
    (film) 242, 243, 244, 246, 247,
    248 n.3
  The Not Knowing of Another
    (video installation) 8, 239–41,
    246, 247

psychiatric drugs 230–1
  impact on voice 226
psychiatric institution abuse 224–5
psychiatry
  criticism of 250–4
  discrimination and stigmatizing
    attitude of 255–7
  and institutional racism 143–4
  medical model 6–7, 263–4
psychic genera 49, 106
psychoanalysis 46–7
'Psychoanalysis +' (event) 47
  'Melancholia' 47–8
psycho-emotional mechanisms 20
psychological mechanisms 18
psychology 252
psychoneuroimmunology 20
psychosis 77, 250
psychosocial affordances 10, 11–12,
  93–5, 101, 103, 107–10
psychosocial mechanisms 18–20, 24
PTSD (post-traumatic stress
  disorder) 22, 23–4
public conversations 113
  Care Café 116–18
  Long Table 113–16
  Porch Sitting 118–20
public engagement 95–101
public testimony 157

radical creativity 55, 56
Rankine, Claudia
  Citizen: An American Lyric 146,
    147, 149
  Don't Let Me Be Lonely 145
  *Just Us: An American
    Conversation* 147, 149
r e a (artist) 153–4, 155
recoverism 269, 272
reflective filmmaking 241–2, 246
reflective self-consciousness 24, 30
refugees. *See also* detention (indefinite)
  arts-based psychosocial
    support 167–8, 176
  Australian policy 127
  disconnection of 172–3
  industry 129, 130
  resilience of 175
  safety and control of 174–5

Somalian 166
Sudanese 166–7
Yezidi 167
refugee writers and artists 126–30
Regan, Daniel 96
relational psychotherapy 187
relief, through animation 186–9
reparations. *See also Parragirls Past, Present*
and EmbodiMap 206
within transitional justice framework 154–5, 157–62
resilience 167–8, 175
resistance
by indefinite detainees 125–37
by Parramatta Girls 103, 106
translation as 128–9
responsibility, poetic 145–6
retributive justice 156
reveries 260–2
Ridiculusmus (theatre company) 69, 71–2, 77–8
Rizzo, Albert 31
Rogers, Carl 82–3
Rose, Nik 101
Rothko, Mark 45
Royal Commission into Institutional Responses to Child Sexual Abuse (UK) 102, 106–7

safety
and blackness 221
and refugees 174–5
Say Her Name movement 143
Schaeffer, Pierre 211–12
Schon, Donald 181
Schore, Allan 23, 25, 187
Schulman, Sarah
Let the Record Show 144–5
sculpture
Baby in a Cage 56, 63
Seidman, Judy
'Art and Memory Workshops' 158–9
Seikkula, Jaakko 70
self
Aboriginal notion of 57
sense of control over 31, 173, 176
and suicidality 30

self-efficacy 31
self-harm 103, 131–2. *See also* suicide/suicidality
self-regulation 186, 188
Sen, Dolly
Bedlamb project 257–8
DSM 69 255
sensible 4, 7, 8, 9
sensorimotor psychotherapy 188
Service for the Treatment and Rehabilitation of Torture and Trauma Survivors (STARTTS) (New South Wales) 167
service user 254
sexual violence 154, 158–60
silence 105, 130
singing 19–20
social media 265–7
social movements 267–72
social support 132–3, 264
Sodell, Thembi
Held Down, Expanding (sound installation) 211, 212, 214–21
Somalian refugees 166
somatic memory 227–8
Songlines 57, 64 n.1
sound installations
Held Down, Expanding 211, 212, 214–21
South Africa 157
reparation measures 158, 159
South African Truth and Reconciliation Commission (TRC) 99–100, 156, 157, 159
State Library of New South Wales (Sydney) 117–18
state patronage 267–8
Stein, Elizabeth 264
Stellenbosch University (South Africa). Studies in Historical Trauma and Transformation 154
stigma 255–7, 264, 269
Stolen Generations 57, 64, 156–7
Stone, Linda 266
storytelling 132
stress 186–7
and indefinite detention 131–2

Strole, James 262
substance use 269
Sudanese refugees 166–7
suicide/suicidality
    child 24
    interventions for 32–5
    and memory 29–30
    in Northern Ireland 49
    online 265–6
    as rational 22–3, 24–5
suicide survivors
    mental imagery of 29
symbolic reparations 158, 161
systemic racism. *See* institutional
    racism

Takotsubo syndrome/Broken heart
    syndrome 185
Tatchell, Peter 270
Taylor-Johnson, Sam
    Still Life (film) 272
tender listening 224–5, 233 n.1
testimony
    dual purpose of 106
    Mental Health Testimony
        Project 224–33
theatre
    *The Eradication of Schizophrenia
        in Western Lapland* 69, 70–1,
        73–7
the third 42
Thunberg, Greta 270
time
    slowing down of 173–4
    vertical time 21
Time to Change campaign 255,
    256–7
Tofighian, Omid
    No Friend but the Mountains 126,
        127
transformative art practices 161–2
transgenerational trauma. *See*
    intergenerational trauma
transitional justice 154–5, 157–62
translation
    as resistance 128–9
trauma 9, 10–13
    and acousmatic gap 218–20
    continuing effects of 104–5

defined 171
and films 50–1
iatrogenic 250–5
and language 171–2
refugees 166–8
shared experiences 133–4
shared experiences and public
    art 48–51
transformation of 96–8, 106–7,
    108–9, 160–1
'trauma informed' 11–12, 167–8
triggering 22, 31, 104–5
trauma awareness workshops 166–7
traumatic memory 73–7
The Trebus Project 87
triggers 22, 30, 31, 104–5
    grief 185–6
Trivelli, Elena 232
truth-telling 7, 155–7, 161

United Kingdom
    *A Policy for the Arts: The First
        Steps* 268
Uti Kulintjaku (artist collective) 154,
    155, 191–2, 193, 194

valence 94, 101
ventricular tachycardia 184–6
verbatim theatre 82–5
vertical time 21
video installations
    It's a Pleasure to Meet You 155
    The Not Knowing of Another 8,
        239–41, 246, 247
violence
    counter-surveillance of 141–3,
        146
    political 159
    sexual 154, 158–60
    silence as 105, 130
virtual embodiment 31–2
virtual reality (VR) 85–6
    Edge of the Present 28–9, 30–5
    EmbodiMap 168–76, 195–207
    The Visit (immersive media) 80–2,
        83–5
visual matrix 33–4, 46
voice/vocalization 226–7, 231
    of fax machine 228–30

von Trier, Lars
  Melancholia (film) 47
vulnerability 198–9

Wart (artist) 96
Wau-mananyi: The Song on the Wind
    (artwork) 154, 192–6
welfare state 267–8
wilderness 242–3
Williamson, Sue
  It's a Pleasure to Meet You (video
    installation) 155
Winnicott, Donald W. 42, 44, 51, 62,
    97, 100–1, 203
  Playing and Reality 51–2
witnessing/witness 203–5
  of acts of injustice 141–3, 146,
    147–9, 155, 156
  enactive 232
Wobcke, Marianne
  Baby in a Cage (sculpture) 56, 63
  Grandmother Dreaming (lino
    cut) 56

women
  hysteric 252
  and police violence 143
Woods, David 69
World Health Organization (WHO)
  International Statistical
    Classification of Diseases
    (ICD) 12 n.2
Wright, Kenneth 94
Wright, Richard 144
writing 127, 146

Yezidi refugees 167
youth and youthfulness 262–3

Zaidi, Ali
  Per te Mamma (film) 269
Zivardar, Elahe (Ellie Shakiba) *135*
  19th July (painting) 137
  Concealed Borders (painting) 134
  Nameless (painting) 137
  Searching for Aramsayesh Gah
    (film) 126, 134–8